The Siege of Vicksburg

D0201812

Pemberton's surrender to Grant on July 4, 1863

THE SIEGE
OF
VICKSBURG

RICHARD WHEELER

HarperPerennial
A Division of HarperCollins*Publishers*

To Kathleen Bross
who is always there
and who shared the enjoyment
of my visit to Vicksburg

A hardcover edition of this book was published in 1978 by Thomas Y. Crowell, Publishers. It is here reprinted by arrangement with Thomas Y. Crowell, Publishers.

THE SIEGE OF VICKSBURG. Copyright © 1978 by Richard Wheeler. All rights reserved. Printed in the United States of America. No part of this book may be used or reproduced in any manner whatsoever without written permission except in the case of brief quotations embodied in critical articles and reviews. For information address HarperCollins Publishers, 10 East 53rd Street, New York, NY 10022.

First HarperPerennial edition published 1991.

Designed by C. Linda Dingler

LIBRARY OF CONGRESS CATALOG CARD NUMBER 90-56429

ISBN 0-06-097414-1

91 92 93 94 95 MB 10 9 8 7 6 5 4 3 2 1

CONTENTS

MAPS

PREFACE

The Siege of Vicksburg is an episode of the Civil War as seen by its participants, with the emphasis on the people themselves rather than on the military technicalities. Though I have given every consideration to factual veracity, the narrative style is intended to be closer to that of an historical novel than to that of the usual compilation of eyewitness accounts. Happily for my purposes, women figured extensively in the Vicksburg campaign, and a number did some lively writing about it. Indeed, many of the book's best contributions are by women.

Because I was unwilling to clutter the narrative with numbers, the sources of the individual quotes are not given. Most of the quotes, however, can be traced through the bibliography. In transposition, some alterations have been made in paragraphing, capitalization, punctuation, and, occasionally, in spelling. Any other tampering that has been done—for the sake of clarity and conciseness, and also to rid certain passages of faulty information—is indicated by brackets and ellipses.

The book's illustrations, except for the maps, are from the war years and the period immediately after, many having been done by artists who were on the spot. Chief sources represented are *Harper's History of the Great Rebellion, Frank Leslie's Illustrated History of the Civil War, The Soldier in Our Civil War,* and *Battles and Leaders of the Civil War.*

I have a number of other debts to acknowledge. Of particular usefulness were the books *Grant Moves South,* by Bruce Catton; *The Web of Victory,* by Earl Schenck Miers; *Vicksburg: A People at War,* by Dr. Peter F. Walker; and *Vicksburg: 47 Days of Siege,* by A. A. Hoehling. These volumes were the product of years of research. Equally helpful was the painstaking scholarship of Edwin C.

Bearss, who not only wrote *Rebel Victory at Vicksburg* but also edited the Morningside Bookshop editions of the memoirs of Confederate soldiers Willie Tunnard and Ephraim Anderson.

Various issues of the *Civil War Times Illustrated* were consulted, with much use being made of the special issue "Struggle for Vicksburg." This contains perhaps the best master map of the campaign to be found anywhere. The ubiquitous Mr. Bearss had a hand in its development.

An unexpected contribution to *The Siege of Vicksburg* came from Walter T. Stockton, of Evanston, Illinois. After reading my article "The Siege of Vicksburg" in the June, 1976, issue of *American Heritage,* Mr. Stockton forwarded, as a gift of interest, a copy of a diary kept during the siege by his grandfather. Mr. Stockton was unaware at the time that the article was being expanded into a book and that such material was being actively sought.

Finally, I wish to offer a very special thanks to the following people I met during my visit to Vicksburg, all of whom I quickly came to regard as friends:

To Mrs. Norma Daughtry, who arranged my visit's itinerary, who obtained for me a typescript of the Emma Balfour diary, and who provided added inspiration for my project with her thrilling vocal renditions of "Dixie" and "Battle Hymn of the Republic" amid the unique acoustics of the battlefield's Illinois Memorial.

To Mrs. Juanita L. Hackett, a licensed tour guide, who directed my investigations of this remarkably well-preserved battlefield, adding much to my knowledge of the siege. I was both astonished and delighted to learn that the sprightly Mrs. Hackett is the daughter of a Confederate veteran.

To Gordon A. Cotton, director of the Old Court House Museum, and to the assistant director and research consultant, Mrs. Blanche S. Terry, for their hospitality, encouragement, and aid. The fine old building itself, which stood during the siege and now contains many fascinating relics of the period, was found to be a treasury of useful information.

To Howard Sit, of the Vicksburg *Evening Post,* for some excellent advance publicity.

R. W.

The Siege of Vicksburg

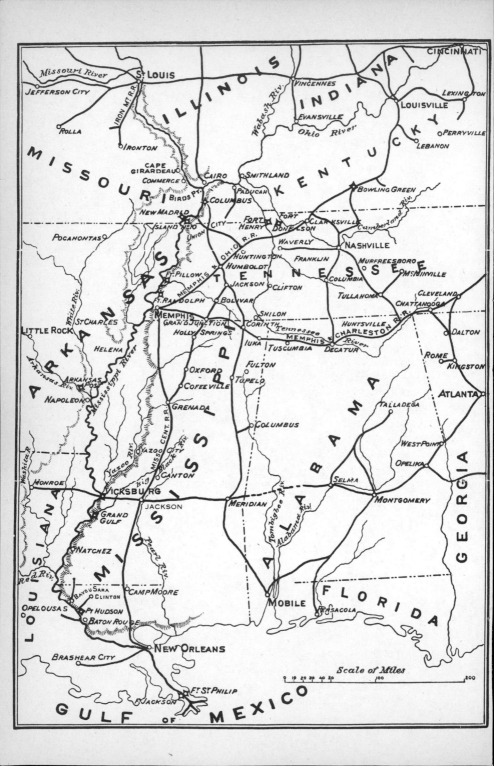

PROLOGUE

As early as mid-November, 1861, seven months after the outbreak of the Civil War, when most Northerners had their
eyes fixed upon Richmond, Virginia, the Confederate capital,
President Abraham Lincoln said at a strategy conference in
Washington: "Vicksburg is the key. The war can never be brought
to a close until that key is in our pocket."

The President was standing before a large wall map, pointing
a long forefinger at the vital spot on the Mississippi River's eastern
bank. His audience of blue-uniformed officers judged the city to
be about 200 miles north of New Orleans, observing also that the
Mississippi reached up past Vicksburg through another 400 miles
of Confederate territory, dividing the East from the West.

Lincoln, who had traveled the river as "bow man" on a flatboat
in his youth, called the group's attention to three of its western
tributaries:

"Here is Red River, which will supply the Confederates with
cattle and corn to feed their armies. There are the Arkansas and
White rivers, which can supply cattle and hogs by the thousand.
From Vicksburg these supplies can be distributed by rail all over
the Confederacy."

The President went on to explain that troops as well as
supplies could be transported eastward in this way.

One of the officers present said later that "Mr. Lincoln's
capacious mind took in the whole subject, and he made it plain to
the dullest comprehension."

Thus it was that winning control not only of Vicksburg but of
the full length of the Mississippi to New Orleans became the chief
goal of the Union forces in the West. Success would bring three

great advantages: the Confederacy would be cut in two, disrupting the flow of supplies and reinforcements from west to east; the Federal army and navy would obtain a convenient highway for further operations; and the farmers and merchants of the Old Northwest would regain the use of a vital trade route to the sea.

Mary Ashton Livermore

1

A TRIP WITH MARY LIVERMORE

*I*T WAS *a cloudy day in early March, 1863. The steamboat* **Magnolia,** *aboard which Union General Ulysses S. Grant had his headquarters, was anchored at Young's Point, on the Mississippi River just above Vicksburg, the "Gibraltar of the Confederacy." Grant stood alone at the rail, quietly smoking a cigar and contemplating the coveted city, now partly hidden by fog. Though only a few miles away, Vicksburg seemed wholly out of his reach.*

Grant was in the midst of his Bayou Expeditions, a set of laborious attempts to work his way through the heavily wooded swamps, in rainy weather, around to the city's rear. An attack on its riverfront defenses was not feasible; they were too strong.

Grant's 50,000 troops, accompanied by a fleet of warships and transports, were strung out along the river from Young's Point to the Yazoo Pass, a waterway about 150 miles to the north.

Complicating Grant's problems was the fact that the powers in Washington were becoming impatient for results. Many strategists considered the goal of opening the Mississippi to be far more important than the goal of the Federal forces in the East, that of capturing Richmond.

Grant was also being pressed by the Union's newspaper editors, who kept the public alerted to the importance of the Western campaign and deplored the pace of its progress. Particularly receptive to the newspaper comments were those people who lived in the states whose commerce the Confederates had disrupted.

Among the Mississippi-oriented Northerners was Mary Ashton Livermore of Chicago, an official of the United States Sanitary Commission, an organization dedicated to looking after the health and welfare of the Union soldiers and their families. Just lately Mrs. Livermore had volunteered to organize a Sanitary Commission task force for a trip down the muddy Father of Waters to Vicksburg.

In addition to Grant's list of wounded, thousands had fallen sick, and it was to be Mrs. Livermore's job to give both the wounded and the sick whatever aid she could, at the same time reporting to the North, in dispatches to newspapers, the extent of the problem.

Wife of a prominent Chicago journalist, Mary Livermore was forty-one years old, sturdily built yet feminine, serious-faced but readily moved to laughter, and abundantly endowed with enterprise. She was a writer, a lecturer, and a lively advocate of temperance reform and woman suffrage. She undertook her mission to Vicksburg with keen anticipation, not in small part because she was curious about Grant and wanted to see for herself what he was like.

Mrs. Livermore learned that some of Grant's sick and wounded soldiers had been sent up the river as far as Cairo, Illinois, where her delegation was to begin its steamboat trip. This was probably some 700 water miles from Vicksburg, though less than 400 by land. Mrs. Livermore relates:

The programme marked out for us was this. We were to visit every hospital from Cairo to Young's Point, opposite Vicksburg; relieve such needs as were pressing; make ourselves useful in any way among the sick and wounded, co-operating harmoniously as far as possible with medical and military authorities. From every point we were to report our movements, the result of our observations, what we had accomplished, and what we found needing attention. . . .

Our assortment of stores comprised almost everything necessary in hospital relief. . . . We also took down about five hundred "private boxes," forwarded by private parties for particular companies, or squads, or individuals, and committed to our care for safe transmission and delivery.

My own personal outfit consisted of a long pair of rubber boots, reaching to the knee, a teapot, a spirit lamp to boil it, with a large quantity of Japan tea, condensed milk, sugar and crackers. . . .

The boat to which we were assigned was a little, rickety, wheezy, crowded, unsafe craft, which poked along down the river at about one-half the usual rate of speed. It towed along three or four barges of hay, which kept us in constant alarm, as they easily took fire from the sparks of the chimney. . . .

Several army officers were on board, who had been home on furloughs. Some of them were accompanied by their wives, who were going as far as Memphis, beyond which point no civilian could pass without special permission. The colonel of the Twelfth Michigan [Regiment] was accompanied by his bride, a beautiful young woman and an exquisite vocalist. . . .

There were also in the company flutists and violinists, and half a dozen members of a brass band attached to one of the regiments stationed down the river. The boat was ringing with patriotic music all the time. Wherever there were military posts or hospitals, the boat stopped for hours. As we steamed to the landings, all our musical force mustered on deck and announced our arrival by a grand chorus of voices and instruments.

They rendered "The Red, White, and Blue," "The Star-Spangled Banner," "Rally Round the Flag, Boys!" and other national songs in a ringing fashion that brought every soldier from his tent flying down the bluffs to welcome us.

The vocalists always accompanied us to the hospitals and made the tour of the wards with us, singing charmingly. . . . It was a great delight to them to observe how the inspiring music brightened the weary, suffering men. . . .

One poor lad, dying of consumption, too far gone to be sent to his home in Iowa, fixed his large, luminous eyes on the fair girl bride, whose voice was like that of an angel, and asked, "Can you sing something for a dying man?"

It was her first acquaintance with hospitals, her first contact with sickness and death. But without hesitation she moved to his bedside, seated herself on a campstool beside him, and, taking one of his thin hands in hers, sang, with great feeling, "Nearer, My God, to Thee."

There was sobbing in the ward when she ended; but the boy to whom she sang only gazed at her with eyes of beseeching.

"Can you sing 'The Sweet By and By'?" he inquired.

That was given, with the chorus, in which all joined. And then, unasked, her tender, sympathetic voice floated again through the long ward in the exquisite melody of *Sweet Home*. Never have I heard it so feelingly rendered.

The scene that followed was alarming. Men buried their faces in the pillows and wept aloud; and others, who were sitting up in partial convalescence, threw themselves on the bed, face downward, in excess of emotion. This would not do.

To change the current of feeling, I called for the stirring song "Rally Round the Flag, Boys!," which was given with a will. Then "America" rang out on the air; and, as the whistle of the boat was calling us to return, the choir took leave of the hospital, singing as they went: "There's a good time coming, boys; wait a little longer!"

... We distributed our sanitary stores with a lavish hand wherever they were needed. Where women were acting as matrons in the hospitals, we committed our benefactions to their care. Where were suspicious-looking stewards or intemperate surgeons we were less bountiful in our bestowments, and lingered to disburse our supplies to individual cases, as far as we could.

At Memphis, there were eleven hospitals containing nearly eight thousand patients, and this number was daily re-enforced by boatloads of sick men, sent up from points below. I went on board one of these newly arrived transports, and was appalled at the condition of the men. Not one in twenty could have been recognized by his kindred or friends, so disguised were the poor fellows by mud, squalor, vermin, rags, and the wasting sickness of scurvy and swamp fever....

Our headquarters while in Memphis were at the Gayoso House [a hotel], which had a great reputation for style, secession proclivities, and discomfort. The last two characteristics were pre-eminent. There were nightly drunken rows and fights in the house, sometimes in rooms adjoining ours, when the crash of glass, the ribald song, the fearful profanity, and the drunken mirth drove sleep from our pillows.

We were detained over two weeks in Memphis, so difficult was it to obtain transportation for ourselves and stores down the river. Strict military surveillance was kept over the boats bound for the South, and none were allowed to leave Memphis without a pass from the Commander of the Department. Our stores were piled on the levee, waiting reshipment, and a guard was placed over them to keep them from thieves.

The Gayoso House was overflowing with *attachés* of the army, waiting a chance to go down the river, like ourselves. A large company of women were also staying there, who made no secret of their sympathy with the South. Some half-dozen were waiting an opportunity to be passed within the enemy's lines, whither they had been ordered by our officers....

One afternoon, while waiting for a chaplain who was to drive me to some of the regimental hospitals outside of Memphis, two of these women came into the parlor and sat down. After we had measured each other with our eyes for a moment, one of them commenced a conversation. She was the wife of a member of the Confederate Congress....

"I am told you are going down below to look after sick Yankee soldiers.... I think it is high time somebody went down to them, for they are dying like sheep.... This city is full of Yankee women, wives of Yankee officers... decked out in cotton lace, cheap silks, and bogus jewelry.... What do *they* care for Yankee soldiers, whether they live or die? We have done wearing silks and jewels in the South until the war is over. I sold my jewels and gave the money to the hospitals...."

"Madam, I honor your devotion to your soldiers, and only regret the badness of your cause. At the North, we are equally solicitous for the welfare of our men. But you make the mistake of supposing that we at the North are as poor as you at the South. The war is not impoverishing us as it is you. Our women can afford to wear silks and jewelry, and yet provide everything needful for the soldiers. Whenever it becomes necessary, we shall be ready to make as great sacrifices as you."

"Ah, *we* have soldiers *worth* the sacrifice we make!" she said with a lofty air. "*Our* men are the flower of our youth... gentlemen, every one of them. But your Yankee soldiers—ugh!.... They are the dregs of your cities—gutter-snipes, drunken, ignorant—"

"Stop!" I interrupted; "Stop! I won't hear such calumny. I know what sort of *gentlemen* your soldiers are; for we have had seven thousand of them at Camp Davis in Chicago, taken prisoners.... And if *they* were the flower of your youth, you are worse off for men in the South than I had supposed."

"And I have seen *your* soldiers, too, to my sorrow and horror. They are barbarians, I tell you. They came to my husband's villa after he had gone to Congress [in Richmond], and I was left alone, with my servants in charge, and they destroyed everything—*everything!* My plate, china, pictures, carpets, even my furniture.... The wretches! They burned up everything!"

"If your manners were as unbearable as they have been during the two weeks I have seen you in this house, I only wonder you escaped cremation with your villa and furniture. It is astonishing the clemency that allows you to be at large in this city...."

"*Allows me to be at large!*" she fairly screamed, almost purple with rage. "Who dares imprison me, I'd like to know? You would like to put me in jail and shut me up with murderers... and thieves, would you? The tables will be turned, by and by. England is going to help us; and we will have our feet on your accursed Yankee necks before you are a year older or wickeder!"

She was standing at her fullest height, her face aflame, her eyes on fire, her voice at its highest pitch. It was useless to talk further, so I rose and left the room, saying at the door, with a low bow, "Until that time, madam, I bid you farewell."

... I learned afterwards that this woman, with her friends and companions, was passed within the Confederate lines at Vicksburg a few days later.... They were as heroic in their endurance of the horrors of the long siege as the Confederate men, and evinced courage as unyielding, and tenacity of purpose as unflinching, as any officer who wore the Confederate gray.

On the evening of the same day as her encounter—a day in mid-March—Mrs. Livermore boarded the steamboat Tigress *and continued her journey down the Mississippi. The next day she got a glimpse of a part of the river rushing through an opening in the earth of the eastern levee. Just lately Grant's troops had shattered the levee with gunpowder in order to gain access to Moon Lake and the Yazoo Pass, starting point for one of the Bayou Expeditions.*

Several warships and troop transports had worked their way eastward from the Mississippi through the tree-crowded waters of the pass to the Coldwater River, having then descended the Coldwater and the Tallahatchie toward Vicksburg's northern flank. The expedition had been brought up short less than halfway to its goal by a Confederate detachment manning an impromptu fort made of earth and cotton bales.

Confederate General William W. Loring won the nickname "Old Blizzards" at this time by striding back and forth behind his artillery crews and shouting, "Give them blizzards, boys! Give them blizzards!"

The Federals would make no further progress with this expedition. In the end, bearing their wounded, they would be obliged to work their way back up the tortuous waterways to their starting point on the Mississippi.

The Yazoo Pass was 150 miles north of Vicksburg by land, but 300 miles by way of the winding river. Mrs. Livermore continues:

The lower Mississippi was on the rampage, and was all over its banks. It was shoreless in some places, and stretched its dull, turbid waste of waters as far as the eye could reach.... Day after day, there was but the swollen, rushing stream before us. And when the banks could be seen, only the skeleton cottonwood trees greeted our eyes, hung with the funereal moss that shrouded them as in mourning drapery.

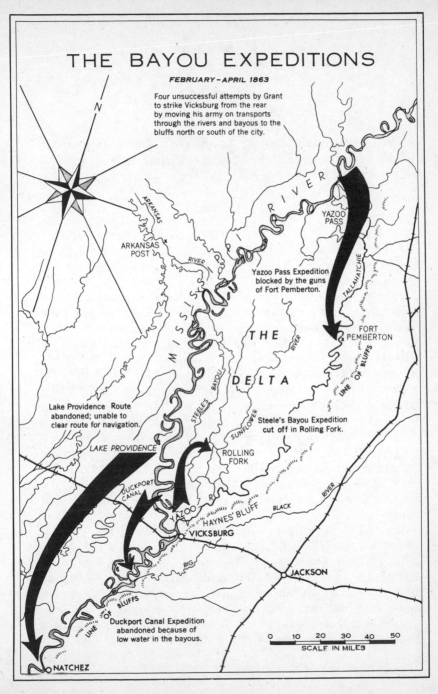

THE BAYOU EXPEDITIONS

FEBRUARY – APRIL 1863

Four unsuccessful attempts by Grant
to strike Vicksburg from the rear
by moving his army on transports
through the rivers and bayous to the
bluffs north or south of the city.

N

ARKANSAS

ARKANSAS
POST

RIVER

MISSI   RIVER

YAZOO
PASS

Yazoo Pass Expedition
blocked by the guns
of Fort Pemberton.

TALLAHATCHIE

THE

RIVER

FORT
PEMBERTON

LINE OF BLUFFS

DELTA

STEELE'S BAYOU

Lake Providence Route
abandoned; unable to
clear route for navigation.

SUNFLOWER

Steele's Bayou Expedition
cut off in Rolling Fork.

LAKE PROVIDENCE

ROLLING
FORK

DUCKPORT
CANAL

YAZOO   RI

HAYNES' BLUFF

BLACK

RIVER

VICKSBURG

BIG

JACKSON

LINE OF BLUFFS

Duckport Canal Expedition
abandoned because of
low water in the bayous.

0   10   20   30   40   50
SCALE IN MILES

NATCHEZ

William W. Loring

The swollen river was in our favor; for the enemy could not plant batteries [i.e., artillery pieces] on the banks and fire into the passing boats until it subsided, especially as the steamers kept very near the center of the stream.

The pilot house of the *Tigress* was battened with thick oak planks to protect the helmsman from the shots of the guerrillas. Dozens of bullets were imbedded in it, which had been fired from the shore on the last trip up the river. And a six-pound shot had crashed through the steamer, not two months before, killing two or three passengers in the saloon, and badly shattering the boat.

The *Tigress* was a large, well-appointed boat, and had been handsome before it entered army service. The officers were understood to be disloyal at heart, but willing to work for the government because of its magnificent, prompt, and sure pay.

The stewardess was a beautiful quadroon [i.e., a person three-fourths white and one-fourth black] of thirty-five, with a catlike grace and suppleness of figure, and was wonderfully attractive in her manners to those whom she liked. I have never seen a handsomer woman.

But what a virulent, vulgar, foul-mouthed rebel she was! There was not a half-hour of the day that she did not grossly insult someone of our party. There was no redress; for we saw that she bore some relationship to the clerk, that she was a great favorite with all the officers, and that they enjoyed our discomfort under her insolence, which they abetted.

She hung her mocking-bird, named "Jeffy Davis," at our door, and then talked *to* him by the hour, but *at* us, calling us by names ... which I cannot [repeat] ... and charging us with the vilest purposes in coming down to the army.

One day, while we were negotiating with the laundress of the boat concerning some work we wished done, Louisa, the stewardess, came along.

"Can I wash for these ladies today?" inquired the laundress of the quadroon....

"*Ladies!*" scornfully echoed the insolent creature "*Ladies!* What's yer talkin' about, gal? Yer hasn't seen no *ladies* sence yer lef' N'Orleans.... Yer may wash for 'em.... But mind yer gets yer pay, gal...."

That day, after dinner, I went into the stern of our boat to read.... Louisa followed to hang up some wet linen to dry, and, as usual, commenced talking *at* me.... She had approached very near and was standing behind me, and we were alone. I turned sharply round, laid my hand heavily on her shoulder, and looked as terrible as possible. I spoke low, but in a very determined tone.

"You will please stop ... your insolent manners towards my friends and myself! We have had enough of it. If it is not stopped *immediately* I will take the matter into my own hands...."

I brought my other hand down heavily on her other shoulder, and spoke yet lower, and in a tone so tragically terrific that I half laughed to hear it.

"I could throw you overboard as easily as if you were a cat, and I have a good mind to do it this minute!"—tightening my grasp on her arms and lifting her from her feet. "Go take that cage down and carry it to your room, and let me hear any more insolent talk if you dare—that's all! You'll see what *one* Yankee woman dares do, for I'll put you where you'll be quiet, I promise you!"

She looked at me ... stammered something, and ... hurried away from me into the saloon.... Whenever we met afterwards, her eyes sought mine with a "comest thou peaceably?" inquiry in them.... There was a marked improvement in her behavior—so great, indeed, that it was the subject of general comment.

Mrs. Livermore and her party headed for Lake Providence, Louisiana, about seventy-five miles up the river from Vicksburg, where thousands of Grant's troops, aided by gangs of newly emancipated blacks, were busy with another of the Bayou Expeditions. They were attempting to turn a part of the Mississippi's flow westward, by means of a channel they were cutting, to navigable bayous leading southward to the Tensas River. The Tensas emptied into the Washita, which, in turn, emptied into the Red River, this last waterway leading back to the Mississippi far below Vicksburg. Had this project succeeded, the Federal vessels could have made so wide a swing west of Vicksburg they never would have come as close as forty miles to the city's guns. Troops might have been transported to the Mississippi's eastern bank below Vicksburg, where the ground was high and dry, for an attack around the city's rear.

About the same time as Mrs. Livermore's arrival at the northern end of the Lake Providence project, a few days past the middle of March, another of Grant's efforts—the Steele's Bayou Expedition—was coming to grief in the same latitude about twenty miles east of the Mississippi. This was a second cooperative move by the army and navy, working among flooded forests, to attack Vicksburg from the north. Not only was the expedition stopped by a Confederate counterattack, but its leading vessels were nearly cut off and captured before a retreat could be effected.

After visiting the Lake Providence hospitals, Mrs. Livermore made a sightseeing tour of the area in an ambulance drawn by two mules:

For hours and hours we rode through the sloughs, finally breaking down in one. Then a score of brawny fellows dropped their work . . . and rushed to our relief with rails and planks, and whoops and yells sufficient for a whole tribe of Indians. The two mules, that had sunk to their bellies, were extricated first. The men were devising ways to lift the ambulance to terra firma when General [John A.] Logan rode up, who was in command at this horrible place.

"What's the matter, boys?" asked the General. . . .

"Oh, the Sanitary Commission's got mired, that's all!"

The General peeped into the ambulance, where I was sitting on the floor, "holding on," as I had been directed. The forward wheels had broken through the rotten logs that formed a corduroy bridge over the slough. The ambulance had pitched forward, and I was "holding on" as well as I could, considering I had laughed at the comical performances and speeches around me until I was exhausted.

The whole thing was so ridiculous that the General laughed too, but set himself to effect my release from the imprisoning mud, and succeeded at the expense of a soiled uniform.

Mrs. Livermore's steamer soon left Lake Providence and headed down the river to Milliken's Bend, the swampy right bank of which held the camps of some 30,000 troops. Milliken's Bend was the northern extremity of Grant's

Duckport Canal project, another attempt to utilize the bayous west of Vicksburg to float vessels to a point south of the city. This was a kind of small-scale version of the Lake Providence project.

Here, as at Lake Providence, blacks with axes, picks, and shovels formed a prominent part of the labor force. The men were fresh from Southern plantations, some having been impressed, and some having entered the Union lines with their families to seek freedom under President Abraham Lincoln's Emancipation Proclamation. The lot of these people hadn't changed. They occupied a segregated camp, with the women, too, earning their keep by doing tasks very much like those they had done before. There were women who turned to prostitution, some not only because it brought them a living but because they considered it a suitable way to reward the men they considered their liberators.

Mrs. Livermore heard one of her companions say: "When this war is over, I never want to see again a Negro or a mule. Both of them are so abused in the army, and both are so dumbly patient and uncomplaining, and receive so little sympathy, that I suffer a perpetual heartache on their account."

Mrs. Livermore adds:

To express pity for, or interest in, a suffering mule . . . was to run the gauntlet of the most stinging ridicule. Everybody beat and neglected the unhandsome brutes; and when they fell into the hands of the ill-treated Negroes, they fared worse than ever. From their own persecution and abuse, they seemed to have learned only lessons of brutality and tyranny.

Among the Federal soldiers encamped at Milliken's Bend was a unit that contained a number of men Mrs. Livermore had known in Chicago before the war:

What a hubbub! What a jubilee! Here was a guest from home who had talked a few days before with their fathers and mothers, sisters and wives. The best "shebang" of the encampment was placed at my disposal, for I was to spend the night with them. . . . Everything in the way of shelter, in camp parlance, that was not a tent was a "shebang." Mine was a rough hut made of boards, with a plank floor, roofed with canvas. . . . We had a lively time in the "shebang" that evening. It was packed with the boys, all eager to hear from home.

At last I broke up the conference. But before withdrawing, George Throop, one of the young men, drew from his breast pocket a copy of the New Testament. . . . All heads were instantly uncovered, all hum of voices ceased, and a portion of the fifteenth chapter of Luke's Gospel was read, when Sergeant Dyer, a very noble man belonging to a Baptist church of Chicago, voluntarily offered a brief and appropriate prayer....

I had a wakeful night. It was my first attempt to sleep in camp.... I was in the enemy's country—I heard the steady footfall of the guard past my tent, and the incessant booming of the great guns at Vicksburg, fifteen miles away....

Long before the drums beat the reveille... I had made my ablutions in the three-legged iron skillet given me for that purpose, and completed my toilet before the little six-by-ten-inch looking glass. I hurried out at roll call and offered to assist in getting the breakfast.

But I was not allowed this gratification of my feminine desire, for the boys confessed that "they didn't do things woman fashion," and that I had better remain ignorant of their *modus operandi*. "The victuals would taste better if I didn't see the cooking!" I thought so too, after I got a glimpse of them making bread in the iron skillet in which I had bathed my face and hands.

For breakfast we had hot biscuit baked in ovens made of Louisiana mud; fried ham; good coffee, to which I added condensed milk and white sugar; potatoes, and pickles.... I honored the *cuisine* of the boys by eating heartily.

The Union camp at Young's Point

Mrs. Livermore spent forty-eight hours with her enthusiastic friends, then went on to Young's Point, the end of her journey.

Two or three miles south of Young's Point the Mississippi made a curve eastward and then northeastward, stopping its northerly course only when it was above the Point, several miles to the east. Next the river made a hairpin curve back toward the southwest.

On the eastern bank of this curve, sitting stably on a set of hills that sloped from the water to a height of about two hundred feet, was Vicksburg. The city was six or seven miles east of Young's Point. Its elevation made it visible across the alternating strips of water and wooded lowlands.

Several Union warships lay on the river just above Vicksburg. From time to time, they opened with shellfire, the discharges reverberating along the winding banks.

Mrs. Livermore viewed the Confederate city with fascination:

It lay stealthily behind its defenses, watching with Argus eyes the movements of the foe in front, belching defiance and protest from its monster guns, which bristled tier above tier, from the river brink to the top of the highest bluff.

None of this fire reached the camps at Young's Point. The danger there was sickness, which was causing many deaths. Funerals were a daily occurrence.

For miles [says Mrs. Livermore], the inside of the levee was sown with graves, at the head and foot of which were rude wooden tablets bearing the name and rank of the deceased, and sometimes other particulars.... In most cases the poor fellows had been wrapped in their blankets and buried without coffins.... In places the levee was broken or washed out by the waters, and the decaying dead were partially disinterred.

Mrs. Livermore was now in a position to seek an interview with General Grant, about whom she was so curious. The curiosity was not based simply on the fact that Grant was a well known figure. At this point he was one of the war's enigmas. He seemed an unlikely candidate for the great task he had undertaken.

The forty-year-old general was barely five feet eight inches tall, had a slight stoop, and weighed only 135 or 140 pounds. His uniform was habitually rumpled, he walked with an unmilitary shuffle, and he was addicted to cigars, puffing them in endless succession. Though his facial lines were good, the skin above his brown beard had an almost feminine clearness. His only really impressive features were a fine set of blue-gray

Ulysses S. Grant

eyes that radiated warmth and humor, and a resonant, penetrating voice. The voice, however, was largely wasted, for Grant never barked classic military profanity, his vocabulary of expletives being limited to "by jinks" and "by lightning."

Grant's background was none too reassuring. Born at Point Pleasant, Clermont County, Ohio, in 1822, he grew up in a rural atmosphere, disliking the work he had to do on the farm and in the tannery which, together, brought his parents their living, a comfortable one for the region and the times.

At the age of seventeen, Grant went east to attend West Point, but only to please his father, for he himself had little interest in becoming a soldier. Finding the training tedious, he often neglected his studies to read novels or to daydream about retiring, on a competence, to the scenes of his boyhood. When he graduated in 1843, he stood twenty-first in a class of thirty-nine, his book knowledge of warfare unimpressive.

A roommate and chum, Rufus Ingalls of Maine, was to say later:

Grant was such a quiet, unassuming fellow when a cadet that nobody would have picked him out as one who was destined to occupy a conspicuous place in history. . . . The principal reputation he gained among his fellow cadets was for common sense, good judgment, entire unselfishness, and absolute fairness in everything he did.

As a lieutenant of infantry, Grant distinguished himself in the war with Mexico, being brevetted twice for "gallant and meritorious conduct." His hazardous adventures were shared by many young officers, citizens of both the North and the South, who shared also his predestination for prominence in the Civil War.

Returning to the States, Grant married Julia Dent, of Missouri, and at once began raising a family. Garrison duty carried him to various parts of the country. In the early 1850s, at a lonely post in Washington Territory, deprived of the company of his wife and children, he began drinking and was soon obliged to resign his commission.

An acquaintance of the time who considered Grant to be a man "of unusual self-control" claimed that his flights into the bottle "did not legitimately belong to his character." Another said that Grant "was not by any means a drunkard," that he merely went on occasional "sprees."

As a civilian, Grant was barely able to support his family. He turned first to farming, building his own home and calling it, appropriately enough, "Hardscrabble." He next tried to sell real estate. At length he became a clerk in his father's leather and hardware store at Galena, Illinois. The outbreak of the Civil War rescued Grant from a doubtful future. Re-entering the service as a colonel, he soon became a brigadier general.

But even as top commander at Vicksburg, with the war near the end of its second twelve-month period, Grant was under a cloud. His troubles had begun a year earlier, when he had allowed a Confederate attack force to surprise his army at Shiloh, Tennessee. Though he had fought back stubbornly and had driven the enemy away, his casualties were horrendous. The people of the North raised a great clamor against him, some accusing him of having been drunk at the crucial moment. The truth was that he just hadn't expected the enemy to attack, and was therefore unprepared.

It had been a very near thing for Grant after Shiloh. As related by Alexander K. McClure, a Pennsylvania journalist who knew President Lincoln well and often visited him at the White House:

I shared the almost universal conviction of the President's friends that he could not sustain himself if he attempted to sustain Grant by continuing his command. . . . So much was I impressed with the importance of prompt action on the part of the President after spending a day and evening in Washington that I called on Lincoln at eleven o'clock at night and sat with him alone until after one o'clock in the morning. He was, as usual, worn out with the day's exacting duties. . . .

I pressed upon him with all the earnestness I could command the immediate removal of Grant as an imperious necessity to sustain himself. As was his custom, he said but little. . . . He sat before the open fire in the old Cabinet room, most of the time with his feet up on the high marble mantel. . . . I could form no judgment during the conversation as to what effect my arguments had upon him beyond the fact that he was greatly distressed at this new complication. When I had said everything that could be said from my standpoint, we lapsed into silence.

Lincoln remained silent for what seemed a very long time. He then gathered himself up in his chair and said in a tone of earnestness that I shall never forget: "*I can't spare this man; he fights.*" That was all he said, but I knew that it was enough, and that Grant was safe in Lincoln's hands against his countless hosts of enemies. The only man in all the nation who had the power to save Grant was Lincoln, and he had decided to do it.

But even Lincoln became unsure of Grant as the Vicksburg campaign foundered. A representative of the War Department, Charles A. Dana—a noted New York editor who had been called into the Federal service—was sent west to investigate Grant and his operations, the findings to be reported to Washington. The mission was given a cover. Grant was supposed to believe that Dana had been appointed "special commissioner of the War Department to investigate and report upon the condition of the pay service in the Western armies." By orders, Dana established himself at Memphis, which was really too far up the Mississippi from the scene of action for his investigations to be very effective.

Back in Washington, the President, in his public statements, continued to defend Grant, stressing his fighting ability. "If his whiskey does it," Lincoln is reputed to have told a group of the general's critics, "I should like to send a barrel of the same brand to every general in the field."

As for Mary Livermore and her delegation, they sought their interview with Grant almost as soon as they reached Young's Point. They found him at his headquarters aboard the steamer Magnolia, *"unsurrounded by any circumstance of pomp or state."*

Our interview was a brief one, and, on the part of the General, laconic. . . . Calling one of his staff officers . . . he requested him to see that any help we might require in the way of escort, passes, ambulances, transportation, etc., was promptly furnished. . . .

In the first five minutes . . . we learned, by some sort of spiritual telegraphy, that reticence, patience, and persistence were the dominant traits of General Grant. . . .[He was a] quiet, repressed, reluctant, undemonstrative man. . . . We instinctively put ourselves on "short rations" of talk with him. . . .

Neither was General Grant a drunkard—that was immediately apparent to us. This conviction gave us such joy that . . . we looked each other in the face . . . and breathed more freely. . . . The clear eye, clean skin, firm flesh, and steady nerves of General Grant gave the lie to the universal calumnies then current concerning his intemperate habits.

The delegation came away from this meeting with the conviction that the people at home "understood neither Grant nor the colossal work on his hands."

A day or two later Mrs. Livermore went to Grant's headquarters vessel alone to ask his aid with one of her problems with the sick. She was ushered into an apartment where he sat by himself, unaware that she was coming:

Through the blue haze of cigar smoke circling through the apartment, I saw General Grant, sitting at the table, wearing his hat, a cigar in his mouth, one foot on a chair, and buried to his chin in maps, letters, reports, and orders. Whatever *mauvaise honte* [i.e., embarrassment] I may have felt in thus obtruding myself upon the modest general was speedily banished by his discompo-

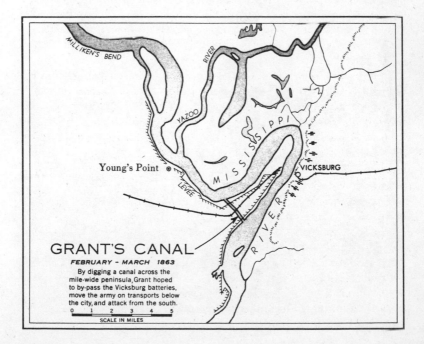

GRANT'S CANAL

FEBRUARY - MARCH 1863

By digging a canal across the mile-wide peninsula, Grant hoped to by-pass the Vicksburg batteries, move the army on transports below the city, and attack from the south.

0   1   2   3   4   5

SCALE IN MILES

sure. For a moment he seemed the most bashful man I had ever encountered. Rising and placing a half dozen chairs at my service, he begged me to be seated, removing his hat and taking his cigar from his mouth, and then quickly and unconsciously replacing both.

Suppressing a smile, Mrs. Livermore stated her errand, received Grant's promise that he would look into the matter, and departed.

While she made her rounds of the Young's Point hospitals, Mrs. Livermore's attention was often arrested by the heavy, vibrating exchanges of gunfire between the Union warships and the Vicksburg defenses. The city was too far away for a clear distinguishment of its details, but she could see that its streets rose sharply from the waterfront to its hilltops. On the skyline were the silhouettes of a few of its buildings, notably that of its large cupola-capped courthouse. Mrs. Livermore was eager for a closer look at the city, and she soon got her chance.

Some of Grant's troops were operating against Vicksburg from a forward position. The city, as has already been explained, was located on the eastern side of a hairpin curve in the Mississippi. Within this curve, pointing toward the northeast, was the De Soto peninsula, low, flat, wooded, about a mile wide and four or five miles long. Across the base of

Origins of Grant's canal at western base of De Soto peninsula

this peninsula a Union engineer corps had been digging a canal, hoping to divert the river through it. Success would have enabled the Federal fleet to pass below Vicksburg outside the range of those worrisome artillery batteries. Moreover, the city would have been left high and dry.

During the first week of Mrs. Livermore's stay at Young's Point, the commander of the engineer corps, Colonel J. W. Bissell, set up a battery of his own on the bank of the peninsula directly across the river from Vicksburg.

Its object [explains Mrs. Livermore] was to destroy the foundries and railroad and machine shops . . . lying near the river, and which were in great activity day and night. The prospecting for the position of the battery, and the planning and marking out of the work had been done in the night, not to attract the attention of the enemy. Now they were to work wholly inside the levee [i.e., the banked earth, which was fifteen feet high at this point], and so were busy in the daytime.

Colonel Bissell himself was in command, and I accepted his invitation to accompany the squad and take a nearer view of Vicksburg than it was possible to gain elsewhere. We steamed down near the mouth of the canal [on the side of the peninsula away from Vicksburg], took a rowboat through one of the creeks

Vicksburg as seen from across the Mississippi

to the point of land opposite the city, and then walked behind the levee.

While the men were working like Titans, the Colonel loaned me a powerful field-glass, and found for me a position where I could look over into the beleaguered city without being seen by their pickets. Here the river was so very narrow that the pickets of the two armies could carry on conversation . . . as they sometimes did.

At the right was the hospital, swarming with gray-uniformed Confederates. They were sitting in the windows, at the doors, on the piazzas, lying on the grass in the yard, coming and going, some on crutches, some led by assistants. A newsboy was selling papers among them, and I could distinguish between the large type of the headings and the smaller print of the columns.

In the belfry of the court house . . . an officer was signaling with flags, of which he seemed to have an immense variety. Beside him stood two ladies, one wrapped in a cloak, and the other in a shawl. I could even see that the bonnet of one was blue in color.

Two Negresses [on a street below], carrying baskets on their heads which looked as if filled with clean clothes, set down their baskets, bowed and curtsied to one another, and then, with arms akimbo, stood and gossiped, laughing convulsively, if one could judge from the motions and gesticulations.

Gray guards were pacing back and forth before the foundries. Officers were galloping to and fro; trains of freight cars were being loaded; new batteries were being placed in position; and other scenes of warlike activity were apparent. But nothing was visible that betokened pleasure or social life, or such proceedings as occupy the people of a city in time of peace. No children were on the streets, no women walking or shopping, no gay equipages [i.e., carriages], no sign of inhabited homes.

But inhabited homes existed. Vicksburg was not nearly so barren of civilian affairs as Mrs. Livermore supposed. It is true, of course, that the military dominated. Some 25,000 soldiers lived in and about the city, the great majority being in tent camps in the outskirts. It is true also that many of the city's original 5,000 inhabitants had moved out, but a considerable number remained, some out of a pure defiance of the Yankees or a desire to protect their property, others for a lack of anywhere else to go. Banks and stores were still in business, the newspapers were publishing, the school system was in partial operation, and the churches were well attended.

On March 26, the day after Mrs. Livermore got her peep into Vicksburg, the bells of the churches sounded up and down the river as they called the city's civilians and soldiers to a special service. President Jefferson Davis had issued a directive from Richmond naming the day one of "fasting, humiliation, and prayer" throughout the Confederacy. Vicksburg's churches were crowded, and some of the hymn-singing that swelled through open doors and windows carried faintly across the river to the peninsula, where groups of Federals paused in their labors to listen.

The people of Vicksburg did not believe themselves to be in any immediate danger from Grant's army, but they found their situation growing more and more inconvenient. Military demands kept the trains off schedule, the mails were irregular, foodstuffs and other goods were in meager supply, and prices soared. A paper shortage caused the newspapers to begin shrinking. The Daily Whig, a woman observed in her diary, "shouts victory as much as its gradually diminishing size will allow."

The woman who wrote this was young Dora Miller, bride of Anderson Miller, a lawyer from Arkansas who was practicing in New Orleans when they met. Unionist in their sympathies, the two were stranded in Vicksburg, where they were renting a house and where Anderson was trying to continue in his profession. Their views made them unpopular, with Anderson being scorned for his avoidance of service in the Confederate army.

On a day in latter March, Dora Miller recorded in her diary:

The slow shelling of Vicksburg goes on all the time, and we have grown indifferent. It does not at present interrupt or interfere with daily avocations, but I suspect they are only getting the range of different points; and when they have them all complete, showers of shot will rain on us all at once. Non-combatants have been ordered to leave or prepare accordingly. Those who are to stay are having caves built. Cave-digging has become a regular business. . . .

The hill called the Sky Parlor has become quite a fashionable resort for the few upper-circle families left here. Some officers are quartered there, and there is a band [for entertainment] and a field-glass. Last evening we . . . climbed the hill to watch the shelling. . . .

Soon a lady began to talk to one of the officers: "It is such folly for them to waste their ammunition like that. How can they ever take a town that has such advantages for defense and protection as this? We'll just burrow into these hills and let them batter away as hard as they please."

The officer agreed with her views, adding gallantly: "When our women are so willing to brave death and endure discomfort, how can we ever be conquered?"

Dora Miller and her husband were now subjected to a stern look by the female speaker: "The only drawback are the contemptible men who are staying at home in comfort when they ought to be in the army if they had a spark of honor."

The woman said more in the same vein. According to Dora Miller:

It was the usual tirade. It is strange I have met no one yet who seems to comprehend an honest difference of opinion, and stranger yet that the ordinary rules of good breeding are now so entirely ignored.

In the same diary entry, Dora stated:

As the spring comes, one has the craving for fresh, green food that a monotonous diet produces. There was a bed of radishes and onions in the garden that were a real blessing. An onion salad, dressed only with salt, vinegar, and pepper, seemed a dish fit for a king; but last night the soldiers quartered near made a raid on the garden and took them all.

It wasn't only Unionists that the soldiers troubled. Said the Whig *in its issue of March 26:*

Yesterday a soldier knocked at the door of a respectable lady . . . and requested her to give him some milk. On the lady's

John C. Pemberton

replying that she regretted her inability to oblige him, he abused her in the most obscene language.... No male protector being present... he escaped the punishment he richly merited.

Actually, relations between the civilians and the soldiers were, for the most part, very good. The soldiers, of course, were recognized as Vicksburg's protectors. Groups of ladies knitted them stockings and other clothing. Parties and dances were arranged. Some of the soldiers found local sweethearts and went riding with them in the moonlight. One man was accused by a comrade of playing sick so that he could nap in his tent all day and run around with the girls at night.

Top commander of the Confederate troops at Vicksburg was Lieutenant General John C. Pemberton, forty-eight years old, a Northerner who had chosen to side with the South. Like Grant, Pemberton was a graduate of West Point and a veteran of the Mexican War. Otherwise, the two were in contrast. Whereas Grant was of Midwestern farm stock, Pemberton was an Eastern aristocrat. He had a slender figure nearly three inches taller than Grant's five feet eight, carried himself very erect, had hair, beard, and eyes of an uncommonly dark brown, and he wore crisp, well-tailored uniforms.

A few months before the outbreak of the Mexican War Pemberton married a girl from Virginia, Martha Thompson, one of whose ancestors was Elbridge Gerry, signer of the Declaration of Independence. It was a union destined to produce five children. In Mexico, Pemberton was twice wounded and twice brevetted for gallantry. After the war he was assigned to garrison duty on the Midwestern frontiers.

During the political turmoil leading to the Civil War, Pemberton's sympathies were entirely with the South. He was in Washington when hostilities began at Fort Sumter, South Carolina, in April, 1861. Having every wish to resign his Federal commission at once, he hesitated only because of the anguish he knew this would cause his kinsfolk in Philadelphia. Shortly his wife wrote him from Virginia, where she was staying with her own family: "My darling husband, why are you not with us? Why do you stay? Jeff Davis has a post ready for you."

During a week of painful suspense, Pemberton's mother wrote a relative:

His ideas of duty and honor are all the other way, and he is perfectly open and honorable in all he does.... We have done all we can. John firmly believes it would be the most honorable and right [course].

The tie broken, Pemberton went to Richmond. A native Southern officer who knew him says that he
offered his sword to the Confederacy without asking for rank. Certainly he must have been actuated by principle alone; for he had everything to gain by remaining on the Northern side.

Pemberton began his new career as a lieutenant colonel. That autumn, promoted to brigadier general, he was ordered to Charleston, South Carolina, to serve as second in command to General Robert E. Lee, then in charge of creating a defense system along the Southern coast from South Carolina to Florida. Three months later, Lee was called to Richmond, leaving Pemberton in top command. This was a responsible job, and Pemberton was handicapped both by Confederate suspicions occasioned by his Northern birth and by a somewhat austere presence.
  Nonetheless, when he was transferred to the war's Western theater in October, 1862, the Charleston Mercury *saw fit to say:*

His stay in South Carolina has been characterized by long months of arduous, incessant labor and devoted energy, and, in that time, although little known when he came here, he has established the reputation of an accomplished and thorough soldier. He has associated his destinies with us, lived with us, and served us faithfully. . . .
  General Pemberton . . . was not a "popular man." His habitual reserve and occasional brusqueness of manner forbid. Yet to those better acquainted with him and his labors, against prejudice and misconception he won greatly upon their confidence and esteem, and leaves many warm friends in South Carolina.
  His independence and directness are marked characteristics worthy of appreciation. . . . His energy of character, keenness of perception, quickness of thought, promptness of action and earnestness in preparation, with the professional knowledge and practical experience he possesses, cannot fail to render him an officer whose services will carry strength in the field wherever he may be assigned.

Pemberton's new command centered upon Vicksburg but embraced the entire Department of Mississippi and East Louisiana. No command in the Confederacy was more important, and many Southerners questioned President Davis's judgment in giving it to a man from the North. But a Vicksburg editor soon informed his readers:

In General Pemberton we have a man worthy of trust and confidence. Free from ostentation, an indefatigable and untiring worker, he has traversed the whole department and overlooked all our works of defense. . . . Where work is needed, he has done it at once. . . . His whole mind is absorbed in the great business before him.

It is said of him that he has no use for a man except to work him; and if he finds that he has about him one unfit for the performance of the duty expected of him he allows no false notions of courtesy to control his action, but drops him at once, and fills his place with someone who knows how and is willing to work. . . .

It is indeed strange how quickly General Pemberton has succeeded in inspiring the most implicit confidence. Brief as has been his command, he has brought order out of chaos, and if . . . it is possible to defend ourselves against the Yankees we believe he will do it.

Pemberton's adversary, General Grant, had known him since both were young men serving in the Mexican War. Grant relates:

I remember when an order was issued that none of the junior officers should be allowed horses during the marches. Mexico is not an easy country to march in. Young officers not accustomed to it soon got footsore. . . . They were found lagging behind. But the order was not revoked, yet a verbal permit was [given], and nearly all of them remounted. Pemberton alone said, no, he would walk, as the order was still extant not to ride—and he did walk, though suffering intensely the while.

This I thought of all the time he was in Vicksburg and I outside of it; and I knew he would hold on to the last.

As March, 1863, drew to a close, all of Grant's Bayou Expeditions were abandoned. Mrs. Livermore saw one of the last of the participating naval vessels make its return to the fleet at Milliken's Bend, a limping symbol of failure:

It had been navigating narrow, tortuous streams . . . through gigantic forests which overarched and interlaced, sweeping away smokestacks and scraping the deck clean of pilot house and every other standing fixture. Abrupt turns . . . had broken her bow and damaged her sides, while snags and fallen trees, and now and then getting aground, had injured the rudder and wheels.... Some of the men had been killed; several were badly wounded.

Grant's efforts against Vicksburg—and his career as well—were now at a crossroads. According to war correspondent Albert D. Richardson, of the New York Tribune:

The people of the East, knowing about as much of the geography of the region of Grant's meanderings as they did of Japan, were utterly bewildered by the fragmentary and mixed-up newspaper telegrams about Lake Providence, Moon Lake, Steele's Bayou, Williams' Cut-off, the Yazoo, the Yallabusha, the Tallahatchie.... They only knew that months dragged wearily by ... that the soldiers were reported dying from disease.... The country was heartsick for victory. Our General ... was ... in deep and growing disfavor. His canal and bayou projects were mercilessly ridiculed. The ever-convenient charges of drunkenness were revived.

Murat Halstead, editor of the Cincinnati Commercial, *who had been keeping a close watch on the Vicksburg situation through a field correspondent, wrote privately to Salmon P. Chase, a member of Lincoln's cabinet:*

General Grant, entrusted with our greatest army, is a jackass in the original package. He is a poor drunken imbecile.... About two weeks ago he was so miserably drunk for twenty-four hours that his staff kept him shut up in a state-room on the steamer where he makes his headquarters.... I know exactly what I am writing about.... Now, are our Western heroes to be sacrificed by the ten thousand by this poor devil? Grant will fail miserably, hopelessly, eternally.

Lincoln agonized as the complaints against Grant reached a new peak, but he soon said with quiet decision, "I think we'll try him a little longer."

Grant himself ignored the complaints. He had begun to spend more and more of his time sitting alone at his headquarters table, enveloped in the usual cigar smoke as he studied his maps, engaged in prolonged periods of frowning concentration, and scribbled a profusion of notes.

Relying entirely upon his own judgment, Grant was planning one of the greatest military maneuvers of all time.

2

TOUGH KNOTS FOR AN OLD SAILOR

*G*RANT'S PLAN *was the climax not only of his own association with the Vicksburg problem but of a struggle that had begun long before either he or John Pemberton had arrived in the area.*

Immediately after Lincoln's strategy conference of mid-November, 1861, preparations were made to move against the line of the Mississippi River both from the north and from the Gulf of Mexico, with Vicksburg the ultimate goal.

From the very beginning, of course, the Confederates were fully aware of the Union's intentions in the West. Upon learning that Washington's overall naval preparations included the building of river warships at a yard near Saint Louis, Missouri, a clerk in the Richmond war offices wrote in his diary:

If they get possession of the Mississippi River, it will be a sad day for the Confederacy. And what are we doing? We have many difficulties to contend against, and there is a deficiency in artisans and material. Nevertheless, the government is constructing . . . several . . . floating batteries in the West.

The Union's first important gains from the north were made in February, 1862, by Grant, then an obscure brigadier. Aided by a fleet under Flag Officer Andrew H. Foote, Grant captured two Confederate forts in north-western Tennessee: Fort Henry on the Tennessee River and Fort Donelson on the Cumberland.

Fort Henry was taken by Foote's gunboats alone, but severe land fighting developed before Donelson. In the end, when the garrison's commander, General Simon B. Buckner, dispatched a note to Grant in which he agreed to discuss terms, Grant wrote back:

No terms except an unconditional and immediate surrender can be accepted. I propose to move immediately upon your works.

David G. Farragut

Fort Donelson's fall opened the whole of western Tennessee to Federal occupation, and a delighted Lincoln promptly nominated "Unconditional Surrender" Grant for promotion to major general. The people of the North deemed it both fitting and auspicious that in addition to a "Father" Abraham they now had a "U. S." Grant. But Grant's new light was only seven weeks old when the Confederates dimmed it at Shiloh.

At the end of April, about ten weeks after the Donelson victory, the Union made another momentous conquest. Flag Officer David G. Farragut, operating from the Gulf with a salt-water fleet, battled his way past the forts at the mouth of the Mississippi and captured New Orleans.

This was to take its place in the war's annals as one of the Federal navy's greatest feats. Curiously, the man who performed it was not only a Southerner but a former resident of the very city he captured. He wrote his wife and son in the North:

It is a strange thought that I am here among my relatives, and yet not one has dared to say "I am happy to see you."

David Farragut was one of the navy's old-timers, his career having spanned more than half a century. An adoptive son of the famed Commodore David Porter, he became a midshipman at the age of nine and saw action in the War of 1812, being with Porter on the Essex during her remarkable cruise against the British whaling fleet in the Pacific. Along with his many other assignments through the years, Farragut took part in the campaign against the last of the West Indies pirates in the 1820s.

David D. Porter

Serving under Farragut at New Orleans was a true son of David Porter, forty-eight-year-old Commander David Dixon Porter, in charge of the fleet's mortar flotilla. Porter, being ambitious, envied his foster brother his high position, but was later to offer this tribute:

On the first sign of war Farragut, though a Southerner by birth and residence, had shown his loyalty in an outspoken manner. The Southern officers [of the naval center at Norfolk, Virginia] had used every argument to induce him to desert his flag, even going so far as to threaten to detain him by force.

His answer to them... [was]: "Mind what I tell you. You fellows will catch the devil before you get through with this business."

Having thus expressed himself in a manner not to be misunderstood, he left Norfolk with his family and took a house on the Hudson River, whence he reported to the Navy Department as ready for duty....

At the time of his appointment to the command of the New Orleans expedition, he was over sixty years of age; but he was as active as a man of fifty, with an unimpaired constitution and a mind as bright as ever.

When the news of Farragut's victory reached Vicksburg by telegraph, the city's 5,000 residents were stunned. They had been assured that New

Orleans was impregnable. With the Union threat from the north not immediate enough to be a real worry, Vicksburg hadn't been fortified. Now, suddenly, there was an unexpected threat from the south. The Federals were 200 miles distant by land and 400 by way of the winding river.

Some of the families promptly tumbled their possessions into horse-drawn vehicles and fled to the country. But even as the exodus was taking place, Vicksburg's consternation gave way to a conviction. According to sternly handsome Brigadier General Martin L. Smith, who took charge of defense preparations on May 12:

The citizens of the town ... made up their minds that its possession ought to be maintained [by the army], even though total demolition should be the result. This determination was enthusiastically concurred in by persons of all ages and both sexes, and borne to my ears from every quarter.

Since the anticipated danger was Farragut's warships, General Smith, who had a reputation for being a cool and efficient leader in times of emergency, turned at once to the emplacement of shore batteries. Troops were assembling, the first arrivals being Louisianans who had evacuated New Orleans, and tent camps began springing up in the city's environs.

Flag Officer Farragut—soon to become the Union's first rear admiral—viewed the task of proceeding against Vicksburg with reluctance. In the first place, he disliked taking his deep-draft ocean vessels among the Mississippi's mudbanks. A second consideration is explained by Colonel Wickham Hoffman, a staff officer with the fleet's land forces:

Martin L. Smith

Farragut was anxious, after the capture of New Orleans, to proceed at once against Mobile [on the Gulf Coast to the East]. I heard him say that, in the panic excited by the capture of New Orleans, Mobile would fall an easy prey. The Government, however . . . was anxious to open the Mississippi. Farragut was ordered against Vicksburg.

In Farragut's words:

Some time was consumed in trying to procure pilots. I mean, by a pilot, one who has a knowledge of the river, for we were totally ignorant.

Soon a division of the fleet under Commander S. Phillips Lee was steaming northward, with some of the vessels not yet fully restored after being damaged in the fight for New Orleans. Farragut himself was preparing to follow with another division. The advance force included two transports carrying 1,500 army men, among them Colonel Hoffman, who found the trip a "delightful excursion."

The plantations along the banks were in the highest state of cultivation; the young cane, a few inches above the ground, of the most lovely green. Indeed, I know no more beautiful green than that of the young sugar cane.

Our flag had not been seen in these parts for over a year [i.e., since the war's beginning, when the Confederates had furled it in favor of their own banner], and the joy of the Negroes when they had an opportunity to exhibit it without fear of their overseers was quite touching.

The river was very high, and as we floated along we were far above the level of the plantations, and looked down upon the Negroes at work, and into the open windows of the houses. The effect of this to one unused to it—the water above the land—was very striking. [The river was held to its course by strong, wide, high-piled levees.]

Natchez, a town beautifully situated on a high bluff, was gay with the inhabitants who had turned out to see us. The ladies, with their silk dresses and bright parasols, and the Negro women, with their gaudy colors, orange especially, which they affect so much, and which, by the way, can be seen at a greater distance than any other color I know of.

One often hears of "setting a river on fire," metaphorically speaking. I have seen it done literally. The Confederate authorities had issued orders to burn the cotton along the banks to prevent its falling into our hands. But as the patriotism of the owners naturally enough needed stimulating, vigilance committees were organized, generally of those planters whose cotton was safe at a distance.

These men preceded us as we ascended the river, and burned their neighbors' cotton with relentless patriotism. The burning material was thrown into the stream, and floated on the surface a long time before it was extinguished. At night it was a very beautiful sight to see the apparently flaming water. We had to exercise some care to steer clear of the burning masses.

According to Charles W. Hassler, a staff officer on one of the gunboats, the expedition approached Vicksburg on Sunday morning, May 18. "The quiet was intense, the atmosphere clear."

The sailors and soldiers crowded the rails of their vessels for a view of the objective, with many of the officers using glasses. It was noted that the houses and other buildings began at the waterfront and climbed the hills, the crests being crowned, as one observer put it, "with elegant private residences." The columned and cupolaed courthouse stood, in all its majesty, above everything else.

Shortly after noon, under a sun that bore brightly on the river's brown surface, Commander Lee put a small boat over the side of his flagship. The oarsmen started pulling toward Vicksburg's wharves, the boat's delegation of officers carrying a white flag and a written demand from Lee that the city surrender at once to Flag Officer Farragut and Major General Benjamin F. Butler, in charge of the occupation forces at New Orleans.

By this time the Confederates under General Martin Smith had armed the city with six or seven artillery batteries. A shot boomed as a warning for the boat to stop. The sound reverberated among the hills, and the heavy missile plunked into the water. A steamer now pushed out from one of the wharves to meet the boat and obtain its message.

Explains General Smith:

The inhabitants had been advised to leave the city when the smoke of the ascending gunboats was first seen, under the impression that the enemy would open fire immediately upon arrival, hence the demand for surrender found the city sparsely populated and somewhat prepared for an attack.

Late that afternoon the Federal demand was answered by notes from three different Confederate authorities.

Wrote General Smith:
Having been ordered to hold these defenses, it is my intention to do so as long as in my power.

Added the city's mayor, Lazarus Lindsay:
Neither the municipal authorities nor the citizens will ever consent to a surrender of the city.

The strongest reply was written by Colonel James L. Autry, the city's military governor:
Mississippians don't know, and refuse to learn, how to surrender to an enemy. If Commodore Farragut or . . . General Butler can teach them, let them come and try.

Four days later, Commander Lee's gunboats began sending their heavy missiles toward Vicksburg's defenses. Little damage was done, but the steady booming and the tremblings of the earth unnerved some of the citizens who had remained in their homes. The result was a new exodus to the country.

Many of Vicksburg's houses now stood with their shutters closed and their doors locked, with some of the doors having been boarded over. These quiet dwellings seemed curiously out of place amid the flowers that bloomed in their well-tended gardens.

Even as the civilian population diminished, military reinforcements filtered in from points to the south and the east. Additional guns were emplaced, and infantry units were deployed against the possibility of a land attack.

The division of the Federal fleet containing David Farragut's flagship joined Lee's division a day or two after Lee began his bombardment. Assuming command of the combined force, Farragut found himself in a quandary. Vicksburg could not be taken by bombardment alone, and Brigadier General Thomas Williams, in charge of the fleet's infantry detachment, had no plan to offer.

According to the army's Colonel Hoffman:
We found no dry place for the soles of our feet. . . . The whole Louisiana side of the river [opposite the city] was flooded. It would have been madness to land on the Vicksburg side with two regiments only. Nothing could be done.

Leaving six vessels lying just below Vicksburg with orders to shell likely targets at discretion, Farragut took the rest of the fleet back down the river.

One of the officers left behind was Charles Hassler, who says that he and others made daily studies of the city with their glasses:

We could see earthworks going up, and steamer after steamer coming down from above the landing, and there unloading men and material.

Farragut, who had launched the expedition against Vicksburg with little faith in its success, was unhappy with the Washington officials who had ordered it. The failure detracted from the reputation he had gained by capturing New Orleans.

"I find the more you do," he complained in a letter to his wife and son, "the more is expected of you."

The old sailor's troubles were only beginning. On his return to New Orleans he found new orders from Washington awaiting him. Their tones were impatient. He was to muster all the force he could and "clear the river," not only as far as Vicksburg but beyond to Memphis, making contact with a Union fleet that was working its way down the river from the north.

"Now they expect impossibilities of me," Farragut wrote home. But he prepared a new expedition at once.

"Early in June," relates Colonel Hoffman,

we started again for Vicksburg.... It was a martial and beautiful sight to see the long line of gunboats and transports following each other in Indian file at regular intervals. Navy and army boats combined, we numbered about twenty sails—if I may apply that word to steamers.

On our way up, the flagship, the famous *Hartford,* was nearly lost. She grounded on a bank in the middle of the river.... The navy worked hard all the afternoon to release her, but in vain. The hawsers [i.e., towropes] parted like pack-thread.

I was on board [during the night] when a grizzled quartermaster, the very type of an old man-of-warsman, came up to the commodore [Farragut] on the quarterdeck, and, pulling his forelock, reported that there was a six[teen]-inch hawser in the hold. Farragut ordered it up....

Two of our army transports, the most powerful, were lashed together, the hawser passed round them, and slackened. They then started with a jerk. The *Hartford* set her machinery in motion, the gunboat lashed alongside started hers, and the old ship came off.

This success wasn't achieved until well after daylight. Says Farragut:

I never left the deck, except to get a drink of tea, until she was off.... It is a sad thing to think of leaving your ship on a mudbank five hundred miles from the natural element of a sailor.

Also working his way up the river at this time, with sixteen mortar schooners and a number of armed steamers, was Farragut's foster brother, Commander David Porter.

Porter, a Pennsylvanian by birth, was one of the war's cavaliers. His gloom over the South's secession was dispelled by the excitement that marked the opening of hostilities. Though not indifferent to the war's tragedy, he revelled in its challenges, its drama, its humor. Aware that he was helping to create some unforgettable history, he made copious notes, which he later expanded into a lively narrative.

The exuberant Porter was surpassed by few of the war's chroniclers in capturing the popular spirit. When it came to depicting the South's blacks, however, he was altogether a product of his own times, preferring, like the majority of white writers, to portray the stereotype, the black of broad dialect and of easygoing and engagingly amusing ways. Porter's stereotypes, however, have an added dimension: they are shrewd and perceptive.

Porter relates:

While ascending the Mississippi ... I had a good opportunity of witnessing the disposition of the people [i.e., the whites] along the river. Notwithstanding our desire to be friends with them, they would have nothing to do with us—they were mad with the secession fever.

Porter goes on to say that one evening he moored his flotilla along the levee that bounded a great plantation:

When I arrived, the levee was all lighted up by the bonfires which the Negroes had kindled, which brought out in relief the dusky forms of four or five hundred of the colored population, together with the mansion of the owner of the estate, and the cabins of the Negroes....

As soon as the vessels were secured to the bank, we landed about a hundred armed sailors and marched them to the rear of the houses as a precaution against an attack by guerrillas or light artillery....

I sent an officer at once to inform the lady of the mansion—for I was told there were only ladies there—that she need be under no apprehensions, as these were only sentries thrown out to keep the sailors from wandering about her place.

In the meantime the Negroes were so jubilant and boisterous that they could not restrain themselves; they danced about like mad, and scattered the fire so that I began to fear the buildings would be ignited from the flying sparks; so I went on shore to have a talk with them.

All the Negroes rushed up to me.... Some wanted to shake hands, some to sell chickens.... Some women wanted to know if I had "any clo' fo' wash...." The pickaninnies were turning somersaults almost into the fire.

"Look here," I exclaimed, "this won't do. You are disturbing the ladies at the house with your noise, and we can't sleep on board the vessels...."

"Oh, de ladies don't mine de noise, Massa Cappen; dis is our night (Saturday), when de work all done," said a dozen voices. "An' we want to ax you, sah, if you won't go coon huntin'?"

"No, I thank you," said I. "But I'll tell you what I would like. Bring your banjos, and sing me a plantation song."

No sooner said than done; three or four banjos, together with bones and other accompaniments, were produced. I knew if I could get the party to singing they would quiet down in a short time....

I sent for the ship's bugler, and told him to stand by to play "Home, Sweet Home" when I gave the order, the Negroes all this time keeping up a great chattering, and seeming unable to agree upon a programme, until a venerable darky, in a voice of authority, sang out, "Look hyar, you niggers! Don' make fools of yerse'fs, an' make dese gemplemens tink yer got no more manners 'an a groun' hog!" At which speech the Negroes all yelled, "Bully fer you, Uncle Moses!"

At that moment the bugler struck up "Home, Sweet Home," and you might have heard a pin drop. The ... darkies ... sat on the ground, eyes ... wide open, while old Moses held up his finger, as if to enforce silence.

The bugler played until he was tired, when an unusually soft "Ah!" came from the crowd....

"Now, bucks," exclaimed Uncle Moses, "dat's wot I calls music.

Better you all shut up shop and put yer ole banjos on de fire dar. Yer can't come nothin' like dat. . . ."

"Uncle Moses," said I, "don't discourage the boys. That bugle music is a signal for all the sailors to go to bed and get some rest, for they must work hard tomorrow. They want to hear you sing 'Mary Blane,' and after that you must all go home and keep quiet."

. . . A hundred voices, men and women, now joined in and sang the Negro melody in glorious fashion. . . .

After the Negroes had finished . . . I said to Uncle Moses, "I have heard music in the best opera houses in the world, but I never heard anything better than that."

"Fo' de Lawd, you done spoil dem niggers, Massa Cappen!" said old Moses. "Dey was wain enuff befo'. . . ."

"Moses," said I, "you seem to have great control over these people. Are you going to lead them out of captivity as your namesake of the Bible led the Israelites out of bondage?"

"Well, Massa Cappen," replied the old Negro, "dese ere niggers . . . talks about fightin' for de Unyum an' Massa Abe Linkum, an' dey knows as much 'bout fightin' as a mule knows 'bout playin' de banjo. . . . You know, sar, what one ob de pocks say . . .: Better bear wid a ole coat . . . full ob holes dan go roun' in your shirtsleebes in wintertime lookin' for a new one. . . ."

"Uncle Moses," said I, "you are wise beyond your generation. But tell me something about your mistress."

"Well, sar," said Moses, "she is a uncommon agreeable pusson, though sometimes a leetle aggravatin'. She likes to hab her own way, an' as I hab charge ob all dese bucks, I likes to hab mine; so occasionally we has disputes. . . . Yesterday missus was real aggravatin'. *She* say dar was a hole in de fence, an' *I* say dar was a hole in de fence, an' we 'sputed about it mor'n a hour."

"Why, Uncle Moses," said I, "that was a silly thing to dispute about."

"P'r'aps so, Massa Cappen; but it ain't no more silly dan what you gemplemens ob de Norf an' gemplemens ob de Souf been a doin'. De *Souf* say dar was a hole in de fence, an' de *Norf* say dar was a hole in de fence, an' after 'sputin' about it a long time, now dey go to shootin' about it."

"Uncle Moses," said I, "you don't understand it. We are disputing about the great principles of universal liberty."

"Yes," said the philosopher, "I knows dat. I hear 'em talkin' a great deal about de niggers will have suffrins [i.e., suffrage] at de poles fo' long, but I seen enough nigger suffrins, an' don't want to see no more of 'em."

"Why, Uncle Moses, you talk doubtfully. . . ."

"Yes, I know, Massa Cappen; dey calls me doubtin' Moses, an' I hab my own 'pinions. If I had my way I'd be on de Canada side. De colored man is safe dar, an' no mistake. As to de equality ob de races I hear 'em talk about, why, some ob our bucks run away an' 'listed board a gun-boat, an' spected to be treated just like white men. Dey put dose bucks to shubbel coal an' workin' before a hot fire, an' didn't eben gib um good hog an' hominy."

"Oh," said I, "that's only a beginning. They'll do better by and by."

"An' in de meantime," said Moses, "dey is to be purified wid fire an' water. Some ob dem fellers from Massa Linkum's gun-boats tells de bucks if dey sabe de Unyum dey'll come out some day in Congress. Yes, I knows, but dey'll be brushin' de white man's coats de same as dey been doin' all dere lives. . . ."

. . . We now walked toward the house. Uncle Moses stepped to the door and announced me. I heard a pleasant voice say, "Ask the gentleman in, Moses," and I entered.

Before me was a stately lady of perhaps forty years of age, still handsome, with large black eyes and dark hair. I excused myself for intruding upon her so late in the evening. . . .

"You are excusable, sir . . . and I am glad you have come, that I might thank you for the precautions you have taken to prevent marauding [by the sailors]. My servants have not been so orderly . . . for a long time. . . . Moses is seventy years old, and is not of much use now in helping govern the Negroes, and he is forever disputing with me about trifles."

At that moment a door opened, and a youth of about nineteen rushed into the room in a great state of excitement.

"Mother!" he exclaimed, "I am too late; they have surrounded the house. . . ."

Just then he caught sight of me, and stood at bay. He was a handsome fellow, with a strong likeness to his mother, and had on a gray suit [i.e., a Confederate uniform], which was nearly concealed by a linen duster.

"What do you want here, sir?" said the youth defiantly. "Why intrude upon unprotected women?"

... "George! George!" exclaimed his mother. "This gentleman has done nothing that we can possibly find fault with.... Excuse me, sir, but he is my only son."

"Who is perfectly safe with me, madam, for I assure you I have not the least idea of molesting him."

"Then let me pass through your lines," said the young man...."I must go or be dishonored."

Just then a young girl entered the room. She looked like a panther about to spring.

"They are not going to take George, mother! What does this mean?"

... There was no need to ask if these young people were brother and sister, their likeness to each other was so striking....

"There is no occasion for alarm, young lady," I said. "I shall not trouble myself to capture unarmed persons, even although they may choose to wear a uniform which is not the most agreeable to Northern eyes."

... I raised the window and signaled to the patrol. "Let this gentleman pass with his horse. —Good-night, sir, and a pleasant journey to you."

The young man took leave of his mother and sister, bowed to me, and in a few minutes his horse's hoofs were heard as he galloped down the road. The mother thanked me for permitting her son to depart.

"I could have done you a greater favor by sending him north as a prisoner," I replied. "It might have saved his life...."

I bade the ladies good-night, hoping I had at least planted one seed toward reconciliation.

Next morning Moses and his "bucks" were at the levee to see us off.

"Keep your bucks in order, Moses," I said.... "And don't dispute with your mistress any more...."

"Well, sar," he replied, "we done had a 'spute already dis mornin'. *I* said you was a Unyum ossifer, an' *she* say you was a Unyum ossifer, an' we 'spute about it ober a hour. God bless you, Massa Cappen, an' see dat dey don' gib us po' niggers any more suffrins at de poles."

We were not molested in our progress up the river, and in due time reached Vicksburg.

It was now latter June, 1862. On the twenty-sixth, David Farragut wrote his wife and son:

Here we are once more in front of Vicksburg [actually, a short distance below], by a peremptory order of the Department and the President of the United States "to clear the river through." With God's assistance, I intend to try it as soon as the mortars are ready.... The work is rough.... It must be done in the daytime, as the river is too difficult to navigate by night.... I think more should have been left to my discretion; but I hope for the best.

According to a field correspondent for Harper's Weekly:

Above and below Vicksburg the hills are crowned with the batteries that the rebels have erected to dispute our advance, the most of them being placed at the lower end of the town.... One tier of batteries is placed near the top of the bluff, and another about halfway from the summit to the water. A single row of water batteries ... is located near the brink of the river.... The batteries above the town are mainly placed on the upper hills, though one ... is placed almost at the very water's edge, in position to sweep the river above and below.

Samuel H. Lockett

Farragut could plan nothing more than to run by the batteries and proceed to his meeting with the fleet coming down the river from the north. No land attack on Vicksburg was feasible, since his army support was still sadly inadequate, the original 1,500 men having been joined by only 1,500 more. Confederate strength was approaching 10,000.

The number of civilians in Vicksburg had risen again, many of those who had fled earlier having returned. Some of the abandoned houses had been reopened, and here and there, in the city's hillsides, the first caves had begun to appear.

Farragut's preliminary bombardment, begun during the afternoon of June 26, got under way in earnest on the twenty-seventh. Particularly unnerving to the Confederates were David Porter's mortars.

Says Samuel H. Lockett, a sensitive-featured, heavily mustached young major who was serving as chief engineer of Vicksburg's defenses:

I measured one of the holes made by the mortar shells in hard, compact clay, and found it seventeen feet deep. It was a difficult matter to make bomb-proofs against such destructive engines.

A few shots were fired from our batteries in answer to the challenge of the mortar boats, but these shots were harmless, and were soon discontinued. The Federal bombardment was likewise nearly harmless. . . . Vertical fire is never very destructive of life. Yet the howling and bursting shells had a very demoralizing effect on those not accustomed to them.

One of my engineer officers, a Frenchman, a gallant officer who had distinguished himself in several severe engagements [earlier in the war], was almost unmanned whenever one passed anywhere near him. When joked about it, he was not ashamed to confess: "I no like ze bomb; I cannot fight him back!"

Confederate General Martin Smith takes up:

At daylight on the 28th the enemy recommenced with the same fury, and soon the gunboats were moving rapdily up in front of the city. . . . The mortars [which covered Farragut's advance from stationary positions below the city] filled the air with shells, and the sloops of war and gunboats [ten in all attempting the passage] delivered broadsides of shot, shell, or grape, according to their distance.

Our batteries opened as soon as they were within range, and for the first time in full force. The roar of the cannon was now continuous and deafening; loud explosions shook the city to its foundations; shot and shell went hissing and tearing through trees and walls, scattering fragments far and wide in their terrific flight.

Men, women and children rushed into the streets, and amid the crash of falling houses commenced their hasty flight to the country for safety.

Killed at this time was a Mrs. Gamble, who was struck in the side by a piece of shrapnel. General Smith speaks of her as deserving "more than a passing notice."

Burning with patriotism, she inspired all around her with the noble spirit of resistance to oppression, and confidence in the success of our cause. Ever present in the hospitals, ministering to the sick and wounded soldiers, she was among the last of her sex to leave the devoted city.... Though but the type of a class of which our Southern land can boast, she is a martyr to the cause she loved.

Mrs. Gamble was the only civilian slain in the fight. Casualties among the combatants themselves remained low, though a few were ghastly enough. David Porter says that serious hits were scored on two of his armed steamers, which had moved upstream from the mortar flotilla to get closer to Vicksburg's lower batteries:

The *Jackson* ... was struck badly with rifle shells, one of which exploded in her wheel-house, disabling the man at the wheel by cutting off his leg.... A 7-inch shot passed in on the *Clifton*'s port bow, going through her boiler. By this catastrophe, six of the men in and about the magazine were scalded to death, and others were scalded severely. The steam drove eight or ten men overboard, one of whom was drowned.

Relates a young engineer (his name was to survive merely as "Albert") who made the passage of Vicksburg aboard Farragut's flagship:

We were so close to the batteries that the men could be seen working the guns and waving their hats in defiance. Most of their shots were too high to disable us, but completely tore our rigging to pieces....

When our fire was directed on any particular battery, the rebels would desert their guns until our attention was directed to others, when they would return and open on us again.

Farragut tells a personal story:

I was in my favorite stand, the mizzen rigging, when all at once the captain of the gun on the poop-deck wished to fire at a battery which would require him to point his gun near me, and requested me to get down, which I did, to avoid the concussion. I was only a moment in doing so when the whole mizzen rigging was cut away just above my head.... I escaped with only a touch on the head, which did not break the skin.... This same shot cut the halyards that hoisted my flag, which dropped to half-mast without being perceived by us. This circumstance caused the other vessels to think that I was killed.

Again in Albert's words:

After being under fire for about two hours in front of the city, and finding that we could not bring our guns to bear any longer, we started ahead fast, the shot still dropping around us, and soon came to anchor out of range of their guns.

Seven of Farragut's vessels completed the passage, three having dropped back, through a misunderstanding of their orders, and rejoined Porter's mortar flotilla.

As it turned out, Farragut did not have to continue up the river to Memphis. The Union fleet coming down the river, with which he had been ordered to make contact, had captured Memphis and was making its way to Vicksburg. Farragut met the advance vessels as he completed his run past the batteries.

Flag Officer Charles H. Davis, commander of the northern fleet, arrived with the main division on July 1. Whereas all Farragut's vessels were wooden ones, some of Davis's were sheathed with iron.

Said Farragut in a letter to his wife and son:

The ironclads are curious-looking things to us salt-water gentlemen; but no doubt they are better calculated for this river than our ships. They draw from six to eight feet of water; we from ten to sixteen. They look like great turtles.

Farragut soon joined the distinguished-looking Charles Davis on his flagship, the Benton, *for a reconnaissance toward Vicksburg. The old salt-water sailor was belowdecks when a heavy shot from one of the enemy's guns crashed through a weak spot in the vessel's iron sheathing and killed a man standing near him.*

Gazing for a moment at the shattered body, Farragut said, "Everybody to his taste. I am going on deck. I feel safer outside." And he continued in this exposed position until the reconnaissance ended.

Farragut and Davis, their fleets merged above Vicksburg, decided there wasn't much they could do except shell the enemy, which they did, with David Porter adding occasional mortar shells from below.

Porter explains:

There was an area of twenty-eight square miles within which the Federals might throw all the shot and shells they pleased. The Confederates did not mind it much, even when the shots fell in the city.

Says Confederate officer Charles E. Hooker:

Even the citizens who remained became accustomed to the steady dropping of shells, and went about their daily business. Women and children who remained sheltered in caves would come out and divert themselves by watching the fiery instruments of destruction, taking refuge again when the shots would concentrate in their neighborhood.

By this time, according to David Porter,

The whole power of the Confederacy had been set to work to save this Gibraltar of the Mississippi. The railroads poured in troops and guns without stint.

"I am satisfied," Farragut wrote Washington, "it is not possible to take Vicksburg without an army of 12,000 or 15,000 men." This estimate was a modest one. But no spare troops at all were available in the war's Western theater at this time.

Since June 27, the 3,000 army men with Farragut's expedition had been encamped on the peninsula opposite the city. They had begun the canal project at the base of the peninsula that was to be continued by Grant's troops six months later.

Relates the army's Colonel Hoffman:

The trees were cut down in a straight line.... Troops were sent to the different plantations both up and down the river, and the Negroes pressed into the service [as pick-and-shovel men].

It was curious to observe the difference of opinion among the old river captains as to the feasibility of our plan. Some were sure that the river would run through the cut; others swore that it would not....

Black laborers beginning work on canal at base of De Soto peninsula

The matter was soon settled by the river itself; for it suddenly rose one night, filled up our ditch, undermined the banks, and in a few hours destroyed our labor of days.

This same period found David Porter, who continued to hold his mortar flotilla in its position below the city, apprehensive that the Confederates would attack him with infantry troops. The mortar schooners and their support steamers were moored in a line that stretched along the river's eastern bank. Porter recounts:

I was one day on shore looking at the defenses against a land attack when a Negro emerged from the woods. . . . He was . . . clad in a good suit of clothes of a scholastic cut. . . . When I asked him what he was doing, he answered, "I'm . . . makin' my escape to the lan' ob freedom. My name is Brutus Munroe. I'm a pastor, sar."

. . . "Well, now, tell me," said I to the preacher, "how many troops have the Confederates in Vicksburg?"

" 'Bout a hunder tousand, sar," he answered promptly. . . .

I saw that . . . it wouldn't do to depend on Brutus's statements.

"Well," said I, "you say you are a Union man?"

"Yes, sar, I prays fo' de President an all oders in autority ebery Sunday befo' my people."

"But which President do you pray for?"

"I prays for 'em bof, sar—Massa Linkum an' Massa Davis—for dey bof stans in need ob prayer."

"But, Brutus," said I, "what side are you on?"

"Well, sar," he answered, "I am just now on de Lawd's side. . . ."

. . . All the time Mr. Munroe was talking, his eyes were wandering in every direction. At length I said to him, "How do you like the looks of things? Do you think you can remember it all?"

The preacher started. . . . "Ise got a werry bad mem'ry, sar. I see you is busy, an' I mought as well be goin'," and he started off.

"Stop!" said I. "You must stay and dine with me."

"No, tank you, sar," said Brutus. "I mus' go to Warrenton [located on the river below Vicksburg], whar I hole a convention wid a pastor ob anodder diocese. I'll call anodder time. . . ."

I beckoned . . . two patrolmen. . . .

"In God's name, sar," exclaimed Brutus . . . "wha' yer gwine ter do ter me?"

"Nothing except shoot you as a spy, Mr. Brutus."

I directed that the preacher should be . . . confined on the berth-deck of one of the schooners. . . . It was not often that the colored men acted as spies, but this was evidently an instance of it.

One of the officers devised a scheme to draw the rascal out. He selected the most intelligent Negro from among our contrabands [a contraband being a slave who had escaped to, or had been brought within, the Union lines] and, after instructing him in the part he was to play, had him conveyed on board the schooner where Brutus was, and tumbled down by his side.

The newcomer began to weep and throw himself about, as if in great agony of mind, until the preacher sternly remarked to him, "Don't yer make a fool ob youse'f. . . ."

. . . "But, mister, dey done gwine ter shoot me tomorrow. . . ."

"Hush!" said Brutus. . . . "Ef dey don't shoot us befo' fo' o'clock dis arternoon, dey'll nebber hab anodder chance!"

"Wot yer mean?" said the other. . . . But Brutus sat silent, not deigning to be more explicit.

At length the colored detective was taken violently ill, and, upon being carried on deck, related all that had passed between him and the preacher. It was not much, but I gathered that we were to be attacked about four o'clock.

It was about four-thirty when a Confederate attack force moved suddenly against Porter's pickets, which were stationed in the woods about a hundred yards from the bank where the flotilla was moored. The pickets, says Porter,

immediately came in to report, the enemy firing on them as they retreated. In a moment all the guns of the mortar vessels and the flotilla steamers opened on the woods with grape, shrapnel, canister, shells, and round shot, the mortars throwing in bombs with small charges. . . .

After the woods were well shelled, the pickets went in and captured three rebel soldiers who were helplessly stuck in the mud . . . and cried out lustily that they had surrendered. They were brought in. . . . These men stated that two regiments, one from Tennessee, the other from Mississippi . . . attempted to pass through the middle of the wood and enfilade us, but got helplessly stuck in the middle of the swamp. . . .

While in this condition, our guns commenced shelling the woods, and the two regiments were panic-stricken. They threw away their knapsacks, cartridge boxes, and everything that would impede their progress. In going over the ground afterwards, our men found evidences of a general stampede throughout the woods. Amongst other things, they picked up from the mud the heavy boots of a general officer, with silver spurs on. There was evidence in the marks that the enemy had been completely bogged or sunk in the mud. . . .

Not wishing to have any mishaps, I landed five howitzers, threw up works, posted fifty marines as pickets, and had a large bell slung up in the woods with lines leading to it from different points so that the pickets might give immediate alarm. . . .

On the 2d of July [two days later] the enemy made another attack on our pickets and drove them in, wounding two of them, and succeeded in getting so close as to fire on our decks; but they soon met with the fire of [the howitzers], which I had placed near the edge of the woods. . . . Five dead bodies [were] found, and evidences of some wounded, from the muskets and other arms thrown away . . . in the retreat.

David Porter's participation in Farragut's expedition was now ending. He had received orders from Washington to withdraw twelve of his mortar schooners down the Mississippi and take them to the Virginia coast for service in that theater of the war.

Before I left Vicksburg [Porter discloses] I sought a final interview with Pastor Brutus Munroe.... A week's close confinement had told on Mr. Munroe, and he did not look so sleek by a good deal.

"Well, sir," said I, "what have you got to say for yourself? Don't you think you deserve hanging as the biggest rascal in the country?"

"Well, sar," said Brutus, "a soff answer turneff 'way raff.... 'Pearances is agin me, sar, but I is innocent, 'deed I is."

"What do you say, then," I inquired, "about going north in this vessel and serving under the Union flag?"

Brutus scratched his head. "But who's gwine to took care ob my flock wen dar pastor done gone to de Norf? Dey'll all go straight to de debbel, sar. Dey forgits in a week all dat I'm a month a teachin' 'em."

"Well, then, Brutus," said I, "go and sin no more, and try to keep your neck out of the halter."

So I dismissed the preacher, who disappeared in the direction of Warrenton, and I never saw him again.

3

THE SAGA OF THE *ARKANSAS*

*T*HE UNION *fleets under David Farragut and Charles Davis remained together above Vicksburg for two weeks, their intermittent shelling of the city's defenses accomplishing next to nothing, and the return fire being equally ineffective. Then the situation changed dramatically, with the Confederates taking the initiative, their means of attack being a single ironclad ram, the* Arkansas.

For the past two months this vessel had been in the process of construction up the Yazoo River, which emptied into the Mississippi about ten miles above Vicksburg. The man chosen to finish the job (about the time David Farragut's first expedition made its appearance below the city) was an uncommonly energetic and resourceful lieutenant in the Confederate naval service, Isaac N. Brown, formerly of the United States Navy. Brown relates:

On the 28th of May, 1862, I received at Vicksburg a telegraphic order from the Navy Department at Richmond to "pro-

Isaac N. Brown

ceed to Greenwood, Mississippi, and assume command of the Confederate gunboat *Arkansas,* and finish and equip that vessel without regard to expenditure of men or money."

... Greenwood is at the head of the Yazoo River [some 200 miles by water from Vicksburg].... It being the season of overflow, I found my new command four miles from dry land. Her condition was not encouraging. The vessel was a mere hull, without armor; the engines were apart; guns without carriages were lying about the deck; a portion of the railroad iron intended as armor was at the bottom of the river [the barge that held these salvaged rails having sunk], and the other and far greater part was to be sought for in the interior of the country.

Taking a day to fish up the sunken iron, I had the *Arkansas* towed to Yazoo City [down the Yazoo in the direction of Vicksburg], where the hills reach the river. Here, though we were within fifty miles of the Union fleets, there was the possibility of equipment.

Within a very short time after reaching Yazoo City we had two hundred men, chiefly from the nearest detachment of the army, at work on the deck's shield and hull, while fourteen blacksmith

Building the *Arkansas*

forges were drawn from the neighboring plantations and placed on the bank to hasten the iron work. Extemporized drilling machines on the steamer *Capitol* [which lay alongside the *Arkansas*] worked day and night fitting the railway iron for the bolts which were to fasten it as armor. This iron was brought from many points to the nearest railroad station and thence twenty-five miles by wagons.

The trees were yet growing from which the gun carriages had to be made—the most difficult work of all, as such vehicles had never been built in Mississippi. I made a contract with two gentlemen of Jackson . . . for the full number of ten. . . .

This finishing, armoring, arming, and equipment of the *Arkansas* within five weeks' working time under the hot summer sun . . . [with] but six hours' steaming between us and the Federal fleets, whose guns were within hearing, was perhaps not inferior . . . to the renowned effort of Oliver Hazard Perry [during the War of 1812] in cutting a fine ship from the forest in ninety days.

We were not a day too soon, for the now rapid fall of the river rendered it necessary for us to assume the offensive without waiting for the apparatus to bend the railway iron to the curve of our quarter and stern [i.e., around the vessel's rear], and to the angles of the pilot house [located just forward of the smokestack, which rose from the vessel's center]. Though there was little thought of showing the former, the weakest part, to the enemy, we tacked boiler-plate iron over it for appearance' sake, and very imperfectly covered the pilot house shield with a double thickness of one-inch bar iron.

Our engines' twin screws, one under each quarter, worked up to eight miles an hour in still water, which promised about half that speed when turned against the current of the main river. We had at first some trust in these, not having discovered the way they soon showed of stopping on the center at wrong times and places; and as they never both stopped of themselves at the same time, the effect was, when one did so, to turn the vessel round, despite the rudder. . . .

The battery was respectable . . . ten guns in all, which . . . could be relied on for good work if we could find the men to load and fire. We obtained over 100 good men from the naval vessels lately on the Mississippi [i.e., those that had retreated southward from Memphis ahead of the Union fleet under Charles Davis], and about 60 Missourians from the command of General Jeff Thompson....

On the 12th of July we sent our mechanics ashore... and dropped below Satartia Bar, within five hours of the Mississippi. I now gave the executive officer a day to organize and exercise his men....

On Monday A.M., July 14, 1862, we started from Satartia. Fifteen miles below... we found that the steam from our imperfect engines and boiler had penetrated our forward magazine and wet our powder so as to render it unfit for use. We were just opposite the site of an old sawmill, where the opening in the forest, dense everywhere else, admitted the sun's rays. The day was clear and very hot.

We made fast to the bank... landed our wet powder... spread tarpaulins over the old sawdust and our powder over these. By constant shaking and turning we got it back to the point of ignition before the sun sank below the trees, when, gathering it up, we crowded all that we could of it into the after magazine, and resumed our way.

Up to this time Union commanders Farragut and Davis, still together just above Vicksburg, were unaware that the Arkansas *was approaching. They knew of her existence up the Yazoo but believed she would stay there rather than expose herself to their merged power.*

According to Albert, the young engineer on Farragut's flagship, the Hartford:

On the night of the fourteenth... two deserters from Vicksburg came aboard and stated that the rebel ram... meditated an attack on the fleet either that night or the following morning. We had heard much of this vessel, and, in order to be on the safe side, the steamers *Carondelet* and *Tyler* [and the *Queen of the West*, an unarmed steamer fitted out as a ram], of Davis's fleet, were despatched up the Yazoo.

Meanwhile, the Arkansas *had made a rest stop about fifteen miles from the junction of the Yazoo with the Mississippi. Again in the words of the vessel's builder and commander, Isaac Brown:*

We... rested till 3 A.M., when we got up anchor.... Before it was light we [accidentally] ran ashore and lost an hour in getting again afloat.

By this time the sun was rising. The three Union vessels were a few miles down the river, moving up at full steam. Their commander was Henry Walke, captain of the Carondelet. *This vessel was an ironclad, though of inferior sheathing. The* Tyler *and the* Queen of the West *were wooden. Henry Walke and the Confederate commander, Isaac Brown, had been friends in the old navy and messmates on a voyage around the world.*

Standing on the deck of the Carondelet, *Henry Walke was impressed by the glories of the morning:*

All was calm, bright and beautiful. The majestic forest echoed with the sweet warbling of its wild birds, and its dewy leaves sparkled in the sunbeams. All seemed inviting the mind to peaceful reflection.

There were openings in the forest, and at some of these stood friendly blacks, the men waving their hats and the women waving leafy branches. Only one white man was seen, and he cupped his hands to his mouth and shouted defiantly: "The Arkansas *is coming!"*

Again in Walke's words:

We had proceeded about six miles up the river when we discovered ... the celebrated *Arkansas*. The *Queen of the West, Tyler* and *Carondelet* at once retreated down the river to avoid being inevitably sunk, firing upon her with our stern and, occasionally,

Henry Walke

with our side guns. The enemy vigorously returned the fire from her heavy bow guns as she pursued, and had greatly the advantage of us from being thoroughly protected by iron.

Relates the Confederate commander, Isaac Brown:

I was on the shield [i.e., on the topmost deck, out in the open] directly over our bow guns, and could see their shot on the way to the *Carondelet*. . . . While our shot seemed always to hit his stern and disappear [within], his missiles, striking our inclined shield, were deflected over my head and lost in air.

I received a severe contusion on the head, but this gave me no concern after I had failed to find any brains mixed with the handful of clotted blood which I drew from the wound and examined.

A moment later a shot from the *Tyler* struck at my feet, penetrated the pilot house, and, cutting off a section of the wheel, mortally hurt Chief Pilot [John] Hodges and disabled our Yazoo River pilot, [J. H.] Shacklett. . . . James Brady, a Missourian of nerve and equal to the duty, took the wheel. . . .

All was going well, with a near prospect of carrying out my first [attempt to use] the ram . . . for the stern of the *Carondelet* was now the objective point, as she seemed to be going slow and unsteady. Unfortunately, the *Tyler* also slowed, so as to keep near his friend, and this brought us within easy range of his small arms. I saw with some concern—as I was the only visible target outside our shield—that they were firing by volleys. . . .

I was near the hatchway . . . when a minie-ball [properly Minié ball], striking over my left temple, tumbled me down among the guns. I awoke as if from sleep, to find kind hands helping me to a place among the killed and wounded. I soon regained my place on the shield. I found the *Carondelet* still ahead, but much nearer.

Federal commander Henry Walke, like Isaac Brown, was directing his operations from his topmost deck:

The *Arkansas* came up, with the evident intention of running us down. I avoided the blow, and as we passed exchanged broadsides at very close quarter. I endeavored to board her, but she passed us too quickly, and I could only fire our bow guns fairly at her stern. . . .

At this moment our wheel ropes were cut off for the third time [with the situation making another quick repair impossible], and we had to run the boat into shore. As she swung round, we gave the rebel vigorous discharges from our bow and starboard guns. Two shot-holes were now seen in her side, when the crew were observed pumping her out. At this juncture a man was observed to be thrown overboard from the *Arkansas*.

Actually, all Walke saw was a pair of legs and the lower part of a torso. During the close-range fighting, a sailor on the Arkansas *had leaned out of a porthole to get a better view of things, and a cannon ball had carried away his head and shoulders. An officer within, seeing no point in saving merely the bottom half of a corpse for proper disposal, and also fearing that the ghastly sight would demoralize the crew, ordered the remains pushed through the porthole to join the pulp in the river. A brother to the victim was among those who watched the deed performed.*

With the Carondelet *aground and virtually defenseless, Walke and the rest of the men on deck retired below.*

Says Isaac Brown:

Though I stood within easy pistol shot, in uniform, uncovered, and evidently the commander of the *Arkansas,* no more notice was taken of me.... Their ports were closed, no flag was flying [the flag had wrapped itself around its staff, giving the Confederates the impression it had been lowered], not a man or officer was in view, not a sound or shot was heard. She was apparently "disabled."

Walke assessed his condition:

We had now received severe damages in our hull and machinery, more than twenty shots having entered the boat. In the engineer's department, three [steam] escape-pipes, the steamgauge, and two water-pipes were cut away. In the carpenter's department, nineteen beams were cut away, thirteen timbers damaged, and three boats rendered useless. Our deck-pumps were cut away also. We had some thirty killed, wounded and missing. When the escape-pipes were cut away [and it was feared the boiler would explode], many of the hands jumped into the water.

On board the Arkansas, *the leaks made by the* Carondelet's *guns required continuous pumping, and a heavy stream of water spurted from the vessel's side. In addition, her smokestack assembly had been damaged, which slowed her speed. But, still formidable, she now turned her attention from the* Carondelet *to the* Tyler *and the* Queen of the West, *both of which were fleeing toward the Mississippi.*

In the words of an unnamed officer on board the Tyler:

We ... managed to keep the ram from two to three hundred yards distant from us, keeping up a rapid fire from our stern-gun and an occasional discharge from our broadside batteries as we could bring them to bear, receiving the fire of her two bow-guns and occasional discharges from her broadside batteries.

The Confederate commander takes up:

On gaining the Mississippi, we saw no vessels but the two we had driven before us. While following these in the direction of Vicksburg I had the opportunity of inspecting the engine and fire rooms, where I found engineers and firemen had been suffering under a temperature of 120 to 130 degrees.

The executive officer ... had organized a relief party from the men at the guns, who went down into the fire room every fifteen minutes, the others coming up, or being, in many instances, hauled up, exhausted in that time. In this way, by great care, steam was kept to service gauge.

Union commanders Farragut and Davis had heard the shooting on the Yazoo, but they were not alarmed, believing that Walke's expedition had merely encountered some Confederate land troops. The two leaders hadn't put much faith in the warning about the Arkansas *given them by the Confederate deserters the night before, not figuring at all on the kind of boldness Isaac Brown was showing.*

Brown continues:

Aided by the current of the Mississippi, we soon approached the Federal fleet—a forest of masts and smokestacks—ships, rams, ironclads, and other gunboats [anchored] on the left side, and ordinary river steamers and bomb vessels along the right. ... We were not yet in sight of Vicksburg, but in every direction except astern our eyes rested on enemies. ... It seemed at a glance as if a whole navy had come to keep me away from the heroic city.

Many of the Federals whom Brown was about to face across gunsights were men of the old navy he had "long known as valued friends."

Albert, of Farragut's flagship, was among those who watched with rising astonishment as the Tyler *and the* Queen of the West *made their desperate approach, the* Arkansas *not far behind:*

We were lying at anchor with fires banked but no steam on. Most of the other vessels in the two fleets were in the same condition, our object being to economize in fuel as much as possible, we having no means to replenish our bunkers should the coal give out.

Great excitement now swept the vessels. With the drummers beating "general quarters," all hands ran to their battle stations. Albert goes on:

As many of our boats as could bring their guns to bear ... immediately opened, and volumes of smoke were soon issuing from the smoke-pipes of the different steamers, as each one was endeavoring to get up steam.

With the air nearly still on this clear summer morning, the gunsmoke began settling around the Federal vessels. The Confederate gunners found themselves obliged to send many of their shots at muzzle flashes rather than at clear targets.

Isaac Brown, his forehead bruised and bloody from the two wounds he

The *Arkansas* running through the Union fleet

had sustained, was still directing the Arkansas *from his position atop her shield:*

As we advanced, the line of fire seemed to grow into a circle constantly closing. The shock of missiles striking our sides was literally continuous, and as we were now surrounded, without room for anything but pushing ahead, and shrapnel shot were coming on our shield deck, twelve pounds at a time, I went below. . . . At this moment I had the most lively realization of having steamed into a real volcano, the *Arkansas* from its center firing rapidly to every point of the circumference.

Some of the Federal vessels, having got up steam, were now in motion, and Brown had scarcely arrived belowdecks when a ram approached from the rear. The bearing guns "blew off" the attack. A moment later a second ram appeared just ahead. Observing through a small port in the pilot house, Brown called to the helmsman, "Go through him, Brady!"

But before Brady could obey, one of the Confederate guns made a hit on the ram's boiler and blew it up. Brown could hear the cries of the crew as they jumped overboard on all sides: "We passed by and through the brave fellows struggling in the water under a shower of missiles intended for us."

From the deck of the Hartford, *Albert saw the sloop of war* Richmond *give the* Arkansas *"a terrible broadside."*

For a moment she was lost in the smoke. . . . As it cleared away, the bow-guns of the vessels lying astern of the *Richmond* commenced firing on her. . . . As she passed us, we gave her the benefit of a broadside. . . . She fired two rifle-shots [i.e., shots from a rifled cannon], which passed harmlessly over our heads.

Lieutenant Reigart B. Lowry, commander of the gunboat Sciota, *says that the* Arkansas
seemed, from her movements, to trust entirely to her invulnerability for a safe run to the cover of the Vicksburg batteries. . . . My eleven-inch gun . . . [struck] him fair, but the shell glanced off almost perpendicularly into the air and exploded.

At the same time I opened a brisk fire with all my small arms against his ports. . . . I observed one man in the act of sponging [the bore of a gun from its muzzle] tumble out of the port, sponge and all, evidently shot by a rifle ball.

Isaac Brown comments: "It was a little hot this morning all around."

The enemy's shot frequently found weak places in our armor, and their shrapnel and minie-balls also came through our portholes. Still, under a temperature of 120 degrees, our people kept to their work.

Relates Lieutenant George W. Gift, a Tennessean in charge of a division of Brown's guns:

We were passing one of the large sloops of war when a heavy shot struck the side abreast of my bow gun, the concussion knocking over a man who was engaged in taking a shot from the rack. He rubbed his hip, which had been hurt, and said, "They would hardly strike twice in a place."

He was mistaken, poor fellow! For immediately a shell entered the breach made by the shot and . . . exploded with terrible effect. I found myself standing in a dense, suffocating smoke, with my cap gone and hair and beard singed. . . . Sixteen were killed and wounded by that shell, and the ship set on fire. . . . In a few

Union gun at moment of firing
(From a sketch by naval officer Henry Walke)

moments the fire was extinguished without an alarm having been created. . . .

The ill luck which befell the crew of the bow gun was soon to be followed by a similar misfortune to the crew of my broadside gun. An 11-inch shot broke through immediately above the port, bringing with it a shower of iron and wooden splinters, which struck down every man at the gun. My master's mate . . . was painfully wounded in the nose, and I had my left arm smashed. . . . Nor did the mischief of the last shot end with my poor gun's crew. It passed across the deck, through the smokestack, and killed eight and wounded seven men at [another] gun. . . .

Stationed on the ladder leading [down] to the berth deck was a quartermaster named Eaton. He was assigned the duty of passing shells from the forward shell room, and also had a kind of superintendence over the boys who came for powder.

Eaton was a character. He had thick, rough, red hair, an immense muscular frame, and a will and a courage rarely encountered. Nothing daunted him, and the hotter the fight the fiercer grew Eaton. From his one eye he glared furiously on all who seemed inclined to shirk, and his voice grew louder and more distinct as the shot rattled and crashed upon our mail.

At one instant you would hear him pass the word down the hatch, "Nine-inch shell, five-second fuse."

"Here you are, lad . . . your rifled shell. Take it and go back [to your gun], quick!"

"What's the matter that you can't get that gun out?" And, like a cat, he would spring from his place and throw his weight on the side tackle, and the gun was sure to go out.

"What are you doing here . . .? Where are you hurt? Go back to your gun, or I'll murder you on the spot!"

"Here's your nine-inch shell."

"Mind, shipmate," to a wounded man, "the ladder is bloody; don't slip; let me help you."

As for Isaac Brown, he remained below for only a short time:
I sought a cooler atmosphere on the shield, to find, close ahead and across our way, a large ironclad displaying the square flag of an admiral. [This was the *Benton;* the banner was that of Flag Officer Davis.]

Though we had but little headway [for the ram's steam pressure was dropping] . . . I ordered the pilot to strike him amidships. He avoided this . . . and, passing under his stern, nearly touching, we gave him our starboard broadside. . . . This was our last shot, and we received none in return.

We were now at the end of what had seemed the interminable line . . . past the outer rim of the volcano. I now called the officers up to take a look at what we had just come through and to get the fresh air; and as the little group of heroes closed around me with their friendly words of congratulation, a heavy rifle-shot passed close over our heads. It was the parting salutation. . . .

We were not yet in sight of Vicksburg [only now heading around the tip of the De Soto peninsula], but if any of the fleet followed us farther on our way I did not perceive it.

The Federals stationed below Vicksburg, both the army and the navy, were now tense and alert. Farragut had rushed a courier across the base of the peninsula to explain what was happening, and the officers feared the Arkansas *would continue down past Vicksburg and attack their forces. A mortar schooner that was aground and could not be moved was readied for demolition. The rest of the naval vessels prepared for action.*

The 3,000 army troops under Brigadier General Thomas Williams were still encamped on the peninsula across from Vicksburg, about three miles below the city, their transports anchored just offshore.

Colonel Wickham Hoffman says that the artillerymen had run their batteries up to the bank, and that the infantry, too, were under arms:

A staff officer said to General Williams, "General . . . let us attempt something, even if we fail."

"What would you do?" said the general.

"Take the *Laurel Hill,* put some picked men on board of her, and let us ram the rebel. We may not sink her, but we may disable or delay her, and help the gunboats to capture her."

"A good idea," said the general. "Send for Major Boardman."

Boardman . . . had been brought up as a midshipman. He was known in China as the "American devil," from a wild exploit there in scaling the walls of Canton one dark night when the gates were closed, climbing them with the help of his dagger only, making holes in the masonry for his hands and feet. . . .

Boardman came; the *Laurel Hill* was cleared; twenty volunteers from the Fourth Wisconsin were put on board, and steam got up. . . . But our preparations were all in vain.

To the north, the Arkansas *had completed her trip around the tip of the peninsula. Isaac Brown and his surviving officers stood upon the shield, their faces darkened by powder smoke and streaked with sweat (and some with blood as well), all absorbing deeply the welcome sight of Vicksburg, gleaming in the sun on the bluffs to their left.*

The Federal activity down the river was also visible. Brown noted in particular the warships whose smokestacks indicated they had their steam up:

With our firemen exhausted, our smokestack cut to pieces [the steam pressure now so low as to barely turn the screws], and a section of our plating torn from the side, we were not in condition just then to begin a third battle. Moreover, humanity required the landing of our wounded—terribly torn by cannon shot—and of our dead.

Brown turned the limping Arkansas *toward the Vicksburg wharves and the cover of the city's artillery batteries. Thousands of soldiers and hundreds of civilians lined the hilltops, having been drawn to these vantage points by the sounds of the action up the river.*

At the approach of the lone vessel, which they knew to be the Arkansas, *and which they realized had prevailed over incredible odds, the Southerners went wild. The hilltops rang with cheers and patriotic songs, the singing accompanied by the music of several regimental bands. Men and women clasped hands and swung into sweeping dance steps.*

Large groups of the spectators streamed to the waterfront, and as Brown and his weary crew stepped from their battered, rust-hued vessel to the wharf, some of them bandaged and bloodstained, they were cheered anew; their blackened hands were pumped; they were grabbed and embraced.

The crowd then swarmed about the Arkansas, *peering through her ports and hatches. Many drew back in horror, for blood was spattered everywhere, some of it mixed with brains, and here and there lay a headless trunk or a dismembered arm or leg. Several of the bloodstained bodies were living men who were removed to the wharf for transfer to a hospital.*

Immediate measures [Brown explains] were taken to repair damages and to recruit our crew, diminished to one-half their original number by casualties and by the expiration of service of those who had volunteered only for the trip to Vicksburg.

We had left the Yazoo River with a short supply of fuel, and after our . . . landing opposite the city hall we soon dropped down to the coal depot, where we began coaling and repairing under the fire of the lower fleet, to which, under the circumstances, we could make no reply. Most of the enemy's shot fell short, but [Commander W. B.] Renshaw, in the *Westfield*, made very fine practice with his 100-pound rifle gun, occasionally throwing the spray from his shot over our working party ... with the benefit of sprinkling down the coal dust.

Getting in our coal, we moved out of range of such sharp practice, where, under less excitement, we hastened such temporary repairs as would enable us to continue the offensive. We had intended trying the lower fleet that evening, but before our repairs could be completed and our crew reinforced by suitable selections from the army, the hours of night were approaching.

Meanwhile, the commanders of the upper fleets, highly mortified by Brown's successful passage of their gantlet, had made plans to renew the contest. Davis was to bombard Vicksburg's upper batteries while Farragut took his fleet down past the city toward his old anchorage, attacking the Arkansas *en route.*

Albert, of the flagship Hartford, *tells how things began:*

At about six o'clock in the evening the fleet got under way.... The Davis fleet had commenced to engage the batteries.... The battcries were firing rapidly, and our boats were returning the fire with good effect. As we approached, shot and shell commenced whistling over us, riflemen were busy at work in the woods along the river ... and bullets chirruped a symphony to the bass voice of the artillery, while the [Union] mortars at either end of the city kept up a roaring accompaniment.

The indomitable Isaac Brown, of course, had lost no time preparing the Arkansas *for action:*

Unfit as we were for the offensive, I told [Lieutenant Henry C.] Stevens to get under way and run out into the midst of the coming fleet. Before this order could be executed, one vessel of the fleet sent a 160-pound wrought-iron bolt through our armor and engine-room, disabling the engine and killing, among others, Pilot [William] Gilmore, and knocking overboard the heroic Brady, who had steered the *Arkansas* through our morning's work. This single shot caused also a very serious leak, destroyed all the contents of the dispensary ... and, passing through the opposite bulwarks, lodged between the woodwork and the armor.

Stevens promptly detailed a party to aid the carpenter in stopping the leak, while our bow and port-broadside guns were rapidly served on the passing vessels. So close were these to our guns that we could hear our shot crashing through their sides, and the groans of their wounded; and ... these sounds were heard with a fierce delight by the *Arkansas*'s people.

Why no attempt was made to ram our vessel, I do not know. Our position invited it, and our rapid firing made that position conspicuous; but as by this time it was growing dark, and the *Arkansas* close inshore, they may have mistaken us for a water-battery.

Says Federal officer R. B. Lowry, commander of the gunboat Sciota:

I ... could see nothing distinctly of the ram, though I received a fire, as from a battery at or near the level with the water. A shell from this battery passed horizontally through [my] vessel.... Several grape and other shots passed through ... and one heavy shot struck under [the] port bow—a plunging, grazing shot from the hill forts.

This fire killed no one, and wounded only two. But on the Hartford, *according to Albert, things were different:*

Poor George Lounsbery ... was killed.... His usual station ... was on the spar-deck, where he had charge of two guns, and in all our engagements we stood side by side; but he was placed on the berth-deck to take the place of the officer of the powder division, who was sick, and thus met his death.

He was in the act of speaking to someone down in the cockpit when a solid shot came through the ship's side and severed his head down to his shoulders. His head was literally torn to pieces, and but fragments of it could be found, while his body fell across the edge of the hatch, and his life's blood gushed in torrents down in the orlop....

The same shot that killed poor Lounsbery also struck a colored cook, taking half of his head off, and also wounding several others. A man named Cameron was also struck in the head and his head partly taken off, on the spar-deck, and but a few feet from where I stood.

The Union gunboat Winona, *while in the process of suffering one man killed and four wounded, experienced another kind of trouble as well. Explains her commander, Lieutenant Edward T. Nichols:*

We ... received a shot on our port side, which started a heavy leak. Started our deck pumps immediately, but finding the water gaining ... pivoted the 11-inch guns to starboard to raise the leak out of water. Water still gaining, pivoted rifle gun to starboard. Shifted port howitzer over, and shifted shot and shells. ...

My orders being to anchor at the old anchorage below Vicksburg, I ran down ... and rounded to, with the intention of anchoring, but finding the leak still gaining fast on the pumps ... I deemed it the safest plan to run the vessel on shore.

With Farragut's entire fleet soon reaching the old anchorage, the action ended. In Vicksburg the night sky was illuminated by a burning house, the victim of a Federal shell. Civilians began to appear on various streets as they emerged from their caves and from behind the city's hills.

Isaac Brown was relieved to find that the Arkansas *had survived her third battle:*

And now this busy day, the 15th of July, 1862, was closed with the sad duty of sending ashore a second party of killed and wounded. ... The rest which our exhaustion rendered necessary was taken for the night under a dropping fire of the enemy's 13-inch shells.

During the following week we were exposed day and night to these falling bombs, which did not hit the *Arkansas* but frequently exploded underwater nearby. One shell, which fell nearly under our bows, threw up a number of fish. ... In time we became accustomed to this shelling, but not to the idea that it was without danger. ...

In three days we were again in condition to move and to menace at our will either fleet [Davis's above Vicksburg or Farragut's below], thus compelling the enemy's entire force, in the terrible July heat, to keep up steam day and night. ... We constantly threatened the offensive; and our raising steam, which they could perceive by our smokestack, was the signal for either fleet to fire up. ...

The result of our first real attempt to resume the offensive was that before we could get within range ... our engine completely broke down, and it was with difficulty that we regained our usual position in front of the city.

July 21 arrived. Brown was concerned, for he had a feeling the Federals were about to make another attack—which they were, with two vessels of the upper fleet, the ironclad Essex, *commanded by heavily bearded*

William D. Porter, brother of David Porter, and the wooden ram Queen of the West, *one of the vessels that had encountered the* Arkansas *in the Yazoo River.*

Brown continues:

They could not have taken us at a more unprepared moment. Some of our officers and all but twenty-eight of our crew were in hospitals ashore, and we lay helplessly at anchor, with a disabled engine. . . .

The following morning at sunrise the *Essex* . . . with the *Queen of the West* . . . ran down under full steam, regardless of the fire of our upper shore-batteries, and made the expected attack. We were at anchor, and with only enough men to fight two of our guns [at a time].

The Essex *began the action. Relates her commander, William Porter:*

I arrived at the ram, delivered my fire and struck her. The blow glanced, and I went high on the river bank with the bows of the ship. . . . I backed off and loaded up.

The enemy had drawn up three regiments of sharpshooters and several batteries of field pieces, ranging from six-pounders to twenty-four pounders. I found it impossible, under these circumstances, to board the rebel boat, though such was my original intention.

After I delivered my fire at but five feet from the ram, we distinctly heard the groans of her wounded. . . . We knocked a very large hole in her side.

The hole was near one of the gun ports. Pieces of railroad iron had been driven among the Confederates, with the shot itself pursuing a deadly course. Eight men were killed and six wounded.

"*The closeness of this contest with the* Essex," *says Isaac Brown,*
may be inferred from the circumstance that several of our surviving men had their faces blackened and were painfully hurt by the unburnt powder which came through our portholes from the assailant's guns.

Officers included, Brown now had a crew of only twenty men. But their work was amply augmented by the batteries on shore. The commander of the Essex *became doubtful about his chances for success:*

I began to look for aid from the fleets, but without result. I ordered the pilots to get the *Essex*'s head upstream, with the intention of holding on until the lower fleet came up, and then make another attack on the ram. At this time I was under the guns of three batteries [on shore], one of which was not over one hundred feet off.

A heavy ten-inch shot from the nearest battery struck my forward casemate [i.e., the forward part of the armor enclosing the gun deck], about five feet from the deck, but fortunately did not penetrate. A rifle seven-and-a-half-inch shot from the same battery struck the casemate about nine feet from the deck. It penetrated the iron, but did not get through [the wood]. . . .

A conical shell struck the casemate on the port side as we were rounding to. . . . It exploded through, killing one man and slightly wounding three. A small piece grazed my head, and another piece tore the legs of the first master's pantaloons. . . .

I held on for a short time longer, but the enemy [on shore] began to fire with such rapidity, and we were so close, that the flashes of his guns through my gun-holes drove my men from the guns. . . .

Seeing no hope of relief or assistance, I now concluded to run the gantlet of the enemy's lower forts and seek an anchorage below the fleet. I therefore reluctantly gave the order to "put her head downstream."

By this time the wooden Queen of the West, *her only weapon a reinforced prow, was moving in to ram the* Arkansas. *She was a curious sight, having hundreds of bales of hay stowed and fastened about her for protection. She had already absorbed several hits by shot and shell from Vicksburg's shore batteries.*

Isaac Brown's twenty men had reloaded all their guns. Brown explains that the Federal vessel came "across, instead of with, the current" and did little damage:

The force of his blow was tempered to us, no doubt, by the effect of our . . . broadside guns, which were fired into him when he was less than fifty feet distant. Apparently blinded by such a blow in the face, he drifted astern [i.e., downstream past the *Arkansas*] and ran ashore under the muzzles of [Lieutenant Charles W.] Read's rifles, the bolts from which were probably lost in the immense quantity of hay. . . .

Getting clear of the bank, the ram wore round . . . and steamed at great speed up the river, receiving in passing a second broadside from our port battery, and in the excitement of getting away . . . he brought himself within range of our deadly bow guns . . . which . . . sent solid shot that seemed to pass through him

from stem to stern. As he ran out of range he was taken in tow and
was run up into the Davis fleet.

*A Federal newspaper correspondent who witnessed the ram's return says
that she presented "a most dismantled and forlorn appearance." Almost
miraculously, her crew escaped with one or two minor injuries.*

 Again in Brown words:

 Thus closed the fourth ... battle of the *Arkansas,* leaving the
daring Confederate vessel ... still defiant in the presence of a
hostile force perhaps exceeding in real strength that which fought
under Nelson at Trafalgar.

The Federals were now in a predicament, and Brown knew it:

 If the *Arkansas* could not be destroyed, the siege must be
raised, for fifty ships, more or less, could not keep perpetual
steam to confine one little 10-gun vessel within her conceded control of six miles of the Mississippi River....

 Soon after our contribution to the *Essex*'s laurels ... the lower
fleet started for the recuperative atmosphere of salt water, and
about the same time the upper fleet ... steamed for the North....

 Vicksburg was now without the suspicion of an immediate
enemy.

*On his way down the Mississippi to New Orleans, David Farragut left
General Thomas Williams and his troops at Baton Rouge, perhaps 250
miles, by way of the river, from Vicksburg. Assigned as support for the
garrison were several naval vessels, including the* Essex.

 *Vicksburg's Confederate leaders, jubilant over their victory, quickly
sent a land expedition against Baton Rouge, the attack taking place on
August 5. Though General Williams was shot through the heart at the
outset, the Confederates were driven away.*

 The Arkansas, *having descended the river, had been expected to sup-
port the attack, but she broke down a few miles above the objective. Isaac
Brown, having fallen ill, was not on board. His place had been taken by
Lieutenant Henry Stevens.*

 On the morning of August 6, with the Arkansas *shakily repaired, the*
Essex *and her consorts approached from Baton Rouge, the* Essex *opening
fire as soon as she came within range. Relates Confederate gunnery officer
Charles Read:*

 The *Arkansas* started for the *Essex*.... Proceeded about three
hundred yards ... and the larboard engine suddenly stopped. She

then makes for the bank . . . the *Essex* pouring a hot fire into her. In this condition we opened fire with the stern. The *Essex* continued to advance.

Henry Stevens, the Confederate vessel's commander, ordered all his guns loaded, then sent the entire crew ashore. Turning the Arkansas *adrift with her colors flying, he set her afire, making sure the job was well done before jumping overboard and swimming to join his men.*

The Federal vessel continued firing, with the Arkansas *seeming to reply as the flames began to discharge her guns. Says Henry Stevens:*

It was beautiful to see her, when abandoned by commander and crew, and dedicated to sacrifice, fighting the battle on her own hook.

The noise of the action had brought many people, both whites and blacks, running to the river bank. A Confederate newspaper correspondent describes the scene as the fire on the Arkansas *at length reached her magazine:*

She . . . exploded with a most terrible uproar. . . . As the burning fragments . . . floated down the river, the Yankee boats speedily fled to get out of harm's way, so that the ill-fated ram was a terror . . . even though a battered wreck.

Her active career had spanned only twenty-three days, but the Arkansas *had made herself a naval legend.*

Most of the vessel's crew managed to elude capture and make their way to Port Hudson, about twenty-five miles up the river (closer by the land route), where the repulsed army units were fortifying. All the Confederates were safe there, for the Federals had no immediate plans to renew the contest.

David Farragut was elated to be able to report to Washington that the Arkansas *had been destroyed, but he admitted that his second expedition up the river had been "fruitless." Its cost in casualties by gunfire had been relatively low, but many of his men had fallen sick. All he could say in favor of his work was that "it showed the enemy that we were prompt and always ready to be upon them with a sharp stick."*

The campaign ended with the Confederates in firm possession of Vicksburg and Port Hudson and the great stretch of the Mississippi that linked them. With the defenses along this vital part of the river being pushed vigorously, connections between the eastern and western halves of the Confederacy were now more secure than when the campaign began.

4

IN THE MISTS OF CHICKASAW
BAYOU

For sixty-seven days [says Confederate garrison officer Charles Hooker] the enemy had been in front of Vicksburg, and during much of the time had been raining shot and shell into the devoted city and defenses. The number of Federal missiles was estimated at from 20,000 to 25,000, yet the casualties in the batteries were only seven killed and fifteen wounded, and but two deaths were reported from the town. Probably 300 guns were used against the defenses, but . . . on the Confederate side not one [gun] was dismounted, and but two temporarily disabled.

Only relatively few of Vicksburg's 5,000 civilians had remained in the city to the end of the campaign, the majority having evacuated by carriage, wagon, and train. Some who used the train went as far as Jackson, Mississippi's capital, some forty miles to the east, a few going even farther. Many others set up camps in the woods just outside the range of the Federal guns.

A Confederate journalist who made a tour of Vicksburg at this time reported that he found the city "deserted and desolate."

Only sentinels and darkies to be seen, and very attenuated cats and dogs. Houses are closed, and though a large number were struck by shells . . . no dwellings seem to be much injured. A few stores, an engine-house, and the Methodist Church are the only severe sufferers, and these may be readily repaired.

In the wake of a general realization that the Yankees were truly gone, at least for the time being, Vicksburg slowly returned to life. Houses were reopened, and the business districts regained much of their normal bustle. But shortages led to stepped-up prices. Choice foodstuffs became hard to get at any price. Even pure water was scarce. This was provided mainly by

Vicksburg as seen from the hills to its north

cisterns, and it had to be shared with the numerous soldiers who were quartered within the city's limits.

The troops assembled in and about Vicksburg were of various origins. According to Major General Earl Van Dorn, the native Mississippian then in overall command:

The power which baffled the enemy resided in the breasts of the soldiers of seven states. . . . Mississippians were there, but there were also the men of Kentucky, of Tennessee, of Alabama, of Arkansas, of Louisiana and of Missouri, as ready to defend the emporium of Mississippi as . . . their own hearthstones.

There was no general relaxation among the defenders when the Yankees departed. Explains Samuel Lockett, chief engineer of the fortifications:

Working parties were at once put upon the river batteries to repair damages and increase their strength wherever recent experience had shown it to be necessary. It was also determined to construct a line of defense in rear of Vicksburg to prepare against an army operating upon land. As chief engineer, it became my duty to plan, locate, and lay out that line of defense.

A month was spent in reconnoitering, surveying, and studying the complicated and irregular site to be fortified. No greater topographical puzzle was ever presented to an engineer. The difficulty of the situation was greatly enhanced by the fact that a large part of the hills and hollows had never been cleared of their virgin forest of magnificent magnolia trees and dense undergrowth of cane. At first it seemed impossible to find anything like a general line of commanding ground surrounding the city; but careful study gradually worked out the problem.

The most prominent points I purposed to occupy with a system of redoubts, redans, lunettes, and small field works, connecting them by rifle pits so as to give a continuous line of defense. The work of construction was begun about the 1st of September [1862] with a force of Negro laborers hired or impressed from the plantations of the adjacent counties. Haynes' Bluff, on the Yazoo River, and Warrenton, about six miles below Vicksburg, were fortified as flank protections to the main position.

Defending the mouth of the Yazoo, about ten miles above the city, was the responsibility of Isaac Brown, lately of the Arkansas. *He decided to equip the river with torpedoes, or mines. He tells how the first was contrived:*

So poor in resources were we that, in order to make a beginning, I borrowed a five-gallon glass demijohn, and, procuring from the army the powder to fill it and an artillery friction tube to explode it, I set . . . two enterprising men to work with a coil of small iron wire, which they stretched from bank to bank, the demijohn . . . being suspended from the middle, some feet below the surface of the water, and so connected with the friction tube inside as to ignite when a vessel should come in contact with the wire.

It was in October, 1862, that General John Pemberton assumed command of the Department of Mississippi and East Louisiana. By a coincidence, this was the same month that General Grant took supreme command of the Department of the Tennessee and focused his eyes upon Vicksburg. From then on, until the struggle for the city ended, it would be Grant versus Pemberton.

As his new assignment began, Grant's front line extended from Memphis, on the Mississippi River, eastward along the full length of Mississippi's northern border. He was some 200 miles north of Vicksburg by land, probably twice that far by way of the winding river.

Commanding Grant's right wing at Memphis was Major General William Tecumseh Sherman, forty-two years old, tall and spare and sinewy, red-bearded, deeply wrinkled, intelligent, nervous, energetic, and, like Grant, an addicted cigar smoker. Unlike Grant, Sherman was brashly outspoken. At this stage of his career he was involved in a running dispute

William T. Sherman

with the correspondents representing the North's newspapers, and, indeed, with the newspapers themselves.

Sherman claimed vociferously that the papers not only published too much information that aided the enemy, but also had too strong an influence upon Washington's war policies:

I feel . . . that our government, instead of governing the country, is led first by one class of newspapers, then another, and that we are mere shuttlecocks flying between.

Sherman's complaints were far from groundless, but he caused himself a great deal of trouble by attacking the press head on. Grant had his own problems with correspondents and editors, but he made no public stir, counting upon his performance in the field to set these problems to rest.

Grant and Sherman, both graduates of West Point but only casual acquaintances before the war, were becoming the firmest of friends. Grant had shown a kindly interest in Sherman during a curious period of depression and lowered competence that required him to take a three-week rest and prompted the press to call him insane. Sherman, his balance fully regained, had provided much of the skill and courage that saved Grant's army after the surprise attack by the Confederates at Shiloh.

The friendship was destined to endure. Much later in the war, when a Northern official came to Sherman and tried to disparage Grant, Sherman responded:

"It won't do, sir; it won't do at all! Grant is a great general. He stood by me when I was crazy, and I stood by him when he was drunk. And now, by thunder, we stand by each other!"

John A. McClernand

While Grant and Sherman were puffing their cigars, consulting their maps, and discussing their plans for moving against Vicksburg, something unfavorable to their efforts was happening in Washington. Major General John A. McClernand, a political general—that is, one who got his commission not as the result of spending long years in the army but through his political connections—was scheming to gain himself an independent command in Grant's department. McClernand, an austere, vain, ambitious, and aggressive man of fifty-one, had visions of capturing Vicksburg on his own.

Since the general was a former congressman from Lincoln's home state of Illinois who supported the administration's war policies, and since he had done an effective job as a division commander under Grant at Shiloh, the President decided to give him his chance. This was possible because Grant had not yet done anything about Vicksburg. The field seemed open.

But McClernand's orders—which he received in secret—were ambiguous. In the first place, they did not place him clearly outside Grant's control. True, he was to use none of Grant's troops, being authorized to recruit a new army at Springfield, Illinois. But as the regiments were formed, he was to send them down the Mississippi to spots in Grant's department. Memphis, the post farthest south, was to be their point of assembly, even as McClernand continued his work in Springfield. In Memphis the regiments, though McClernand's on paper, would automatically come under Sherman's jurisdiction.

Naval officer David Porter, now an acting rear admiral, was in Washington at the time of the talks between McClernand and Lincoln. Porter was about to leave for Cairo, Illinois, to replace Charles Davis as commander of the Mississippi Squadron.

The President told Porter of the plans being formed; and Porter, who wasn't acquainted with McClernand, was at first sympathetic to the idea. He himself had made his way up through the ranks, never having attended Annapolis, and he was at this time prejudiced against West Point officers, finding those he knew "too self-sufficient, pedantic, and supercilious." He had not yet met the unpretentious Grant and Sherman.

Porter tells of his final meeting with Lincoln:

"Now," said the President, "I will give you a note of introduction to McClernand. I want you to talk the matter over with him before you leave Washington."

He wrote the note, gave it to me, and I left with Mr. Fox [i.e., Gustavus V. Fox, Assistant Secretary of the Navy].

"What do you think of that plan?" I said to Fox when we were outside.

"Well, I don't know," he replied. "But after you have talked with McClernand, suppose you stop in and tell me what you think of him."

I found the general at his hotel, and he talked in the most sanguine manner of taking Vicksburg in a week [of campaigning]!

... I left him after he informed me he had already received orders to enlist an army at Springfield, Illinois. . . .

I stopped in to see Fox, who said, "Well, what do you think of General McClernand?"

"I could form no opinion of him," I said. "Good by. . . . I leave for Cairo, Illinois, in two hours to see Grant. McClernand is going to Springfield to raise troops. He is shortly to be married, and if he proposes to recruit an army in that way, I think it will be hardly worthwhile to wait for him."

... Soon after my arrival at Cairo, I sent a messenger to General Grant informing him that I had taken command of the naval forces [on the Mississippi]. . . . I also informed him that General McClernand had orders to raise troops at Springfield, Illinois, prior to undertaking the capture of Vicksburg. I thought it my duty to tell him this, as it was not information given to me in confidence.

Several weeks later Captain McAllister, quartermaster at Cairo, gave a supper party to me and the officers of the station on board the quartermaster's steamer, a large, comfortable river boat.

Supper had been served when I saw Captain McAllister usher in a travel-worn person dressed in citizen's clothes. McAllister was a very tall man, and his companion was dwarfed by his superior size. McAllister introduced the gentleman to me as General Grant, and placed us at a table by ourselves. . . .

Grant, though evidently tired and hungry, commenced business at once. "Admiral," he inquired, "what is all this you have been writing me?"

I gave the general an account of my interviews with the President and with General McClernand, and he inquired, "When can you move your gunboats, and what force have you?"

"I can move tomorrow with all the old gunboats and five or six other vessels; also the *Tyler, Conestoga,* and *Lexington.*"

"Well, then," said Grant, "I will . . . write at once to Sherman to have thirty thousand infantry and artillery embarked in transports ready to start for Vicksburg the moment you get to Memphis."

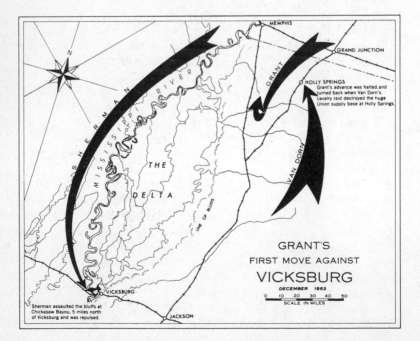

GRANT'S FIRST MOVE AGAINST VICKSBURG
DECEMBER 1862
0 10 20 30 40 50
SCALE IN MILES

Grant went on to explain the campaign that he and Sherman had been hatching. It was to be a cooperative affair. While Sherman's force, along with Porter and his fleet, descended the river, Grant was to lead a land expedition down through central Mississippi toward Vicksburg's rear. Grant's intent was to draw so great a number of Pemberton's troops away from Vicksburg to confront his march that Sherman would be able to make a lodgment on the hills just north of the city and then press into the city itself. It was hoped that Sherman would get the additional support of an expedition from New Orleans under Admiral David Farragut and General Nathaniel P. Banks.

In twenty minutes [David Porter continues] Grant unfolded his plan of campaign, involving the transportation of over one hundred thousand men; and, with a good supper staring him in the face, proposed to ride back again over a road he had just traveled without tasting a mouthful, his cigar serving, doubtless, for food and drink.

Three days after, with all the naval forces, I started down the Mississippi, and at Memphis found General Sherman embarking his troops on a long line of river steamers, and sent word to the general that I would call upon him at his headquarters.

Thinking it probable that Sherman would be dressed in full feather, I put on my uniform coat, the splendor of which rivaled that of a drum-major. Sherman, hearing that I was indifferent to appearances and generally dressed in working clothes, thought he would not annoy me by fixing up, and so kept on his blue flannel suit; and we met, both a little surprised at the appearance of the other.

"Halloo, Porter," said the general, "I am glad to see you. You got here sooner than I expected.... Devilish cold, isn't it? Sit down and warm up." And he stirred up the coal in the grate.... "How's Grant?"

This was the first time I had ever met General Sherman, and my impressions of him were very favorable. I thought myself lucky to have two such generals as Grant and Sherman to cooperate with.

I soon returned to my flagship, the *Black Hawk,* and gave Captain Walke orders to proceed with several vessels to the Yazoo River, take possession of the landings in order to prevent the erection of batteries, and drag the river above Chickasaw Bayou for torpedoes. Captain Walke was directed to use all possible expedition, so as to reach the Yazoo at least a day in advance of us.

It was now mid-December, 1862. General McClernand was still at his recruiting headquarters in Springfield, more than 300 miles to the north. He had sent many regiments to Memphis, obligingly swelling Sherman's ranks. Presently awaiting orders from Washington to close the recruiting office and go himself to Memphis to launch his campaign down the river to Vicksburg, McClernand, a widower, was busy preparing for his wedding—an event that Springfield's gossips delighted in discussing because the bride-to-be was the sister of his deceased wife.

Sherman made great haste to complete his embarkation, fearing that McClernand would arrive before he sailed. Countless mix-ups occurred, and the general din along the wharves and aboard the steamers was punctuated by profanity of an eloquence unusual even for the military.

In the minds of many men, the expedition took on an extra importance when news arrived of a Union setback in the East. General Ambrose E. Burnside had attacked General Robert E. Lee at Fredericksburg, Virginia, on December 13 and had suffered a staggering repulse, ending Federal efforts against Richmond for the winter. A success in the West would help make up for this.

Among the newspaper correspondents with the army at Memphis was a keen observer and a skillful writer representing the Missouri Democrat; *he signed himself simply "D." Having a pretty good idea of why Sherman was embarking so hurriedly, D. noted that the situation was worsened by the fact "that on the day previous the army had been paid off for the first time in several months, and the men and officers were nearly all lively with drink."*

The scene of confusion which characterized this embarkation [D. goes on] was probably never paralleled except by an army making a precipitate retreat. Companies were separated from their regiments, and officers from their companies; batteries were on one boat, and caissons [i.e., ammunition wagons] belonging to them on another; and the horses and artillerymen on still another.

The case was just as bad with the cavalry regiments, if not worse. There seemed to have been no places provided for them, and so they and their horses were scattered about on various boats, in little squads, wherever room could be found, and not the slightest attention was paid to putting the men on the same boats with their horses. In case of emergency, to have put a single company of cavalry on shore, mounted and equipped, would have involved the necessity of landing half a dozen boats.

Late in the afternoon on December 20 the fleet, some seventy vessels strong, steamed out of the Port of Memphis with drums beating and colors flying.

Ships' whistles tooted, some deeply and some shrilly, as Unionist crowds on shore cheered and waved and swung their hats. Groups of the city's Confederate sympathizers watched solemnly, fearing for the outcome of so strong an effort.

The departure was made in plenty of time to escape General McClernand. It would be a week before he, his new bride, and their entire wedding party, still celebrating, came steaming down the river to Memphis. Having anticipated taking charge of his legions while his wife and friends watched with admiration, the general would be filled with mortification and anger to find the camps empty and the fleet gone. He would soon steam in pursuit.

Newsman D. accompanied Sherman and Porter:

All the transports were crowded to their utmost capacity, and as they had all been hastily pressed into the service without preparation . . . there were no adequate accommodations for the troops, either for comfort or cleanliness. The men were all huddled between-decks and on the guards [i.e., the wooden frames shielding the paddle wheels] like so many sheep, and at night were compelled to sleep in a space scarcely sufficient for them to stand comfortably in in the daytime.

To make a bad matter worse, nearly every soldier had managed to get a canteen of whisky, enough to keep him drunk for two days, with what they had already taken, and for that space of time such a scene of riot and filthiness was scarce ever witnessed.

I was shut up on a small boat with such a crowd, and never before realized the full force of the expression "hell broke loose." In the cabin, among the officers, affairs were but little better, so far as sobriety was concerned. A large proportion of the officers were drinking and gambling day and night during the entire trip, and their behavior was unbecoming in the extreme. Their conduct excited any other idea rather than that of a band of patriots going down to fight the battles of their country. Of course, there were many noble exceptions, but neither their example nor influence could restrain their more unruly companions.

The steamers were using wood for fuel, and stops had to be made to send parties ashore to cut new supplies. On the second day out of Memphis the expedition approached the right-bank town of Helena, Arkansas, a Union outpost that was to contribute additional troops and transports.

Again in D.'s words:

As we reached this point . . . very little of the city could be seen for the long line of tents stretched along the bank. The fleet stopped there for the night and took on the troops that were to accompany the expedition, and next morning started for Friar's Point, the first place of rendezvous. It lay there all night . . . and about nine o'clock next morning again started down the river, and reached Gaines's Landing, 150 miles below Helena, about two o'clock P.M., where it stopped to wood.

As the fleet approached this point, the bank appeared to be lined with Negroes . . . hurrahing and shouting and jumping and cutting all kinds of antics. I learned from some of them that they thought the fleet was going down to set all the slaves free.

When the boats landed, a Negro gave information of a large store of wood of the best quality, amounting to more than 2,000 cords, secreted in the timber near the bank, in a place where it would not readily have been found. This was a great prize. . . . Every soldier able to do his duty was sent on shore to pack wood, and by nightfall all the boats were well supplied for nearly the whole trip.

Near the wood were some ten or twelve houses, one of them a very fine frame. The Negroes said the owners had gone to join the Southern army, and the soldiers, without more ado, burned them all down. Many of the Negroes . . . came on the boats . . . under the protection of the army.

At early light the next morning the fleet moved on again, and as General [George W.] Morgan's division came opposite a little village known as Wood Cottage Landing, some guerrillas secreted in a clump of undergrowth fired a volley at one of his transports. To teach them a lesson for the future, General Morgan sent some troops on shore and burnt every house in the neighborhood.

General Sherman and Admiral Porter naturally assumed that Grant was making good progress with his own part of the campaign, his overland thrust toward Vicksburg's rear. Unfortunately, Grant's eager and optimistic marchers had jested and sung their way only a few miles past their advance base at Oxford, Mississippi, when the stunning news came that some fast-moving Confederate cavalry units had swung around behind them and cut their supply lines. As Grant tells it:

General Van Dorn appeared at Holly Springs, my secondary base of supplies, captured the garrison of 1,500 men . . . and destroyed all our munitions of war, food and forage. . . . At the same time [General Nathan Bedford] Forrest got on our line of railroad between Jackson, Tennessee, and Columbus, Kentucky, doing much damage to it. This cut me off from all communication with the North.... I determined, therefore, to abandon my campaign....

The news of the capture of Holly Springs and the destruction of our supplies caused much rejoicing among the people [i.e., the Confederate citizens] remaining in Oxford. They came with broad smiles on their faces, indicating intense joy, to ask what I was going to do now without anything for my soldiers to eat. I told them that I was not disturbed; that I had already sent troops and wagons to collect all the food and forage they could find for fifteen miles on each side of the road.

Countenances soon changed, and so did the inquiry. The next was, "What are *we* to do?" My response was that we had endeavored to feed ourselves from our own Northern resources while visiting them; but their friends in gray had been uncivil enough to destroy what we had brought along, and it could not be expected that men with arms in their hands would starve in the midst of plenty.

Unaware that Grant's columns were turning back, Sherman's expedition neared the end of its trip down the river. According to D.:

Milliken's Bend ... was to be the last rendezvous of the fleet before it started out for active operations on Vicksburg, and we

Black refugees boarding a Union steamer

Dabney H. Maury

arrived there about dark on the evening of the twenty-fourth December. The next day would be Christmas, and many of the soldiers had the idea that the fleet would sail right in without difficulty, and that they would take their Christmas dinner in Vicksburg.

Having no knowledge that the Yankees were so near, Vicksburg celebrated Christmas Eve with a grand ball. The ballroom was filled with officers in their smartest uniforms and ladies in elegant floor-length gowns. Shortly after midnight, a bedraggled and breathless messenger hurried in from the darkness, pushed his way through the dancers to the side of General Martin Smith, and whispered into his ear. Smith, turning somewhat pale, signaled for the music to stop and announced in a loud voice: "This ball is at an end. The enemy are coming down the river."

From then on, Vicksburg's yuletide was to be bleak and fear-filled. "It is earnestly recommended," began a notice issued by General Pemberton, "that all the noncombatants, especially the women and children, should forthwith leave the city." Every soldier fit for duty was put on the alert, with full crews manning the artillery batteries and keeping a grim watch on the river.

Because Grant's columns had retreated, Pemberton was able to bolster his numbers with many of the troops that had been standing in Grant's way

at Grenada, about 135 miles northeast of Vicksburg. Among the com-
manders at Grenada was Major General Dabney H. Maury, of the
Virginia family that produced the famed oceanographer Matthew Fon-
taine Maury. The general relates:

On Christmas Day, a prominent and prosperous gentleman of
Grenada, Mr. Mister . . . gave a grand dinner to General [Sterling]
Price and his generals, and a sumptuous table it was that we sat
down to. All were in fine humor to enjoy it, for Grant was gone
and there was no one to make us afraid.

We had just taken our seats when a courier arrived with a
telegram from General Pemberton, ordering [my] division to
march at once to reinforce General Stephen D. Lee at Vicksburg
[or, more precisely, in the defenses just north of Vicksburg, where
Lee commanded and where Sherman was expected to attack]. . . .

I arose at once, bade farewell to Mr. Mister and his brilliant
company of generals and colonels, and proceeded to put the First
Division in motion to succor Lee. . . . We had to go by rail to
Jackson, thence to Vicksburg, over the very worst line of road in
the state.

As for the Union expedition on the river, newsman D. says that it lay at
anchor at Milliken's Bend, with Sherman and Porter developing their
plan of attack, all through Christmas Day:

A few ineffectual attempts were made to get up Christmas
festivities; but the usual staples were *non est,* and the day
dragged . . . as dismally as can be imagined. At length, as evening
approached, an order was received from General Sherman to
prepare to move up the Yazoo early the next morning. Immediately all was life and activity. Long faces disappeared, and the
joyful anticipation of at length commencing operations on the
enemy was manifest in every countenance. At daylight next morning all was ready, and the fleet started for . . . the Yazoo.

This river had been dragged for Isaac Brown's torpedoes, and the greater
part of them had been destroyed. During the progress of the work, however,
one of Porter's vessels had come to grief. In the admiral's words:

The *Cairo* encountered a floating torpedo. Two explosions in
quick succession occurred, which seemed almost to lift the vessel
out of the water. . . . She sank in twelve minutes . . . with nothing
but the tops of her chimneys showing above the surface. All the
crew were saved.

Union guns of the Yazoo expedition

When Sherman's transports had proceeded about ten miles up the Yazoo,
D.'s attention was captured by
the ruins of a large brick house and several other buildings, which
were still smoking. On inquiry I learned that this ... plantation ...
was an extensive establishment working over 300 Negroes. It contained a large steam sugar refinery, an extensive steam sawmill,
cotton gins, machine shop, and a long line of Negro quarters.

The dwelling was palatial in its proportions and architecture,
and the grounds around it were magnificently laid out in alcoves,
with arbors, trellises, groves of evergreens, and extensive flower-
beds. All was now a mass of smouldering ruins. Our gunboats had
gone up there the day before, and a small battery planted near the
mansion announced itself by plugging away at one of the
ironclads, and the marines went ashore after the gunboats had
silenced the battery, and burned and destroyed everything on the
place.

If anything were wanting to complete the desolate aspect ... it
was to be found in the sombre-hued pendent moss peculiar to
Southern forests.... As on almost every Southern plantation,
there were many deadened trees standing about in the fields,

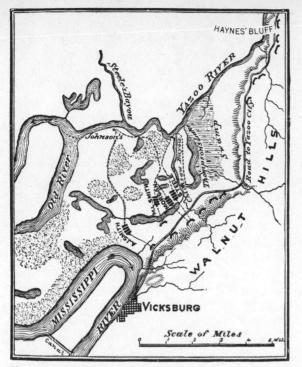

Sherman's attack at Chickasaw Bayou

from the limbs of all of which long festoons of moss hung, swaying with a melancholy motion in every breeze.

The owner of the devastated plantation was an ardent secessionist, W. H. Johnson, now absent. Along the plantation's banks the great fleet came to a stop. Three or four miles to the right, or the southeast, across swampy lowlands, were the fortified Walnut Hills, where Sherman hoped to make his lodgment. Success would place him only a few miles above Vicksburg, on a road that led directly to the city.

As the troops prepared to land, a heavy rain came up. D. explains that another problem was posed by the nature of the Yazoo's banks:

Along the edge of the water . . . is a dense undergrowth of willows, briers, thorns, vines, and live oaks, twined together in a most disagreeably promiscuous manner. To effect a landing of the troops and trains [i.e., supply wagons], a way had to be cut through this entanglement from every boat, and this caused such a delay that it was quite dark before all the troops were got on shore. Tents were pitched for the night, pickets sent out, and the army encamped, anxiously awaiting the dawn of the next day.

On the following morning a scene of confusion ensued which fully equalled that of the embarkation, and, in fact, resulted from it. Companies seeking their regiments, officers seeking their companies; men hunting for missing horses; wagoners seeking their teams, and everybody looking for something which could not be found.

While the troops deployed along an irregular front facing the vast swampland that led to the Walnut Hills, Admiral Porter sent several of his warships farther up the Yazoo to bombard the Confederate right flank at Haynes' Bluff.

During this time [Porter discloses] the *Benton* received many heavy blows from the enemy's shot and shells.... Although the *Benton* was much cut up, her efficiency was not impaired.... Lieutenant-Commanding [William] Gwinn stood on the upper deck during the whole action.... This ... cost him his life, for he was struck with a fifty-pound rifle shell which tore away the muscles of his right arm and breast.

Sherman's right flank now embraced the ruins of Johnson's plantation, while his left was just beyond Chickasaw Bayou, about three miles farther up the Yazoo. According to Thomas W. Knox, field correspondent for the New York *Herald:*

To approach the enemy's position ... bridges ... had to be constructed at various points to enable the troops to cross. In constructing them, we first met with opposition from the enemy. Their skirmishers and sharpshooters [sent out from the foot of the Walnut Hills] were placed ... behind logs, trees, and stumps, and kept up a constant and galling fire upon our working parties.

Still our men did not suffer much from their fire, our own picked marksmen giving them a good deal of annoyance and rendering them careful of showing themselves long enough to get accurate aims.

In addition to this annoyance ... the enemy opened their batteries in the face of the bluffs upon us. But in this they were decidedly the losers, as our heaviest field artillery was brought on to the ground wherever this occurred, and in several instances silenced their batteries and compelled them to withdraw their guns up the hill.

"By nightfall," says the Missouri Democrat's D.,
the enemy had been driven a quarter of a mile from where they
were first encountered, and the contest then ceased, both forces
resting on their arms, ready to renew the contest in the morning.
During the night . . . darkness prevailed in both camps. Not a fire
was lighted . . . by which either would betray its position to the
other.

In the night a light wind sprung up, blowing toward the river
from the enemy's position, and the night became clear and frosty.
Amid the prevailing silence, and aided by the wind, the sound of
cars constantly running could be heard on the Jackson and
Vicksburg Railroad, no doubt bearing reinforcements to the
enemy.

During the night the enemy was . . . busily engaged in erecting
rifle pits and breastworks [in the lowlands near the base of the
Walnut Hills]. . . . On the following morning long lines of them
could be seen where none were visible the night before. Several
new batteries were also seen on the heights beyond.

It now became a matter of interest among the troops to know
where General Grant was. It had been understood all along that
he was to cooperate with General Sherman, and as it was now
manifest that the enemy was much stronger than had been anticipated, his presence was anxiously looked for, and all kinds of
rumors began to spread in camp as to his whereabouts.

*Sherman was to be deprived of help not only from Grant but from the New
Orleans expedition as well. General Banks's troops, supported by three of
Admiral Farragut's warships, had come up the Mississippi as far as Baton
Rouge, but next in their path stood Port Hudson, now heavily fortified,
which they did not feel strong enough to attack.*

*With the gunboats on the Yazoo covering his flanks with an intermit-
tent fire from their big guns, Sherman spent the second day struggling
through the swamps and pushing back the enemy's skirmishers. Sherman's
intent was to establish a line from which he could make an assault on the
hills. By late morning of the next day, December 29, he was ready. But, as
D. points out, so were the Confederates:*

Batteries were seen planted at every assailable point, and it was
evident that the rebels had exerted a most commendable industry
during the night and had prepared to make the most determined
resistance to our anticipated assault. . . .

Far back on the highest peak of the hill they had erected a
signal station, overlooking all the battleground, and far removed

from the reach of shot or shell. By the aid of a glass the persons in charge of the station could be easily seen; and . . . every movement of our troops was signaled to the commanding general. Many spectators were also posted there with glasses, among whom were a number of women.

While Sherman's troops awaited the signal to begin their attack, General George Morgan, who was standing near Captain Jacob T. Foster's First Wisconsin Battery, noted a movement on a roadway that ran along the fortified hillside. He raised his glass:

I saw approaching from the enemy's right, about a mile away, a caisson, with gunners [seated] on the ammunition boxes and a few horsemen in front. I asked Foster if he could blow up that caisson.

He replied, "I can try, sir."

He waited until the caisson came within fair range, and fired. The report of the gun and the explosion of the caisson seemed to be instantaneous; caisson and gunners were blown into the air; every man and horse was killed, and a shout went up from around Foster and his battery.

. . . I learned [later] that one of the victims of the explosion was Captain Paul Hamilton, assistant adjutant-general on the staff of General S. D. Lee. He was but twenty-one years of age, was distinguished for his gallantry, and had gone through several battles without a scar.

Sherman's attack opened with a furious cannonade, which was answered at once by the Confederates, many of their shells plummeting into watery areas and raising silver spouts.

Again in the words of Union General Morgan:

With a wild shout, the troops . . . advanced to the assault. . . . The assaulting forces came under a withering and destructive fire. A passage was forced over the abatis [i.e., the barrier made of felled trees] and through the mucky bayou and tangled marsh to dry ground. All formations were broken; the assaulting forces were jammed together . . . and were mowed down by a storm of shells, grape and canister, and minie-balls which swept our front like a hurricane of fire.

Newsman D. relates that Brigadier General Frank P. Blair, who was on horseback, led his brigade upon the first line of rifle pits, and after a hard but brief struggle drove the enemy to their second line. Between the two lay a sort of ditch or small slough, with mud and quicksand in the bottom. As General Blair advanced, his horse got inextricably mired, and the General coolly slid down his head and led his brigade the remainder of the way on foot. The other mounted officers, seeing the difficulty, abandoned their horses also.

On arriving at the second line of rifle pits, another charge was made . . . and the enemy was again routed. . . . The enemy . . . commenced retreating up the hill, General Blair's brigade pursuing them, when all of a sudden the enemy, from a masked battery, opened a most deadly and destructive fire upon them with grape and canister. In a few minutes the ground was covered with the dead and dying. . . . This ended the assault on the hill at this point, and General Blair, with the remainder of his brigade, fell back.

Thomas Knox, of the New York Herald, *who was situated on another part of the field, made notes even as the action progressed. Looking toward the Confederate lines, he wrote:*

On our right a Negro sharpshooter has been observed whose exploits are deserving of notice. He mounts a breastwork regardless of all danger, and getting sight of a Federal soldier, draws up his musket at arm's length and fires, never failing of hitting his mark. . . . It is certain that Negroes are fighting here, though probably only as sharpshooters.

Several hours passed, with the attack making no solid gains. Men shouted, horses whinnied, and mules brayed. The crackle of muskets and the crash of artillery were almost continuous, with the warships on the Yazoo adding deeper discharges. Each time a Federal unit was thrown back, the Confederates on the hills sent up a round of cheers.

General Sherman tells how one of his boldest regiments propelled itself into a predicament:

The Sixth Missouri Infantry, at heavy loss . . . crossed the bayou . . . but could not ascend the steep bank. Right over their heads was a rebel battery, whose fire was in a measure kept down by our sharpshooters . . . posted behind logs, stumps, and trees on our side of the bayou. The men of the Sixth Missouri actually scooped out with their hands caves in the bank, which sheltered them against the fire of the enemy . . . right over their heads.

Adds newsman D.:

Our sharpshooters ... kept up a fire to prevent firing from the bank, and in some instances their aim was too low, and the consequence was that they shot dead two of our own men. The men sent up a shout, "Fire higher," and the rebels on the bank attempted to drown their voices by superior numbers, shouting: "Fire lower."

The parties were so close together that when the rebels reached their guns over the bank and depressed them, those below could easily have crossed bayonets with them. Conversation could be easily carried on, and one rebel cried out: "What regiment below?"

On being answered that it was the "Sixth Missouri," he replied: "It is too brave a regiment to be on the wrong side."

It was now nearly evening, and the men had tasted no food since before day, and one of them called out: "Have you got anything to eat up there? I'm hungry."

Immediately a large loaf of corn bread was thrown on the bank to them, and was welcomed heartily.

As soon as darkness fell, the Federals slipped from their holes and retreated to safety. D. goes on:

Not until the night was pitchy dark did the firing all cease, and floods of rain were now descending as if we were to have a second edition of Noah. The ground where the fighting was done was all low and marshy, and soon the water and mud were several inches deep.... The wounded lay in their agony on that oozy bed, under a soaking rain, uncared for, and many who had fallen on their faces and were unable to turn themselves smothered in the mud, and many more died from the exposure.

Sherman's attack had failed at all points. The next day, according to Knox of the Herald, *the troops rested:*

The enemy occasionally threw a shell into our lines to keep us awake, and once in a while their sharpshooters would creep up and open a slight skirmish. The lines of the two armies were parallel and scarcely a mile apart.... This field was swept by the musketry as well as the artillery of either party, and hence the impossibility of venturing upon it to bury the dead, or even bring off ... the helpless wounded. Occasionally one and another of those unhappy fellows... would crawl into the lines and find succor; but to many the long day wore wearily away, leaving them still unrelieved upon that miserable plain.

Sherman and Porter, extremely loath to abandon their efforts, made plans for a new attack to take place the following morning, but a heavy fog set in, and the venture was thwarted.

Now, says newsman D.:

General Sherman sent out parties with flags of truce to bury the dead and bring away the wounded, and the whole day was consumed in the discharge of this melancholy duty. It was discovered that the enemy had carried off all the slightly wounded as prisoners of war, leaving only those who were unable to walk. All the dead had been robbed of their haversacks, and many of the bodies stripped of their outer clothing.

During the day, many rebel soldiers came down to the flags of truce and manifested a disposition to be quite friendly . . . in some instances assisting in burying the dead. They also brought a few Vicksburg papers of that morning containing a glowing account of the battle, and jubilating over the repulse of the Yankees. . . .

The weather had cleared off . . . and the beauty of the day . . . illy harmonized with the mournful work in which our army was engaged. By night the last sad office of burying the dead was completed, and the wounded were borne from the field to the hospital boats.

The troops with whole skins, too, had begun withdrawing across the swamps, having been ordered back to their transports. Darkness brought a new surge of rain, which added to the general disheartenment.

In Admiral Porter's words:

The current ran so strong in the river that the vessels had to be fastened securely to the trees. The wind howled like a legion of devils, though which side it was howling for I have no idea.

That night General Sherman came on board my flagship, drenched to the skin. He looked as if he had been grappling with the mud and got the worst of it. He sat down and remained silent for some minutes. . . .

I said at length, "What is the matter?"

"I have lost seventeen hundred men, and those infernal reporters will publish all over the country their ridiculous stories about Sherman being whipped, etc."

"Only seventeen hundred men!" I said. "Pshaw! That is nothing; simply an episode in the war. You'll lose seventeen thousand before the war is over.... We'll have Vicksburg yet before we die. —Steward, bring some punch for the general and myself."

"That's good sense, Porter!" exclaimed the general, "and I am glad to see you are not disheartened. But what shall we do now? I must take my boys somewhere and wipe this out."

I informed the general that I was ready to go anywhere.

"Then," said he, "let's go and thrash out Arkansas Post."

This was a Confederate fort on the Arkansas River that the Union expedition had bypassed on its way down the Mississippi. Also called Fort Hindman, it held a garrison of about 5,000 men and was equipped with eleven heavy guns.

Porter thought Sherman's idea a good one, and plans were made to leave the Yazoo. The embarkation of the troops was about complete early the next morning when the Federals who were milling around on the decks saw a large party of armed Confederates approaching through the swamps. In their surprise, none of the Federals raised their muskets. The Confederates, too, hesitated to fire. General Stephen Lee, commander of the party, says that it was led by a regiment of Texans:

I ordered the fire to open. This most gallant regiment, with a dash, rushed almost up to the boats, delivering their fire with terrible effect on their crowded transports. Never have I seen so sudden a disappearance from crowded vessels, nor vessels move off so hurriedly. The gunboats at once opened ... with about twenty boat howitzers from their upper decks and with rifles from their plated decks.... As nothing was to be gained by firing on their ironclads, [the Texans] withdrew.

About this same time, Admiral Porter explains, something of a different nature was happening on board his flagship, lying farther down the Yazoo toward the Mississippi:

A colonel, dressed in a new suit of uniform, sought an interview with me. I knew he could not belong to Sherman's army, for all his officers had long ago worn the brightness from their accoutrements.

"I come," said he, "from General McClernand, who is at the mouth of the Yazoo River, and wants you to call and see him as soon as possible."

"Well," thinks I to myself, "that's cool!"

"You can tell the general," I said, "that my duties at present are so engrossing that I am making no calls, and that it is his place to come and see me. . . ."

"He has come," said the officer, "to take command of the army. . . ."

Here was a pretty kettle of fish! I bade the officer good morning, and he took his departure. Just then I saw General Sherman in a small boat pulled by two soldiers. I hailed him, and when he was near enough I said, "Sherman, McClernand is at the mouth of the Yazoo, waiting to take command of your army!"

Sherman looked serious as he inquired, "Are you going to call on him?"

"No," I replied. . . .

"But I must," said Sherman, "for he ranks me."

In two hours General Sherman returned with General McClernand, and I received the latter on board the flagship with all due courtesy, and inquired if he had brought an army with him. . . .

"No," replied McClernand, "but I find this army in a most demoralized state, and I must do something to raise their spirits. . . . If you will let me have some of your gunboats, I propose to proceed immediately and capture Arkansas Post."

Sherman made a remark . . . [and] McClernand made a discourteous reply, whereupon Sherman walked off into the after cabin. . . .

I informed General McClernand that the proposition to capture Arkansas Post had been broached by General Sherman the previous evening, and that I never let my gunboats go on such an important expedition without me.

"If," I said, "General Sherman goes in command of this army, I will go along with my whole force and make a sure thing of it; otherwise I will have nothing to do with the affair."

Just then Sherman beckoned to me, and I went in to him. "My God, Porter!" he exclaimed. "You will ruin yourself if you talk that way to McClernand. He is very intimate with the President, and has powerful influence."

"I don't care who or what he is, he shall not be rude to you in my cabin," I replied.

"Did you understand my proposition, General McClernand?" I inquired on my return to the forward cabin. . . .

"Yes," said McClernand, "I understand it and agree to it. There is no objection, I suppose, to my going along?"

"None in the world," I answered.

In spite of Porter's stipulations, McClernand was now in official command of Sherman's troops, having orders from Washington to take over. However, McClernand had no authority to make demands of Porter. To ensure the admiral's cooperation, McClernand played a somewhat subdued role in the events that followed.

Porter continues:

We started [up the Mississippi] as soon as possible and arrived at the Post . . . on the Arkansas River. I attacked it with three ironclads and several smaller vessels, and in three hours disabled all the guns. General Sherman surrounded the place with his troops, and, after heavy losses [on the Federal side], it surrendered—the fort, in charge of naval officers, to me, and the Confederate army . . . to General Sherman. Our flag was . . . hoisted over Arkansas Post [on] January 11, 1863.

Immediately after the battle, Sherman reported to McClernand on the vessel he was using as his headquarters. Sherman explains:

I found General McClernand . . . in high spirits. He said repeatedly: "Glorious! Glorious! My star is ever in the ascendant!" He spoke complimentarily of the troops, but was extremely jealous of the navy. He said: "I'll make a splendid report! I had a man [watching] up a tree!" etc. I was very hungry and tired, and fear I did not appreciate the honors in reserve for us, and asked for something to eat and drink.

As soon as the work at the fort was completed, the Federal expedition retired down the Arkansas River and anchored off Napoleon, where the river joined the Mississippi.

"From here," says General Grant, who was then in Memphis,

I received messages from both Sherman and Admiral Porter, urging me to come and take command in person, and expressing their distrust of McClernand's ability and fitness for so important and intricate an expedition [as that against Vicksburg].

On the 17th I visited McClernand and his command at Napoleon. . . . By this time I had received authority [from Major General Henry W. Halleck, general-in-chief under Lincoln in Washington] to relieve McClernand or to assign any person else to the command of the river expedition, or to assume command in person.

I felt great embarrassment about McClernand. He was the senior major general after myself within the department. It would not do, with his rank and ambition, to assign a junior [such as Sherman] over him. Nothing was left, therefore, but to assume the command myself. . . .

On the 20th I ordered General McClernand, with the entire command, to Young's Point and Milliken's Bend, while I returned to Memphis to make all the necessary preparations for leaving the territory behind me secure. . . . On the 29th of January I arrived at Young's Point, and assumed command the following day.

McClernand was reduced to the status of corps commander, the Mississippi army having four such units. Grant goes on to explain that the outraged general protested to him in writing:

His correspondence . . . was highly insubordinate, but I overlooked it, as I believed, for the good of the service. General McClernand was a politician of very considerable prominence. . . .

McClernand wrote also to Lincoln, his protests aimed mainly at General-in-Chief Halleck, who had worked with Grant against him, not entirely with the President's knowledge. "Do not let me be clandestinely destroyed," the general urged, adding the request that he be given the independent command against Vicksburg that was originally promised him.

Lincoln wrote back:

I have too many *family* controversies (so to speak) already on my hands to . . . take up another. You are now doing well—well for the country and well for yourself—much better than you could possibly be if engaged in open war with General Halleck. Allow me to beg that for your sake, for my sake, and for the country's sake, you give your whole attention to the better work.

McClernand had no choice but to settle into the job of corps commander. But he did not regard the demotion as being final. He had hopes of replacing Grant.

It was at this time—at the beginning of February, 1863—that Grant, aided very actively by Sherman and Porter, undertook his Bayou Expeditions, the failure of which, after two grueling months, forced him to decide upon the bold maneuver that finally brought the epic struggle for Vicksburg to a climax.

5

FIREWORKS AT MIDNIGHT

SIMPLY STATED, *Grant's plan was this: His army was to pick its way through the swamps on the western side of the Mississippi to a point some miles below Vicksburg. Admiral Porter was to take a squadron, which was to include three ordinary river steamers carrying army supplies and towing barges of coal to keep the navy in fuel, directly past the city's batteries in the night. Once the army and the navy were reunited down the river, the army was to be ferried across for a campaign, on dry terrain, around Vicksburg's rear.*

Before launching this campaign, however, Grant intended to cooperate with General Banks, operating out of New Orleans, in reducing Port Hudson, Louisiana, the Confederate stronghold on the eastern bank of the Mississippi, about 120 direct land miles below Vicksburg, perhaps twice as far by way of the river. Banks was then supposed to help Grant with the main effort.

Admiral Porter listened to Grant's ideas and agreed to render full cooperation, though he had some private reservations. To begin with, it seemed highly unlikely that the three ordinary, unarmed river steamers would make it past the batteries; this was something previously undreamed of. Most of Grant's other associates were openly against the whole maneuver. In Porter's words:

They urged that to move his army below Vicksburg was to cut himself off from his base of supplies at the North, to cut his own communications, and ... to place himself in a position where, if defeated, the defeat would be overwhelming.... Some of the most accomplished soldiers in his army, men who had won their way to fame, urged him, with all the power of eloquence, not to undertake the rash movement.

"It is an interesting commentary upon its military nature," adds Lieutenant Colonel William F. Vilas, of the Twenty-third Wisconsin,

that his warmest friend and ablest general, Sherman ... endeavored to dissuade him, both by personal interview and written communication, representing how grossly he was overriding the fundamental axiom of strategy in exposure of his army. . . . Grant, however, remained unshaken.

By this time Charles Dana, the special commissioner sent from Washington to check on Grant, had secured permission from Secretary of War Edwin M. Stanton to leave Memphis, where he had gleaned only secondhand information, and attach himself to Grant's headquarters. Grant had realized from the start why Dana was in the West. Now the general decided simply to absorb the special commissioner.

Dana explains that he reported to Grant on April 6, 1863:
He received me cordially. Indeed, I think Grant was ... glad to have me with his army. He did not like letter writing, and my daily dispatches to Mr. Stanton relieved him from the necessity of describing every day what was going on in the army. From the first, neither he nor any of his staff or corps commanders evinced any unwillingness to show me the inside of things.

In the first interview at Milliken's Bend, for instance, Grant explained to me so fully his new plan of campaign—for there was now but one—that by three o'clock I was able to send an outline of it to Mr. Stanton. From that time I saw and knew all the interior operations of that toughest of jobs, the reopening of the Mississippi.

Grant was in no danger of being diminished by Dana's reports to Washington. Though a man of a different mold than Grant, being superior in intellect, culture, and refinement, Dana soon came to understand the general's worth:
Grant was an uncommon fellow—the most modest, the most disinterested, and the most honest man I ever knew, with a temper that nothing could disturb, and a judgment that was judicial in its comprehensiveness and wisdom. Not a great man, except morally, not an original or brilliant man, but sincere, thoughtful, deep, and gifted with courage that never faltered. When the time came to risk all, he went in like a simple-hearted, unaffected, unpretending hero, whom no ill omens could deject and no triumph unduly exalt.

A social, friendly man, too, fond of a pleasant joke and also ready with one; but liking above all a long chat of an evening, and ready to sit up with you all night. . . . Not a man of sentimentality,

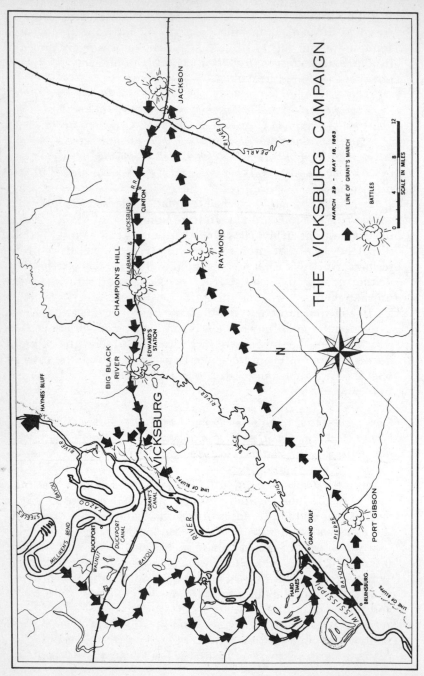

THE VICKSBURG CAMPAIGN

MARCH 29 – MAY 18, 1863

LINE OF GRANT'S MARCH

BATTLES

SCALE IN MILES

0 4 8 12

not demonstrative in friendship, but always holding to his friends; and just, even to the enemies he hated.

Grant opened his campaign by starting a portion of his troops—those under McClernand—down through the swamps on the west side of the river. They were to build roads and prepare the way for the rest of the army so that no time would be wasted in making a junction with the fleet. McClernand, incidentally, was one of the few commanders in the army who supported Grant at this time, no doubt seeing in the hazardous movement a chance for personal advancement. McClernand did not lack courage.

About twenty-five miles down the river from Vicksburg, on the west bank, was a Confederate outpost commanded by Colonel Francis M. Cockrell. Among the men under Cockrell was Corporal Ephraim McDowell Anderson. Born and raised in Kentucky but now a member of a Confederate regiment from the border state of Missouri, where his father had been farming, Anderson was twenty-one years old and was described on his enlistment papers as being five feet eight inches tall, with a fair complexion but with dark hair and eyes.

The corporal had just returned from a week's leave at a village some miles east of the river, a week he had spent in courting a girl, "listening to the soft accents of her silvery voice, basking in the light of her smiles, and breathing the intoxicating atmosphere of love."

"Did you ever go fishing," Anderson asks,
when it was immaterial whether the fish nibbled or pulled the cork under?. . . I have, and this was the occasion. Setting our poles upon the edge of the bank, we withdrew to a little mossy knoll, shaded by the gorgeous foliage of a magnificent magnolia, laden with its wealth of fragrance . . . and beautiful bloom. Under that gigantic old tree, and in the presence of the girl I loved, was there anything more to desire?

The brief week had ended with Anderson hoping that "destiny might open the way for something beyond." Now, in camp with his unit on the west side of the river, he remembered the week as the "dearest and happiest epoch" of his life.

Anderson says of the troops at the outpost:
This force was bivouacked in the yard and upon the premises of a gentleman whose name was Perkins [i.e., Judge John Perkins], a representative in the Confederate Congress. He was now in Richmond, and had burned his handsome mansion, with every-

thing in it, before leaving [just prior to Farragut's first arrival from New Orleans]. It was stated that his object in doing this was to keep the Federals from having that pleasure themselves. The grounds around were ornamented with the now neglected remains of wealth and refinement. . . .

Federal forces were already moving down upon this side of the river, and their advance was at New Carthage, only a few miles above. The roll of the drums was within hearing distance. Their strength was not accurately ascertained, nor was the design of the movement they were making as yet apparent or obvious. . . .

During the stay here, our company was on picket duty most of the time, or reconnoitering the enemy's movements, the situation of their camp, and ascertaining if their advance was in force. This service was mostly discharged in small boats . . . as the country was generally under water. . . .

During a part of the time I stood picket with three or four of the boys . . . upon the plantations of President Davis and his brother, Joseph Davis. These estates were on the opposite side of the river from our command, and had once been in a fine state of improvement, but were now utterly in ruins, having been visited several times by Federal gunboats and Northern soldiers [during Farragut's expeditions]. A few half-starved old Negroes, unable to get away, were the only inhabitants left upon the premises.

Corporal Anderson soon got the chance to participate in a raid against a forward detachment of the Yankees who were coming down the west bank. Anderson's commander, Colonel Cockrell, learned through an area woman that this detachment had been collecting Negroes ("contrabands") and was holding them at a house on a nearby plantation. The house was encircled by only a light picket, or guard, with the main body of the detachment being encamped about a quarter of a mile away.

Anderson explains:

Cockrell determined to capture these Negroes, and the picket with them, if possible. . . . Taking our regiment and a few [other] companies . . . he left camp about three o'clock in the night. His design was to get there, secure his booty, and be off again before the enemy, in such close proximity, would be aroused.

Most of the route lay through a vast sheet of water, covering the surface of both woods and fields, from knee to waist-deep, through which the men had to wade, and, at the same time, carefully protect their guns and ammunition.

A somewhat protracted and cautious march brought us, about daylight, within sight of the house, when the colonel's dispositions were made so as to capture the parties [making up the picket] without delay. The men were ordered not to fire unless attacked from the direction of the camp.

The picket was surrounded and cut off, our men receiving a few shots from it as we advanced. It surrendered immediately, however, and was placed under guard. The shots aroused the darkies, who jumped up from their beds, in and around the house, and went yelling in every direction, badly frightened.... When they found there was no intention to kill them, they became less noisy and clamorous.

The colonel now ordered some of the boys to go upstairs and see if anyone was there. Several of us rushed up the steps, and, upon entering one of the rooms ... [surprised and captured] a tall, spare, grave-looking personage, accompanied by a young, full-grown, athletic ... Negress.... It was not long before we discovered that this live and interesting sybarite was the chaplain ... of an Illinois cavalry regiment....

This occurrence and the principal actor in it were a source of rare amusement ... to the picket we had captured, the men of which ... belonged to the same regiment with the chaplain.

The firing and melee had roused the soldiers in camp, who ... were rapidly assembling in arms. Our expedition was thus far successfully accomplished, and we moved off with the ... Negroes, besides the picket and chaplain, who were all safely conducted to camp.

Meanwhile, up the river above Vicksburg, Admiral Porter was completing his preparations for the passage of the city's batteries. Grant says that Porter found the supply transports a particular problem:
The great essential was to protect the boilers from the enemy's shot, and to conceal the fires under the boilers from view. This he accomplished by loading the steamers ... with bales of hay and cotton ... adding sacks of grain.... Before this, I had been collecting, from St. Louis and Chicago, yawls and barges to be used as ferries when we got below.

Grant's plans were unknown to the Confederates. The relative ease with which General Pemberton had frustrated Grant's attempts to attack Vicksburg from the north had lulled them into a feeling of invulnerability.

They were not careless or unalert, but they were devoting more time to life's amenities.

In the words of Confederate General Dabney Maury, who was living with his wife and baby in a house in the city's outskirts:

We desired to have our little son baptized, and the good Bishop [William M.] Green of Mississippi, who was in the city, kindly consented to perform the ceremony at my headquarters.... The members of my staff all assembled for the occasion.... While the ceremony was progressing, Grant opened a new battery upon my headquarters, and throughout the baptismal service the shriek of the falling shells sounded in our ears. One of them actually fell in the stable near at hand and exploded there; but the bishop went calmly on to the end, for Vicksburg had been under bombardment so long, and without fatal results, that all were accustomed to it.

A grand spring ball was being arranged for the night of April 16. The city's Christmas ball had been interrupted by Sherman's expedition from Memphis, but this one seemed on secure ground.

Nor did the occasional shellings interfere with other social plans. Late in the day on April 15, Mary W. Loughborough, the young wife of a Confederate officer stationed in Jackson, the state capital, about forty miles to the east, "set off with a party of friends for a pleasant visit to Vicksburg." The group traveled by train.

Employing an imagery that is both overdrawn and sometimes confusing, Mary relates:

How beautiful was this evening. The sun glowed and warmed its mellow tints over the rough forest trees; over the long moss that swung in slow and stately dignity, like old-time dancers scorning the quick and tripping movements of the present day!

Glowing and warming all over, this evening sun, this mellow, pleasant light, breaking in warm tints over the rugged ground of the plantations, showing us the home scenes as we passed; the sober and motherly cows going home for the evening's milking through the long lanes between the fields, where the fences threw shadows across the road; making strange, weird figures of the young colts' shadows, lean and long-limbed and distorted; the mothers, tired of eating the grass that grew so profusely, were standing in quiet contentment, or drank from the clear runs of water.

And so we passed on by the houses, where the planter sat on his veranda listening to the voice of his daughter reading the latest paper, while round her fair head, like a halo, the lingering beams of the sun played.

It was dark by the time the train rolled into Vicksburg, announcing its arrival with several toots of its shrill whistle. Mary went directly to the house where she was to be a guest. The next day dawned bright blue and mild, with the Vicksburg Whig *making the reassuring announcement that it anticipated "no immediate danger" from the Yankees. After breakfast, Mary set out on a sightseeing tour in her host's carriage:*

I had thought . . . that the town must have been a ruin; yet very little damage has been done, though very few houses are without evidence of the first trial of metal. One I saw with a hole through the window. . . . The corner of the piano had been taken off, and on through the wall the shot had passed. One, also, passed through another house, making a huge gap through the chimney.

. . . The inhabitants live in their homes . . . not knowing what moment the house may be rent over their heads by the explosion of a shell.

"Ah!" said I to a friend, "how is it possible you live here?"

"After one is accustomed to the change," she answered, "we do not mind it. But becoming accustomed, that is the trial."

. . . I looked over this beautiful landscape, and in the distance plainly saw the Federal transports lying quietly at their anchorage. Was it a dream? Could I believe that over this smiling scene in the bright April morning the blight of civil warfare lay like a pall? . . . Verily, war is a species of passionate insanity.

While standing and thinking thus, the loud booming of the guns in [our] water batteries startled me, the smoke showing that it was the battery just below me that opened, I was told, on what was thought to be a masked battery on the opposite shore. No reply was elicited, however.

Mary goes on to tell how she closed her day:

Our ride that evening had been delightful. We sat long on the veranda in the pleasant air, with the soft melody and rich swell of music from [a military] band floating around us, while ever and anon my eye sought the bend of the river . . . where the Federal transports, brought out in bold relief by the waning crimson light of the evening, lay in seeming quiet.

On a vessel farther up the river, General Grant was at this moment entertaining his wife, Julia, and their children, who had come down from

Memphis for a brief visit. Earlier in the day Julia, a plain, intelligent, cheerful woman to whom Grant was deeply devoted, had told the general pertly that he had better get his campaign in full swing at once or President Lincoln would surely put another general in his place. Grant had smiled and promised her a good show as David Porter took his squadron past the city.

The admiral was now ready for his perilous trip: "We knew they were to have a grand ball that night in Vicksburg, and thought the sounds of revelry would favor us in getting the transports past the batteries." No one in Vicksburg seems to have had any inkling of what was coming.

As recounted by a correspondent for the New York Times:

The plan decided upon was that the ironclads should pass down in single file, with intervals between the boats . . . and that when in front of the batteries they should engage them with their broadside guns, making as much smoke as possible, under cover of which the transports should endeavor to pass unseen.

A warm, cloudless day was succeeded by a clear twilight, beneath which boats [filled with spectators] from all points up the river began to assemble at the Lower Landing, a place about four miles in a direct line from Vicksburg, and which in daylight affords an extended and detailed view of the city and its fortifications.

The *Von Phul,* having on board General Grant and wife [and children], General McClernand and wife, together with several other military officials and ladies, also came down from Milliken's Bend, and took a position just at the head of the canal, where her passengers had a most excellent view of the whole operation. . . .

Other parties proceeded down in skiffs, yawls, tugs, etc., and placed themselves wherever they imagined the best view of the coming spectacle could be obtained. In short, by nine o'clock the audience was all seated, waiting and impatient for the opening of the performance.

There were in all perhaps thirty boats . . . each of which was black with spectators, of whom not a few were ladies. These, and the stars, were the witnesses. . . . I am bound to say that the stars were the more serious and quiet portion of the gathering. The balance passed the hours of waiting in jokes, laughter, choruses, and love-making—which, together with a running fusilade of champagne corks, indicated anything but an appreciation of the fact that the drama about to open was a tragedy instead of a roaring farce.

Lights twinkled busily from the Vicksburg hillsides until about ten o'clock, when they disappeared. And about the same moment song and laughter on our side were hushed, as a shapeless mass of what looked like a great fragment of darkness was discerned floating noiselessly down the river. It was the *Benton* [Admiral Porter's flagship]. It passed and disappeared in the night, and was succeeded by another bank of darkness—the *Lafayette* [a second gunboat, with a wooden naval steamer and a coal barge lashed, for their protection, to its side—the one away from the enemy]. . . .

Ten . . . noiseless shapes [including the three transports, or ordinary river steamers, loaded with supplies] revealed themselves and disappeared, and then we knew that all the actors in the play had given us the first scene of the first act.

According to Vicksburg's chief engineer, Samuel Lockett:

The movement of the boats was soon discovered by the Confederate pickets who nightly patrolled the river in small boats. They immediately crossed the river and fired several houses in the village of De Soto, so as to illuminate the river. To appreciate the boldness of this action, one must try to put himself in the place of these pickets, who ran great risks of being captured in landing on the opposite shore, which was occupied by the Federal forces. In addition, as soon as their work was accomplished they were exposed to the enemy's sharpshooters, [being] on the now brightly lighted river, and were in the direct line of fire of the batteries of their friends. Yet they neither failed nor faltered.

The beginning of the action found only a relatively few of Vicksburg's soldiers and citizens attending the grand ball. The great majority of the people were in bed. General Dabney Maury was sound asleep beside his wife, their newly christened baby in a crib nearby. Mrs. Maury snapped to a sitting position at the sound of the first shot. As others quickly followed, she shook her husband, calling him by his nickname, "Dab!"

Dab relates:

I sprang up and called to Jem [a slave] to saddle my horse. He seemed to be always awake, no matter at what hour he might be called, and he could "catch a horse" quicker than anyone I ever saw. By the time I was booted and spurred, the horse was ready at the door, and I mounted and galloped off towards the firing.

All of my staff were at [the] ball; but as I passed my couriers' quarters I shouted for them to turn out and follow, and as I

Passage of Porter's squadron as Vicksburg saw it
(From a sketch by Confederate engineer Samuel Lockett)

crossed [a] bridge I heard the clatter of horses' feet behind and
found one of my smartest Texans was close at hand. He joined
me, and together we mounted the hill overlooking the river in
time to see ... Porter's whole fleet as he came around the bend
above the city and past its front. ...

It was the grandest spectacle of my life. ... Our batteries were
in full play, blazing away at the line of gunboats making their way
past them and giving shot for shot. ... The whole landscape was
as light as day. ... Porter gamely led, and hove-to off the town to
send a few shots along its streets, which stampeded the entire
population, especially the ball, whence the gallant young officers
dashed away to their posts, leaving the ladies to their own devices. ...

Believing that Porter's whole fleet would join in the bombardment of the city, I sent a courier back to my wife, with instructions to get at once in the ambulance and drive out of the town
until she reached a position beyond the reach of the enemy's guns,
but she decided to remain where she was, and stayed serenely

there, explaining to me afterwards that she did not wish to take the baby into the night air.

A further word about the ball is provided by Mary Loughborough, though she herself did not attend:

Some young lady friends of mine were [there] . . . one dressed in a corn-colored silk, trimmed with black lace; another in blue silk, trimmed with white point; and still another in white lace. . . .

. . . As the first shot fell, one of the young girls, who was dancing with a brigadier general, clasped her hands and exclaimed, "Where shall we go?"

. . . He said, "To the country for safety."

. . . In the confusion that ensued, she told her young friends. They set out alone with all speed, frightened and trembling. . . .

A gentleman friend, discovering their absence, overtook and proceeded with them. As a shell would be heard coming, he would cry, "Fall!" And down they would drop in the dust, party dresses and all, lying until the explosion took place; then up, with wild eyes and fiercely beating hearts, flying with all speed onward.

After running about a mile in the fewest moments possible, and falling several times, they stopped at the first house, and remained.

One of these girls was to tell Mary later: "If you could have seen our party dresses . . . and our hair, and the flowers, full of dust, you would never have forgotten us!"

Though Mary herself was in a deep sleep when the action began, in a few moments she was in her robe and slippers, running to the veranda:

Our friends were already there. The river was illuminated by large fires . . . and we could discern plainly the huge black masses floating down with the current, now and then belching forth fire from their sides, followed by the loud reports, and we could hear the shells exploding in the upper part of town. . . .

Each [vessel], on passing the track of the brilliant light on the water, became a target for the land batteries. We could hear the gallop, in the darkness, of couriers upon the paved streets; we could hear the voices of the soldiers on the riverside. The rapid firing from the boats, the roar of the Confederate batteries, and, above all, the screaming, booming sound of the shells as they exploded in the air and around the city, made at once a new and fearful scene to me.

The... shells were beginning to fly unpleasantly near. My heart beat quickly as the flashes of light from the portholes seemed facing us. Some of the gentlemen urged the ladies to go down into the cave at the back of the house.... While I hesitated... a shell exploded near the side of the house. Fear instantly decided me, and I ran, guided by one of the ladies, who pointed down the steep slope of the hill, and left me to run back for a shawl.

While I was considering the best way of descending the hill, another shell exploded near the foot, and, ceasing to hesitate, I flew down, half sliding and running. Before I had reached the mouth of the cave, two more exploded on the side of the hill near me. Breathless and terrified, I found the entrance and ran in, having left one of my slippers on the hillside.

I found two or three of our friends had already sought refuge under the earth; and we had not been there long before we were joined by the remainder of the party, who reported the boats opposite the house.... I was sorry to find myself slightly fluttered and in a state of rapid heart-beatings as shell after shell fell in the valley below us, exploding with a loud, rumbling noise, perfectly deafening.

The cave was an excavation in the earth the size of a large room, high enough for the tallest person to stand perfectly erect, provided with comfortable seats, and altogether quite a large and habitable abode (compared with some of the caves in the city), were it not for the dampness and the constant contact with the soft earthy walls.

While Mary and her friends sat in their cave, eyes wide in the lamplight, and with Mary keeping her slipperless foot drawn modestly back beneath her robe, the uproar outside increased. Many people were still in the streets. In the firelight, they ran about, some of them shouting and gesticulating. Galloping horses pulled fieldpieces into position alongside the heavy guns already firing, and bodies of infantry sent to the wharves began to harry the Federals with small-arms fire.

Watching from the Von Phul, *General Grant found the sight "magnificent but terrible." An aide to Grant, James Harrison Wilson, was curiously engaged:*

"One of the Grant children sat on my knees with its arms around my neck, and as each crash came, it nervously clasped me closer, and finally became so frightened that it was put to bed."

Frederick Dent Grant, twelve years old at the time, was later to recall: "My father and I stood side by side on the hurricane deck. He was quietly smoking, but an intense light shone in his eyes."

Among the ladies on board the Von Phul *was a "sanitary agent," or nurse, from Iowa, Mrs. Annie Wittenmyer, who was experiencing "the most exciting night" she had ever known:*

Our boat swayed with the concussion of sound. . . . Each shot and shell had a voice of its own, and could be heard in thunder tones with awful distinctness. And running through the bass and treble of solid shot and screaming shells, the click of the musketry of the sharpshooters on the wharves of Vicksburg could be heard as, by the light of the bonfires blazing high, they aimed the deadly bullets at the captains and pilots who stood up unarmed in full view. . . .

Shells were flying in every direction. With their burning fuses they made their [semi]circles, dropping down out of the sky like stars of the first magnitude, now and then . . . bursting in mid-heaven with a million scintillations of light. . . .

. . . Mrs. Grant and I stood together . . . shivering with agony. We . . . were overwhelmed with anxiety for the safety . . . and the success of the expedition. . . .

"Our men are all dead men." "No one can live in such a rain of fire and lead," we said to each other.

Actually, casualties remained minimal. As related by an unnamed officer on board the Federal gunboat Lafayette:

A perfect tornado of shot and shell continued to shriek over our deck and among all the vessels of the fleet . . . but not more than one in ten struck or did any damage. . . . They mostly went over. . . . A good view could be had, through the ports, of the rebel batteries, which now flashed like a thunderstorm along the river as far as the eye could see.

But the incessant spatter of rifle balls, the spray from falling shot, the thunder of steel-pointed projectiles upon our sides, did not incline one to take a very protracted view of the scenery.

A few discharges of grape, shrapnel, and percussion shell was all we could afford at the time to bestow upon our rebel friends in exchange for their compliments. At each round the Confederate artillerymen gave a shout, which seemed surprisingly near. At one time we could not have been one hundred yards from the Vicksburg wharves.

Our vessel, with the steamer and barge lashed to our starboard side, became almost unmanageable, drifted in the eddy and turned her head square round, looking the batteries in the face. At this time we seemed to be receiving their concentrated fire at less than a hundred yards from the shore. The smoke from our own and the rebel guns, with the glare of the burning buildings from the opposite shore, rendered it difficult for the pilots to make out the direction we were going.

The enemy, supposing we were disabled, set up a fiendish yell of triumph. We soon, however, backed round and once more presented our broadside to them, and slowly drifted past, as if in contempt of their impotent efforts. Shells burst all around the pilot house, and at one time John Denning, our pilot, was literally baptized with fire. He thought himself killed, but he brushed the fire from his head and found he was unhurt.

A second Federal newspaper correspondent who was among the spectators says that after "an interval of maddest rage," the gunfire on both sides began to slacken:

Just as the . . . longer and longer intervals of silence gave intimation that the exciting scene was nearly over . . . a new glow of light . . . climbed gently toward the sky.

"They are lighting another beacon!" shouted many voices.

But . . . the speakers were mistaken. The light . . . with slow and equal pace, was moving onward, passing down the stream! There was no disguising the truth—one of our own boats [a transport] was on fire!

Mary Loughborough, still in her cave, was aware only that the terrifying sounds and vibrations had diminished:

One of the gentlemen came down to tell us that all danger was over, and that we might witness a beautiful sight by going upon the hill, as one of the transports had been fired by a shell and was slowly floating down as it burned.

We returned to the house, and from the veranda looked on the burning boat, the only one, as far as we could ascertain, that had been injured, the other boats having all passed successfully by the city. We remained on the veranda . . . the gentlemen speculating on the result of the successful run by the batteries. All were astonished and chagrined. . . .

The lurid glare of the burning boat fell in red and amber light upon the house, the veranda, and the animated faces turned toward the river.... I sat and gazed upon the burning wreck of what an hour ago had thronged with human life; with men whose mothers had this very night prayed for them; with men whose wives tearfully hovered over little beds, kissing each tender, sleeping lid for the absent ones. Had this night made them orphans?

As a matter of fact, only the cargo of supplies was lost with the transport. All hands including a white chambermaid who had insisted on sharing the adventure with the men, had escaped, chiefly by means of the vessel's small boats. The pilot, who had remained on board as long as possible, had been plucked out of the water by a detail of rescue boats under General Sherman. He and his party of volunteers had worked their way across the swamps of the De Soto peninsula, with some of the men staying on the levee and others pushing out into the river below Vicksburg to be on hand for just such an emergency as had occurred.

Relates Admiral Porter:

I had just passed the last battery... when I was hailed by someone in a boat, "*Benton* ahoy!"

"Halloo!" I replied, and presently I recognized the voice of General Sherman.

"Are you all right, old fellow?"

"Come on board and see," I replied, and Sherman came over the side to hear about our fortunes.

The *Benton*, in lead, clears last battery and is hailed by Sherman, who has been watching the show from small boat depicted in foreground

"One man's leg cut off by a round shot; half a dozen shell and musket ball wounds," I said.

". . . There are a lot of my boys on the point ready to help you if you want anything. . . . Good night! I must go and find out how the other fellows fared."

The whole squadron passed Sherman and moved on to Warrenton, on the east bank about five miles below. A few more guns were encountered, but the fighting was anticlimactic.

For the federal spectators in their boats above Vicksburg, the show ended with the knowledge that the passage had succeeded. Saya Annie Wittenmyer:

General Grant came down from the upper deck with the glad news, for he had been watching for the signals or rockets that the boats, one by one, sent up as they got safely through.

The beacon fires died, and their smoke, mingled with that of the gunfire, drifted away. A deep silence settled over the river. Julia Grant was aware that "the stars looked down tenderly upon Union and Rebel alike . . . and the frogs began again their summer songs."

Admiral Porter was elated:

Although the squadron was under fire from the time of passing the first battery until the last vessel got by, a period of two hours and thirty minutes, the vessels were struck in their hulls but sixty-eight times by shot and shells, and only fifteen men were wounded.

At 2:30 A.M. all the vessels were safely anchored at New Carthage . . . where was encamped the advanced division of the army under General McClernand. [These men had heard the gunfire at Vicksburg and Warrenton, and now some of them came to the bank and shouted their jubilation at the squadron's safe arrival.]

The plantation at this place was owned by an ultra-Confederate who exulted over the expected loss of all the gunboats . . . but when at two o'clock he saw them one after another heave in sight . . . signaling to the flagship "all's well," he went off in despair, got drunk, set fire to his house . . . and departed to parts unknown.

During the next few days many of the other people living in the threatened areas made hasty evacuations. The detachment of Confederate troops to which Corporal Ephraim Anderson belonged slipped across the Mississippi

*to the east bank, its destination Grand Gulf, the point some miles below
where the Big Black River, which flowed down from the north about ten
miles east of Vicksburg, made its ingress.*

Anderson recounts:

Slaves from the ... plantations were seen flocking off in the
direction of the Federal forces. They went by hundreds, each
carrying a bundle of some description. Old and young—men,
women, and children—seemed to be making a general hegira....

... Beautiful habitations ... were being broken up and abandoned, and nearly everything about them was left to the mercy of
the enemy. The families removed with such valuables as jewelry
and plate, and the few trusty servants disposed to follow them.
Personal safety and security made this course indispensable, as the
war on the part of the Federal forces had become one of general
plunder and indiscriminate conflagration.

*The Confederates at Vicksburg, as Samuel Lockett explains, now turned
an anxious watch on New Carthage:*

Here there was a fleet of formidable gunboats, and transports
and barges enough to ferry a large force across the river. This
gave a serious and threatening aspect to the movement.

*It wasn't only the imminence of an attack that worried the Confederates.
When Porter took control of the river below Vicksburg, he cut off the boat
traffic on which the city depended for a part of its supplies. Among many of
the residents, the supply problem was already serious. Dora Miller, the
bride from New Orleans, admitted to her diary:*

I never understood before the full force of those questions—
What shall we eat ... and wherewithal shall we be clothed?

... Such minute attention must be given the wardrobe to pre-
serve it that I have learned to darn like an artist. Making shoes is
now another accomplishment. Mine were in tatters.... A pair of
old coatsleeves saved—nothing is thrown away now—was in my
trunk. I cut an exact pattern from my old shoes, laid it on the
sleeves, and cut out thus good uppers and sewed them carefully;
then soaked the soles and sewed the cloth to them.

I am so proud of these home-made shoes; think I'll put them
in a glass case when the war is over, as an heirloom.

*At first the only Union troops with the fleet at New Carthage were those
under McClernand. While Grant lingered at Milliken's Bend to tie up*

loose ends, other units began to make their way down the river's west bank. David Porter says their march was a slow one.

The roads were in wretched condition, and the artillery and wagons were continually stalled. The soldiers had therefore to corduroy the roads [i.e., to cover the muddy spots with logs laid side by side] so that those coming after could get along faster, but it was terrible marching at the best.

From the little damage that had been inflicted on the gunboats, General Grant felt satisfied that he could send transports [with additional supplies] by the batteries of Vicksburg, and shortly afterwards six of these, on a dark night, passed down in charge of their pilots.... Only one steamer was sunk by the enemy's shot.

A sufficient number of gunboats had been left at the mouth of the Yazoo River to take care of the upper Mississippi.... Sherman remained with his division at Young's Point, ready to make another attack from the Yazoo if opportunity offered, and also to protect the supplies at Milliken's Bend.

The protection of these supplies was about to be turned over to a special detachment not scheduled to join the campaign around Vicksburg's rear—a detachment that included some of the first Southern blacks to become soldiers in the Union army. President Lincoln had sent General Lorenzo Thomas from Washington to organize black regiments on the Mississippi, and Grant had given the move his cooperation. Thomas's work, however, was proceeding slowly. The great majority of blacks associated with Grant's campaign would continue to be laborers and servants.

Admiral Porter continues:

General McClernand had been ordered by Grant to push forward ... and, with the help of the navy, to seize upon Grand Gulf [where Grant hoped to make his crossing].... McClernand had been given the advance to satisfy his ambition, but he was not equal to the occasion....

Grant, in the company of Charles Dana of the War Department, moved his headquarters to the New Carthage area on April 23. Dana explains that an "irritating delay" now occurred:

McClernand's corps was not ready to move.... There was apparently much confusion in McClernand's command, and I was astonished to find, now that he was ordered to move across the

Mississippi, that he was planning to carry his bride with her servants and baggage along with him, although Grant had ordered that officers should leave behind everything that could impede the march.

On the 26th, the day when it was hoped to make an attack on Grand Gulf . . . [McClernand's] steamboats and barges were scattered about in the river and in the bayou as if there was no idea of the imperative necessity of the promptest movement possible. . . . Grant sent for McClernand, ordering him to embark his men without losing a moment.

In spite of this order, that night at dark . . . not a single cannon or man had been moved. Instead, McClernand held a review of a brigade of Illinois troops . . . about four o'clock in the afternoon. At the same time a salute of artillery was fired, notwithstanding the positive orders that had repeatedly been given to use no ammunition for any purpose except against the enemy. . . .

. . . The next morning . . . Grant . . . wrote a very severe letter to McClernand, but learning that at last the transport steamers and barges had been concentrated for use he did not send the rebuke.

That same morning, according to Colonel William Vilas,

Grant wrote Sherman [who was still above Vicksburg] of his desire to have a seeming attack on Haynes' Bluff to distract the enemy's attention from his operations. Yet it looked hard to ask Sherman to undergo again an apparent repulse, who had been so sorely abused in Northern newspapers and derided in the South for his failure there in the Christmas season before. And so Grant's letter to him ran:

"The effect of a heavy demonstration in that direction would be good so far as the enemy are concerned, but I am loth to order it, because it would be so hard to make our own troops understand that only a demonstration was intended, and our people at home would characterize it as a repulse. I therefore leave it to you whether to make such a demonstration. . . ."

Sherman's reply the next day was characteristic: "I will take ten steamers and ten regiments and go up the Yazoo as close to Haynes' as possible without putting the transports under the rifled guns of the enemy. We will make as strong a demonstration as possible.

"The troops will understand the purpose, and will not be hurt by the repulse. The people of the country must find out the truth as they best can; it is none of their business. You are engaged in a hazardous enterprise, and, for good reasons, wish to divert attention. That is sufficient for me, and it shall be done."

Grant points out:

My object was to compel Pemberton to keep as much force about Vicksburg as I could until I could secure a good footing on high land east of the river. [Sherman's] move was eminently successful, and, as we afterwards learned, created great confusion about Vicksburg, and doubts about our real design.

At this same time, Pemberton and his troops—now numbering about 45,000 effectives—were confused also by Federal cavalry commander Benjamin H. Grierson, who led a raid down through Mississippi from the Tennessee border.

Relates Mary Loughborough, now back in the capital city of Jackson, about forty miles east of Vicksburg, after her hair-raising visit to the beleaguered city:

Our quiet was destined to be of short duration. We were startled one morning by hearing that Colonel Grierson, of the Federal army, was advancing on Jackson. The citizens applied to General Pemberton [then in Jackson] to protect them. He answered that there was no danger.

Suddenly the ladies' carriage and saddle horses were pressed [into service], and the clerks and young men of the town were mounted on them, and started out to protect us! I was told that the first time they met the Federal troops most of them were captured, and we heard of them no more.

As it turned out, Grierson passed well to the east of Jackson, continuing on to Baton Rouge, Louisiana, and joining the Federal forces there. He had not only drawn attention from Grant but had torn up many miles of railroad tracks and had destroyed engines, cars, stations, factories, and other public property, the total worth of which was several million dollars. This was one of the great cavalry raids of the war.

Admiral Porter took his fleet against the batteries of Grand Gulf, where Grant hoped to make his landing, on the morning of April 29. The Confederate guns were securely placed on a commanding bluff. In Grant's words:

For nearly five and a half hours the attack was kept up. . . . All this time McClernand's 10,000 men were huddled together on the transports in the stream, ready to attempt a landing if signalled. I occupied a tug from which I could see the effect of the battle on both sides.

One of those fighting on the Confederate side was Ephraim Anderson, the corporal who had helped to capture the sinning chaplain. Anderson says that some of the Federal vessels came close under the bluff:

The fire from all the boats was ... furious, and our guns were skilfully handled. ... One of the gun carriages of the lower battery was injured by a very heavy discharge of powder [the gun having been overloaded] ... while one of the upper battery was disabled by a shot from the enemy. Colonel [William] Wade was killed at one of the guns of the lower battery, his head torn off by an immense shell. ... A shell also fell and exploded in the rifle pits ... and killed and wounded eleven men. A few other casualties also occurred.

Considering that Porter's big guns threw more than a hundred tons of metal at the Confederates, little was accomplished. Grant explains that the fleet withdrew up the river about half-past one:

The enemy ceased firing as soon as we withdrew. I immediately signalled the Admiral and went aboard his ship. The navy lost in this engagement eighteen killed and fifty-six wounded. A large proportion of these were of the crew of the flagship. ... The sight of the mangled and dying men which met my eye as I boarded the ship was sickening.

Porter takes up:

General Grant ... decided that it would be too hazardous to attempt to land troops, as it did not appear that the guns in the enemy's works were dismounted. ... For the same reason the general concluded not to send the transports past the batteries with the soldiers on board but to march the latter around by land.

The troops disembarked on the river's west bank near Hard Times. Porter's squadron tied up nearby to bury its dead, "who were followed mournfully to their graves by their messmates and friends."

Three hours afterwards [Porter goes on] the squadron got underway and again attacked the batteries, while the transports all passed in safety. ... Some of the Confederate gunners fired at the gunboats but did no damage.

It was dark when the fleet tied up at De Shroon's plantation, on the west bank a few miles below. The troops made a night march to the same spot with a minimum of confusion.

Relates the "special commissioner" from Washington, Charles Dana:

Late in the evening I left Hard Times with Grant to ride . . . to De Shroon's. The night was pitch dark, and, as we rode side by side, Grant's horse suddenly gave a nasty stumble. I expected to see the general go over the animal's head, and I watched intently . . . to see . . . if he would show any anger.

I had been with Grant daily now for three weeks, and I had never seen him ruffled or heard him swear. His equanimity was becoming a curious spectacle to me. When I saw his horse lunge my first thought was, "Now he will swear."

. . . But Grant was a tenacious horseman, and instead of going over the animal's head, as I imagined he would, he kept his seat. Pulling up his horse, he rode on . . . without a word or sign of impatience.

Looking down the river from the dark heights of Grand Gulf that night, Confederate Corporal Anderson and his comrades saw many tiny lights moving about on the west bank and also on the decks of Porter's warships and the other vessels in their company. The Federal troops had begun embarking as soon as they reached De Shroon's.

Late that night Admiral Porter entertained a special guest from Washington on board his flagship. Lorenzo Thomas, the general who was recruiting Negro regiments on the Mississippi, was traveling with Grant's advance in company with two other officials. Looking somewhat less than dignified as he sat in a long nightshirt taken from his carpet bag, Thomas informed Porter that he had a secret to impart.

In Porter's words:

"Wait a moment," I interrupted, "your throat sounds dry; try this glass of toddy; it will make you sleep like a top, and you won't feel the mosquitoes."

The general drank it down without winking. "You would have made a fortune, Admiral, as a barkeeper," he said; "you have such a talent for mixing drinks. But don't mention what I'm going to tell you. I carry in my bag full authority to remove General Grant and place whomsoever I please in command of the army."

And the old general drew himself up and looked at me as much as to say, "What do you think of that?"

I reflected for a moment, and then asked whom it was proposed to put in Grant's place.

"Well," replied General Thomas, "that depends. McClernand is prominent."

"General," I said, "no doubt your plans are well considered, but let an old salt give you a piece of advice. Don't let your plans get out, for if the army and navy should find out what you three gentlemen came for, they would tar and feather you, and neither General Grant nor myself could prevent it."

"Is it possible?" exclaimed the general. "But I don't intend to do anything. We are delighted with all we have seen, so there will be no change...."

General Thomas apparently related this story about his secret orders for effect alone. If he really had such orders—and it is more likely that he had only the power to suggest Grant's removal to Lincoln—they were a month old and had become essentially obsolete as soon as Grant launched his grand movement past Vicksburg.

On the morning of April 30, says Grant,

the enemy [at Grand Gulf] saw our whole fleet, ironclads, gunboats, river steamers and barges, quietly moving down the river ... black, or rather blue, with National troops. ... A colored man [had] informed me that a good landing would be found at Bruinsburg ... from which point there was a good road leading to ... the interior. The information was found to be correct, and our landing was effected without opposition.

Bruinsburg was merely a boat landing at another deserted plantation, and the only audience as the thousands of men poured ashore with cheers and shouts and amiable jostlings were a few blacks who saw in the great blue tide a vision of the Promised Land.

Grant states that the debarkation brought him a vast feeling of relief:

Vicksburg was not yet taken, it is true, nor were its defenders demoralized by any of our previous moves. I was now in the enemy's country, with ... the stronghold of Vicksburg between me and my base of supplies. But I was on dry ground on the same side of the river with the enemy. All the campaigns, labors, hardships and exposures from the month of December ... to this time ... were for the accomplishment of this one object.

6

GRANT ATTACKS TOWARD JACKSON

BRUINSBURG AND the surrounding country [explains Admiral Porter] was the great depot for livestock, grain, etc., and in twenty-four hours . . . fresh meat abounded in camp. . . . Foraging was not prohibited; in fact, the soldiers were cautioned to save the government rations for an emergency; so that the squealing of pigs, and the bleating of calves and sheep, and the cackling of poultry were common sounds in camp, and many a fence rail was burned to cook [the foraged] provisions.

At this time, Grant points out, the army's wagon train was still on the Mississippi's west bank:

My own horses, headquarters transportation, servants, mess chest, and everything except what I had on, was with this train. General A. J. Smith happened to have an extra horse at Bruinsburg, which I borrowed, with a saddle-tree without up-holstery further than stirrups. . . .

It was necessary to have transportation for ammunition. . . . I directed, therefore, immediately on landing, that all the vehicles and draft animals, whether horses, mules, or oxen, in the vicinity should be collected and loaded to their capacity with ammunition.

Quite a train was collected . . . and a motley train it was. In it could be found fine carriages loaded nearly to the top with boxes of cartridges that had been pitched in promiscuously, drawn by mules with plough harness, straw collars, rope lines, etc.; long-coupled wagons, with racks for carrying cotton bales, drawn by oxen, and everything that could be found in the way of transportation on a plantation, either for use or pleasure.

Grant was now about thirty miles south of Vicksburg. To make his landing secure, he headed McClernand and his troops eastward toward Port Gib-

McClernand's advance on Port Gibson

son, a dozen miles from the river, on the afternoon of the day they disembarked. The men were in a new kind of country now, with the road to Port Gibson winding over a set of bluffs. According to an unnamed correspondent:

The route over these bluffs differs so materially from that over the dead levels of the preceding days that we were continually finding something to wonder at and admire. The abrupt acclivities, the deep ravines, the waving corn, the beautiful flowers and magnificent magnolias . . . diffusing most delicious perfumes, and the long line of soldiers winding along the green trees, formed a truly beautiful picture.

Darkness fell, and McClernand continued his march, though now with greater caution. It was a pleasant, starlit night, and the troops retained their daytime cheer. Every now and then the artillerymen sent shells bursting over the woods on both sides of the road as illuminations seeking a hidden foe.

It was about 1 A.M., and the head of the column was still a few miles west of Port Gibson, when the first Confederate muskets sparkled and crashed, to be followed by the flash and roar of artillery. These were the advance troops of a 7,500-man force under General John S. Bowen, which had hurried from Grand Gulf to Port Gibson in an attempt to block the Yankee penetration.

The invaders drew up and rested on their arms until dawn, at which time they deployed and moved forward to the attack. Elements of the

Confederate force were still approaching the field, among them the Third and Fifth Missouri infantry regiments, marching together. As related by Colonel Robert S. Bevier, of the Fifth:

It was early in the day when we moved through Port Gibson, and the noble people of the old town were up and out to cheer us to the contest. Already it could be heard . . . the mingling echoes of cannon and musket. . . . Soft-eyed women looked at us through their tears, and strong old men sobbed their farewells, knowing it was the last day for many of us.

About two miles beyond the town we struck the . . . hills that bristle all along this portion of the Mississippi, and, climbing up and down one rugged acclivity after another, we at length came to a halt in an old cornfield in front of a thick canebrake, and at the foot of a steep, cane-covered hill. Here we lay for some hours, waiting for orders and listening to the semicircle of firing that appeared to be enlarging. . . .

In his camp at Bruinsburg, General Grant had waked to the sounds of the battle and had ridden speedily toward the scene. On the way he passed units of the corps led by Major General James B. McPherson, who was following closely behind McClernand. In all, about 20,000 Federals were available for the attack. Grant recounts:

I was on the field by ten A.M., and inspected both flanks. . . . On the right [where McClernand was commanding in person] the enemy, if not being pressed back, was at least not repulsing our advance. On the left, however, [Brigadier General Peter J.] Osterhaus was not faring so well. He had been repulsed with some loss. . . . I ordered up McPherson . . . with two brigades of Logan's division. This was about noon.

I ordered him to send one brigade . . . to support Osterhaus, and to move [the other] to the left and flank the enemy out of his position. . . . Osterhaus was directed to renew his front attack. It was successful and unattended by heavy loss. The enemy was sent in full retreat on their right. . . .

The Confederate left, which faced McClernand, held on a little longer, though, like the right, it was strongly outnumbered. The Third and Fifth Missouri, after their lengthy pause in the old cornfield, had been thrust into the thick of this action, where leaves and twigs, clipped from the trees by zinging bullets, showered to the ground. Confederate Colonel Bevier says that "the continuous roll of small guns was appalling, almost drown-

ing the fierce discharge of the artillery. The noise was so incessant that no orders could be heard."

At last a courier arrived and informed the regiments that a general retreat was commencing. Bevier continues:

By signs only could the retreat be *sounded.* . . . All semblance of organization was lost. The rush to the rear was active and speedy; and over the low brow of the hill, for fifty feet sheer down, the two regiments tumbled, each man plowing his individual furrow through the canebrake, to the sore distress of his person and his uniform.

At the very place where we lay so long in the cornfield, our flags were again unfolded and the rallying point established. Out of the three hundred and fifty men that went into the fight, we lost over one hundred. The remnant promptly rallied round the flag. . . . Here we remained until near sundown, the enemy not seeming disposed to follow us up or push their advantage. We retired slowly, and with precision. . . .

The social festivities of Port Gibson [enjoyed during previous months of duty in the area] had endeared it to us. The elegant hospitality of its people had constituted the place an oasis in the desert of our military career. It was, therefore, with sad hearts that the remnants of our regiments slowly, and for the last time, marched through the streets. Again the terrified friends were out to greet us, with tearful eyes and pale faces, wishing us God speed, and apprehending the worst of fates in their own future.

We were compelled to abandon them to it . . . and just as the sun was sinking below the horizon . . . its last lingering rays decking the church steeples and adorning the court house cupola, we turned from the last fond gaze at them and plunged [northward] into the deepening shades of the woods that bordered the bayou.

These men, along with the rest of General Bowen's small army, were heading back up the Mississippi to Grand Gulf, their starting point; but they would quickly abandon that place also and retreat north toward Vicksburg.

Bowen had been obliged to leave his dead and the worst of his wounded on the Port Gibson battlefield. Confederate casualties in the day-long struggle totaled about 790 killed, wounded, captured, and missing. The Federals lost about 850.

A glimpse of conditions behind the Union lines that day is given by Charles Dana, who left Bruinsburg for Port Gibson an hour or two after

Grant. Dana says that he was on foot:

I had not gone far before I overtook a quartermaster driving toward Port Gibson. He took me in his wagon. About four miles from Port Gibson we came upon the first signs of battle, a field where it was evident that there had been a struggle. I got out of the wagon as we approached, and started toward a little white house with green blinds, covered with vines. The little white house had been taken as a field hospital, and the first thing my eyes fell upon as I went into the yard was a heap of arms and legs which had been amputated and thrown into a pile outside. . . .

As the army was pressing the Confederates toward Port Gibson all that day I followed in the rear, without overtaking General Grant. While trailing along after the Union forces I came across Fred Grant [the general's twelve-year-old son] . . . who had been left asleep by his father on a steamer at Bruinsburg, but who had started out on foot like myself as soon as he awoke and found the army had marched.

Fred had shortly mounted a mule with one of the army's improvised wagon trains; then he switched to a seat on a caisson belonging to an artillery battery; finally he began walking again. He made a curious picture, for he was wearing the sash and sword his father never bothered to use. Fred relates:

The horrors of a battlefield were brought vividly before me. I joined a detachment which was collecting the dead for burial. Sickening at the sights, I made my way with another detachment, which was gathering the wounded, to a log house which had been appropriated for a hospital. Here the scenes were so terrible that I became faint, and making my way to a tree, sat down, the most woebegone twelve-year-old lad in America.

Soon an approaching horseman hailed me, an orderly from my father's escort, and, dismounting, he proceeded to make me comfortable, putting down his saddle for a pillow, and advising me to go to sleep. This I did, but suddenly I heard the orderly cry out: "Your father has come."

About fifty yards off sat my father, drinking coffee from a tin cup. I went to him, and was greeted with an exclamation of surprise, as he supposed I was still on board the boat.

Grant was pleased at the enterprise the boy had shown, but had little time to devote to him, for the battle was only now being concluded. The general moved on; and it was then that Charles Dana came up and joined Fred. In Dana's words:

We tramped and foraged together until the next morning, when some officers who had captured two old horses gave us each one. We got the best bridles and saddles we could, and thus equipped made our way to Port Gibson, which the enemy had deserted and where General Grant now had his headquarters.

Detachments of Grant's army spent this day hastening the retreating Confederates north toward Vicksburg, though Grant did not intend to press far in that direction at this time.

On the next day, May 3, according to Dana,

General Grant started with a brigade of infantry and some twenty cavalrymen for Grand Gulf. I accompanied him on the trip. . . . Grant made inquiries on every side about the food supplies of the country we were entering. He told me he had been gathering information on this point ever since the army had crossed the Mississippi, and had made up his mind that both . . . cattle and corn were abundant in the country.

Reaching the Gulf, Grant found all the Confederates gone and Admiral Porter there with his fleet. The general explains:

I had not been with my baggage since the 27th of April and consequently had had no change of underclothing, no meal except such as I could pick up sometimes at other headquarters, and no tent to cover me. The first thing I did was to get a bath, borrow some fresh underclothing from one of the naval officers, and get a good meal on the flagship. . . .

While at Grand Gulf I heard from Banks [commander of the Department of the Gulf of Mexico] . . . who said that he could not be at Port Hudson before the 10th of May and then with only 15,000 men. Up to this time my intention had been to secure Grand Gulf as a base of supplies, detach McClernand's corps to Banks, and cooperate with him in the reduction of Port Hudson [afterward moving against Vicksburg with Banks's help].

The news from Banks forced upon me a different plan of campaign from the one I intended. To wait for his cooperation would have detained me at least a month. . . . The enemy would have strengthened his position and been reinforced by more men than Banks could have brought. I therefore determined to move independently of Banks, cut loose from my base [at Grand Gulf], destroy the rebel force in rear of Vicksburg, and invest or capture the city.

Grant's campaign, influenced by frequent reassessments of the situation, was to develop in such a way that he moved first toward the Confederate garrison at Jackson, the state capital, which lay about sixty miles northeast of Grand Gulf and, as stated before, about forty miles eastward along the railroad from Vicksburg.

With Sherman now coming down the west bank of the Mississippi after his demonstration at Haynes' Bluff, Grant would shortly have about 40,000 men on the east bank. Confederate General Pemberton's forces more than matched that number, but they were widely scattered, since Pemberton was still unsure of Grant's intentions. Some of the Confederates were tied to vital garrisons, including Vicksburg itself. Pemberton had less than 20,000 men available for maneuver.

Since Grant wanted to have as many supplies as possible on hand as he cut loose from Grand Gulf, he ordered another expedition from Milliken's Bend to be sent past the Vicksburg batteries. The quartermaster, who had remained at the Bend, could muster only three vessels, the steam tug Sturgess *and two barges which he loaded with foodstuffs and bales of hay.*

The crews numbered about thirty-five men in all, mostly soldiers; but also included were three news correspondents: Junius H. Browne and Albert D. Richardson, both of the New York Tribune, *and Richard T. Colburn, of the New York* World. *Spirited young bachelors, they belonged to a fraternity of newsmen who called themselves the "Bohemians." Though the trio could have made the trip to Grant's army by way of the west bank, they chose to join the river expedition because it offered a greater chance for excitement.*

The little tugboat, with the two barges in tow, started from Milliken's Bend during the moonlit night of May 3. In the words of newsman Junius Browne:

As we sat smoking our cigars on the barges, we could see every tree on the banks of the mighty river; and as we neared the peninsula opposite Vicksburg we could observe the different streets and buildings of the city that had so long defied the combined power of our army and navy.

An officer with us had a bottle of Catawba, and as there was some probability that, in the storm of shot and shell which awaited us, its flavor might be damaged, we quaffed its contents to the speedy downfall of the hostile stronghold and the early suppression of the Rebellion, to the women we loved . . . and to the consolation of the unfortunately married. . . . Ours was indeed a merry party. . . .

We were moving very little faster than the current of the stream; and as we began to round the peninsula . . . the Rebel pickets, who had . . . very unwisely been permitted [by the diminishing Union troops in the area] to cross the river and take position on the Louisiana shore, gave the alarm by discharging their muskets at us—without detriment, however—followed by a signal rocket from the city. . . .

Now the heavy guns opened with their thunderous roar, and the first struck one of the barges, as we knew from the jar. . . . The round shot howled, and the shells shrieked over our heads, and sometimes cut . . . the hay bales in a manner calculated to give . . . something of a sensation. . . . All along the shore we saw the flashes of the guns. . . . Clouds of smoke rose along the river like a dense fog, and the water and the atmosphere shook with reverberations. . . .

. . . At times we were not more than three or four hundred yards from the ten-inch guns. It did seem strange our frail vessels, which were struck again and again, were not blown to pieces. But the little tug—semi-occasionally we heard its quick, sharp puff—passed on and we were yet unharmed. . . .

. . . The Rebels, as if disappointed and enraged, seemed to augment their efforts. Faster and heavier the batteries thundered, and louder howled the shot and shrieked the shell, above, below, around. . . .

For three-quarters of an hour we were under the terrible fire, and were near the lower end of the city. Another quarter would put us out of danger, for we had passed the heaviest batteries. . . . In the occasional pause of the artillery . . . we could detect the rapid puff, puff, puff of the little tug, which was the sure sign that we still floated.

Suddenly a huge crash, by our side, of wood and iron. A deep and heavy and peculiar report. A rush of steam and a descending shower of cinders and ashes that covered our persons. We heard the puff of the tug no more. . . .

The boiler . . . had been exploded by a plunging shot from one of the upper batteries. The shot . . . wrecked our expedition at once. After passing through the boiler, the shell exploded in the furnaces, throwing the fires upon the barges and igniting the loose hay immediately.

"The play is over," said Richardson.

"Hand in your checks, boys," exclaimed Colburn.

"A change of base for the Bohemians," [I] remarked. . . .

And we glanced around, and heard the groans and sharp cries of the wounded and the scalded. We rushed forward to try and trample out the flames, but they rose behind us like fiery serpents . . . and lit up the dark waters of the Stygian river far and near.

The Rebels, who had ceased firing for a moment [to raise a wild huzza at their success], now bent themselves to their guns once more, and the iron missiles swept over and around us, and several of the soldiers on board were wounded by fragments of bursting shells.

Everyone was now bent on saving himself. A few of the privates and some of the tug's crew plunged madly overboard . . . and in three minutes none but the wounded and the journalistic trio remained on the burning barges. We threw the bales of hay into the river for the benefit of the wounded and those who could not swim. . . .

Richardson went off first on a bale of hay. . . . Colburn followed; and I . . . answered his summons and dived—after divesting myself of all superfluous clothing. . . . Several bales of hay were floating below, but I swam to the one nearest Colburn, and there we concluded to . . . make our way as best we could back to the army.

The Rebels had then ceased firing . . . and . . . were evidently coming to capture us. My companion and myself believed if we kept very quiet and floated with our faces only out of the water, we would not be discovered.

A yawl full of armed men passed near us, and we fancied we would escape. . . . Just as we were internally congratulating ourselves, a small boat darted round the corner of the burning barge, and we were hauled in by a couple of stalwart fellows, after the manner of colossal catfish. . . .

In fifteen minutes we were under guard on shore, where we found our collaborateur Richardson safe and sound. About half our small crew had been killed and wounded. . . . We were all reported lost, we learned afterward; though General Sherman's humorous comment, when apprised that three of the Bohemians had been killed ("That's good! We'll have dispatches now from hell before breakfast.") did not prove a veracious prediction. . . .

The Bohemians lost all their baggage; and I, having prepared myself for Byronic exercise [i.e., for swimming], went ashore with nothing on but shirt and pantaloons. Barefooted was I also ... as I walked in company with the others through the moonlit streets of the town....

A number of the captives were either wounded with fragments of shell or scalded by the steam, and groaned and wailed piteously as we walked along.... [The rest] of us ... were in the best of spirits; and we marched merrily through the streets, chatting and laughing at our mishap ... and gayly speculating upon what would be the next turn of Fortune....

One of my journalistic companions, when we were examined by the provost marshal ... remarked, in a rather pompous and exacting tone: "Captain ... we would like to have as comfortable quarters as you can give us."

The officer replied that they were rather short of accommodations just then....

After our examination, we were marched out under guard through several streets; and at last, about dawn, were stopped before a dingy iron gate and a dingier brick wall.... There a bell was pulled, and we were admitted ... by an ill-favored turnkey.... We soon found he was in harmony with his surroundings.

The courthouse in Vicksburg

The jail-yard was filled with thieves and malefactors of every kind. . . . They were filthy, ragged, coarse-featured, vile-spoken, and every way disgusting. They slept on the ground, with very little, if any, covering, and cooked their fat bacon on sticks in the fire. . . .

To complete the delightfulness of the place, I should say the ground seemed covered with vermin, and the prisoners there swarmed with them. . . . We were afraid to sit down, or even to stand still, lest we should be overrun; and so we continued to walk backwards and forwards. . . .

Before noon . . . the three correspondents, and two officers of the Forty-seventh Ohio captured with us, were transferred to the court house, whose dome we had so often seen from our camps across the river. . . . At the court house we had fresh air and a fine view of the Mississippi and much of the surrounding country from the altitude of our position. We could see our transports across the Louisiana peninsula and our camps up the river . . . and we felt not a little annoyed that we were captives almost within musket range of our friends. . . .

The three days we remained in Vicksburg we were visited by a great many officers and citizens who showed us all the courtesy we could have expected. We were even taken out at night to the headquarters of general officers, to be catechised about the opinions of the people of the North respecting the duration of the war . . . and, especially, what disposition the Yankees proposed to make of the Negroes. . . .

During our brief sojourn in the Southern stronghold we were rather lionized than otherwise. The papers there spoke favorably of us and complimented us upon what they were pleased to term our singular fearlessness in volunteering without any particular motive to go upon so perilous an expedition. The editors paid us several visits. . . .

On the evening of the 5th of May, the two Ohio officers and the Bohemians, with a number of privates, were sent to Jackson [on the first leg of a trip to Richmond, Virginia, for internment in Libby Prison]. . . . We were permitted to visit the *Appeal* office . . . with whose editors we were personally acquainted before the war—and to write notes to our friends in the North that we were still among the living. . . . The editors of the *Appeal* and one or two others treated us very kindly, lent us money, and gave us such articles as we most needed. . . .

Great excitement prevailed in the Mississippi Capital at the time of our arrival, on account of the report that General Grant... was marching on the town. At the street corners were knots of excited men.... It was evident they were at a loss what to do; and you can imagine we rather enjoyed the trepidation of the Rebels.

We saw a number of vehicles of various kinds, loaded with household furniture, and men, women, children, and black servants, all greatly excited, moving rapidly out of town. A panic of the most decided kind existed among all classes of society; but we had no difficulty in perceiving that the Negroes of both sexes, young and old, enjoyed the quandary of their masters and mistresses. Whenever we passed, they recognized us as Yankee prisoners and glanced at us with a meaning smile....

The mayor had put forth a gasconading handbill... which was posted in prominent parts of the capital, informing the citizens that there was not the least cause for alarm; calling the people of Mississippi to arms to repel the barbarous invader from the soil he polluted with his footsteps....

The bellicose poster, so far as our observation extended, did not seem to have the desired effect. If the citizens were flying to arms, they must have concealed them somewhere in the country, and have been making haste in that direction to recover them. They were certainly leaving town by all possible routes, and by every obtainable means of conveyance.

Newsman Browne and his fellow prisoners were shortly placed on a train headed for the East.

Among the Jackson citizens still in their homes at this time was Mary Loughborough. Her soldier husband had been sent to Warrenton, below Vicksburg, and she, with a two-year-old daughter to care for, was on her own and in a state of indecision. She had heard that Jackson was to be defended, but was disturbed when General Pemberton, who had been operating from a headquarters in the city, sent his wife to Mobile, Alabama, and transferred his headquarters to the Vicksburg area.

Mary relates:

Batteries were being erected in different parts of the town— one directly opposite the house I was in. I stood considering one morning where it was best to go, and what it was best to do, when a quick gallop sounded on the drive, and a friend rode hastily up and said, "Are you going to leave?"

"Yes," I answered, "but I have not yet decided where to go."

"Well, I assure you there is no time for deliberation. I shall take my family to Vicksburg as the safest place, and, if you will place yourself under my charge, I will see you safely to your husband."

So the matter was agreed upon, and we were to leave that evening. Still, I was in doubt. The Federal army was spreading all over the country, and I feared to remain where I was. Yet, I thought, may I not be in danger in Vicksburg? Suppose the gunboats should make an attack? Still, it was true, as my friend had said, we were in far more danger here from the rabble that usually followed a large army and who might plunder, insult, and rob us. No—to Vicksburg we must go!

Very hurriedly we made our arrangements.... Our friends, also, were in as great a panic and dismay as ourselves. Mrs. A. had some chests of heavy silver. Many of the pieces were such that it would have taken some time to bury them. Her husband was absent, and she feared to trust the Negro men with the secret. Another friend feared to bury her diamonds, thinking in that case she might never see them more; feared, also, to retain them, lest, through Negroes' tales, the cupidity of the soldiers [of Pemberton's command] might become excited and she be a sufferer in consequence.

Every tumult in the town caused us to fly to the doors and windows, fearing a surprise at any time. And not only ladies, with pale faces and anxious eyes, met us at every turn, but gentlemen of anti-military dispositions were running hither and thither with carpet bags and little valises, seeking conveyances, determined to find a safe place, if one could be found, where the sound of a gun or the smell of powder might never disturb them anymore....

The depot was crowded with crushing and elbowing human beings ... baggage being thrown hither and thither—horses wild with fright, and Negroes with confusion.... We found ourselves ... amid the living stream that flowed and surged along—seeking the Mobile cars, seeking the Vicksburg cars—seeking anything to bear them away from the threatened and fast depopulating town.

Leaving the ... teeming town behind us, we moved slowly on—our friends, my little one, and myself—toward Vicksburg. Ah! Vicksburg, our city of refuge.... Yet, is there any place where one is perfectly safe in these terrible times?

As we travelled along, the night air blowing so refreshingly upon us through the open window—our seats so quiet—the motion of the cars so soothing, my friends soon gave unmistakable signs of the deep sleep that had fallen upon them. . . . I leaned my head against the window and looked into the darkness. . . .

As we passed along . . . we could see camps and campfires, with the dim figures of men moving around them. We could see the sentinel guarding the Black River bridge, silent and erect, looking in the darkness like a dusky statue. . . . And farther, masses of men in the road marching quietly in the nighttime, followed by the artillery; long lines of wagons, too. . . . We heard the shout of the teamsters, the crack of the whip . . . and the occasional song of a wagoner.

At the depot [in Vicksburg] soldiers were crowded, waiting to go out. And on our arrival at our friend's, we, so weary with the excitement and turmoil of the day, were glad to rest our tired heads. . . .

Upon reading the papers the next morning, almost the first article that caught my eye was an order from General Pemberton, insisting on all noncombatants leaving the city. . . .

"Ah!" cried I, "have we no rest for the sole of our foot? Must we again go through the fright and anxiety of yesterday?"

"We cannot leave here," replied my friend. . . . "We *must* stay . . . even if the gentlemen [of the military] say go. . . ."

When the gentlemen came, we talked of the order with them. At first they said we must leave. . . . We declared . . . that we would meet any evil cheerfully in Vicksburg, where our friends were. . . .

So, laughingly, they said they were completely overcome by our distress, and would arrange it so that we could stay if we wished.

"But remember," they said, "if trouble comes, you must meet it with your eyes open."

. . . We settled ourselves. . . . With our sewing in the morning, and rides in the evening, our home was very pleasant. . . . Almost every day we walked up the Sky Parlor Hill and looked through the glass at the Federal encampment near the head of the abandoned canal. . . . Altogether, the Federal encampment and movements were far more stirring and interesting than the quiet, fortified life of Vicksburg. . . .

The gunboats that stood out in the stream above seemed to be acting as sentinels, or on a kind of picket duty, I might call it, as a man in uniform constantly paced the deck with a large glass under his arm, which he frequently raised and took a survey of the city.

Now and then the gunboats sent in a few shells. Dora Miller, the young bride from New Orleans, was sitting in her living room, sewing—her black cook, Martha, being in the kitchen—when one of the bombardments began:

Listening to the distant sound of bursting shells, apparently aimed at the court house, there suddenly came a nearer explosion. The house shook, and a tearing sound was followed by terrified screams from the kitchen.

. I rushed thither, but met in the hall the cook's little girl America, bleeding from a wound in the forehead and fairly dancing with fright and pain, while she uttered fearful yells. I stopped to examine the wound, and her mother bounded in, her black face ashy from terror.

". . . My child is killed and the kitchen tore up!"

Seeing America was too lively to be a killed subject, I consoled Martha and hastened to the kitchen. Evidently a shell had exploded just outside, sending three or four pieces through.

When order was restored, I tried to impress on Martha's mind the necessity for calmness. . . . Looking round at the close of the lecture, there stood a group of Confederate soldiers laughing heartily. . . .

They chimed in with a parting chorus: "Yes, it's no use hollerin', old lady."

During these days in early May, 1863, something of great moment happened in the war's Eastern theater. The Union army in northern Virginia, led now by "Fighting Joe" Hooker, was defeated by Robert E. Lee and Stonewall Jackson at Chancellorsville. This was Stonewall's last battle, for he was fatally wounded by his own men while returning from a reconnaissance in front of his lines at dusk. But the victory gave Lee the opportunity to plan an invasion of the North that was to lead to the fateful Battle of Gettysburg.

The two great campaigns—Gettysburg in the east and Vicksburg in the west—were destined to culminate at the same time.

General Grant began pushing his army northeastward from Grand Gulf on May 7. According to Charles Dana:

This march toward Jackson proved to be no easy affair. More than one night I bivouacked on the ground in the rain after being all day in my saddle. The most comfortable night I had, in fact, was in a church of which the officers had taken possession. Having no pillow, I went up to the pulpit and borrowed the Bible for the night. . . .

In spite of the roughness of our life, it was all of intense interest to me, particularly the condition of the people over whose country we were marching. A fact that impressed me was the total absence of men capable of bearing arms. Only old men and [boys] remained. The young men were all in the army or had perished in it. The South was drained of its youth. . . .

Another fact of moment was that we found men who had at first sympathized with the rebellion, and even joined in it, now of their own accord rendering Grant the most valuable assistance, in order that the rebellion might be ended as speedily as possible, and something saved by the Southern people out of the otherwise total and hopeless ruin.

"Slavery is gone, other property is mainly gone," they said, "but, for God's sake, let us save some relic of our former means of living."

Marching with Grant's army at this time was a talented young diarist, Sergeant Osborn H. Oldroyd of the Twentieth Ohio Infantry. At the time the war broke out, Oldroyd was thinking more in terms of becoming an independent bookseller than a Union soldier, but he decided to volunteer soon after First Bull Run. Slight of frame and in delicate health, he was uncertain of his ability to endure; but the outdoor life toughened him until he was able to march and fight with the strongest.

An avid reader, the sergeant noted in his diary on May 8:

The boys frequently bring in reading matter with their forage. Almost anything in print is better than nothing. A novel was brought in today, and as soon as it was caught sight of, a score or more had engaged, in turn, the reading of it. It will soon be read to pieces.

Oldroyd kept his diary with faithful regularity, later pointing out that each day's march, battle, or life in the camp was recorded upon the spot—now at the close of a hard day's march; again, when tired and hungry after a hotly contested battle; and again, in the camp, while the cross-firing of the contending lines made it impossible to find a place secure enough to write [with concentration]. . . . I have brushed the powder of a bursting shell off my paper, and changed my position in order to escape the range of the enemy's guns.

Oldroyd's regiment was a part of Logan's division, McPherson's corps. The sergeant made the following entries during the march toward the village of Raymond, which lay along the route to Jackson:

May 9th: ... O, what a grand army this is.... I shall never forget the scene of today, while looking back upon a mile of solid columns, marching with their old tattered flags streaming in the summer breeze, and hearkening to the firm tramp of their broad brogans keeping step to the pealing fife and drum, or the regimental bands discoursing "Yankee Doodle" or "The Girl I Left Behind Me."

... Camped a little after dark.

May 10th: ... This forenoon my bunkmate, Cal Waddle, and I went to a house near camp to get some corn bread, but struck the wrong place, for we found the young mistress, who had just been deserted by her Negroes, all alone, crying, with but a scant allowance of provisions left her. She had never learned to cook, and in fact was a complete stranger to housework of any kind. Her time is now at hand to learn the great lesson of humanity....

But although I am glad the Negroes are free, I don't like to see them leaving a good home.... They have caught the idea from some unknown source that freedom means fine dress, furniture, carriages, and luxuries....

This lady's husband is a Confederate officer now in Vicksburg, who told her when he left she should never see a Yankee "down thar." Well, we had to tell her we were "thar" though. And to our question what she thought of us, after wiping her eyes her reply was we were very nice-looking fellows.

We were not fishing for compliments, but we like to get their opinions ... for they have been led, apparently, to expect to find the Lincoln soldier more of a beast than human....

May 11th: We drew two days' rations and marched till noon.... General Logan thinks we shall have a fight soon. I am not particularly anxious for one.... As we contemplate a battle, those who have been spoiling for a fight cease to be heard. It does not even take the smell of gunpowder ... a rumor being quite sufficient....

May 12th: Roused up early and before daylight marched, the 20th in the lead. Now we have the honored position, and will probably get the first taste of battle.

The column was now a few miles southwest of Raymond. Three thousand Confederates under Brigadier General John Gregg had reached the town from Jackson the day before. According to Captain William E. Cunningham of the Forty-first Tennessee:

Early on the morning of the 12th the town was overrun with [Confederate] soldiers having what we called a "high old time." In the midst of fun and feasting the long roll sounded, and every man answered promptly. As General Gregg moved through the town, hundreds of people eagerly watched him, little dreaming of the carnage so soon to follow.

Gregg marched his command two or three miles in the direction of the Federal approach, then deployed along a front about a mile wide.

"We were expecting nothing but cavalry, which we felt we could whip," explains Captain Cunningham. "Skirmishers were advanced."

Sergeant Oldroyd and his comrades were still in column formation on the road. "At nine o'clock," Oldroyd recounts,

slight skirmishing began in front, and at eleven we filed into a field on the right of the road, where another regiment joined us on the left of the road and a battery on the road itself. In this position our line marched down through open fields until we reached the fence, which we scaled, and stacked arms in the edge of a piece of timber.

No sooner had we done this than the boys fell to amusing themselves in various ways, taking little heed of the danger about to be entered. A group here and there were employed in euchre, for cards seem always handy enough where soldiers are. Another little squad was discussing the scenes of the morning.

One soldier picked up several canteens, saying he would go ahead and see if he could fill them. . . . He returned with a quicker pace, and with but one canteen full, saying . . . "While I was filling the canteen I heard a noise, and, looking up, discovered several Johnnies behind trees, getting ready to shoot; and I concluded I would retire at once and report."

Meanwhile my bedfellow had taken from his pocket a small mirror and was combing his hair and moustache. Said someone to him, "Cal, you needn't fix up so nice to go into battle, for the Rebs won't think any better of you for it."

Just here the firing began in our front, and we got orders: "Attention! Fall in—take arms—forward—double-quick, march!"

And we moved quite lively as the Rebel bullets did likewise. We had advanced but a short distance . . . when we came to a creek, the bank of which was high, but down we slid; and wading through the water . . . dropped upon the opposite side and began firing at will. . . . The enemy were but a hundred yards in front of us. . . . They fought desperately, and no doubt they fully expected to whip us before we could get reinforcements. . . .

The regiment to the right of us was giving way, but . . . Logan dashed up, and with the shriek of an eagle turned them back to their places, which they regained and held. . . .

The booming of artillery had joined the rolling musket fire, and the fury increased as the Federal reinforcements arrived. Though soon heavily outnumbered, the Confederates continued to make a strong showing. On both sides visibility became a problem as the smoke and dust thickened.

One of the more conspicuous figures in the haze was Confederate Colonel Randall W. MacGavock, who strode about shouting orders, flourishing his sword, and revealing the bright red lining of his cloak. MacGavock was shot dead while launching a charge that made a temporary break in Logan's line.

"For two hours," says Union Sergeant Oldroyd,
the contest raged furiously. . . . The creek was running red with precious blood spilt for our country. My bunkmate and I were kneeling side by side when a ball crashed through his brain. . . . With the assistance of two others I picked him up, carried him over the bank in our rear and laid him behind a tree, removing from his pocket [his] watch and trinkets and the same little mirror that had helped him make his last toilet. . . .

We then went back to our company after an absence of but a few minutes. Shot and shell from the enemy came over thicker and faster. . . . One by one the boys were dropping out of my company. The second lieutenant in command was wounded; the orderly sergeant dropped dead, and I found myself . . . in command of the handful remaining. . . .

Into another part of the line the enemy charged, fighting hand to hand, being too close to fire, and using the butts of their guns. . . . They were . . . forced to give way.

Only now did the Confederates become fully aware of the size of the force they were fighting. According to Captain Cunningham:
General Gregg . . . by examining captured prisoners, found that they represented eighteen different regiments. A whole corps was in our front. There was a choice of two things left

us—to retreat in the face of such numbers or to wait until we were entirely surrounded. He decided upon a retreat, and this we accomplished successfully. . . .

On our retreat through Raymond, we saw ladies with quilts and bandages tenderly caring for our wounded. They would not leave even after the enemy's shells were flying and crashing through the streets and houses.

The day's casualties came to about 500 in killed, wounded, captured, and missing on both sides.

"I am very sad on account of the loss of so many of my comrades," wrote Union diarist Oldroyd. "I suppose this will be named the Battle of Raymond."

Oldroyd's regiment joined a column that moved up near the town and halted. Says the regimental commander, Colonel Manning F. Force:

In a few minutes the earth was sparkling with fires, over which coffee was making in tin cups, and little chunks of salt pork were [broiling on sharpened sticks]. The sweet savor told that supper was nearly ready, when orders came to march through the town and go on picket on the farther side. Every man picked up his smoking cup and the stick which bore his sizzling bit of salt pork, and we incensed the town with the savory odor as we marched through.

The Union triumph at Raymond was the signal for new hordes of "contrabands" of both sexes and all ages to make their way to the army's encampments. If there was any doubt before that the Yankees had come to stay, it had now vanished, and the blacks sought their succor and protection.

Many of the refugees were on foot, struggling under the weight of their possessions and the goods they had plundered from abandoned plantations. Others appeared in wheeled vehicles ranging from mule-drawn carts to the most elaborate rigs boasting matched teams with silver-studded harnesses. Carts, wagons, and carriages held jumbles of fine furniture, beautiful tapestries, and luxuriant feather beds. A spirit of jubilee prevailed, with the adults beaming and praising the Lord, and the children skipping and dancing.

General Grant was still some miles west of Raymond on the day of the battle. News of the victory reached his headquarters camp at sundown. As a bright moon rose, Grant sat on a log by his bivouac fire and dictated dispatches to an orderly while an artist from Harper's Weekly *sketched the scene.*

Late that night Grant slipped into the tent of his artillery commander, Colonel William Duff, and asked for a drink of whisky, citing an extraordinary fatigue as the creator of his need. Duff drew a canteen from beneath his pillow, and the general took two or three heavy drinks from a tin cup, then went quietly back to his tent. There was little danger of Grant's overindulging at this time, for liquor was scarce.

Again in the words of Sergeant Oldroyd, who was encamped at Raymond:

May 13th: Up early, and on the march to Jackson, as we suppose.

I dreamed of my bunkmate last night. Wonder if his remains will be put where they can be found, for I would like, if I ever get the chance, to put a board with his name on it at the head of his grave.

When we enlisted we all paired off, each selecting his comrade—such a one as would be congenial and agreeable to him—and as yesterday's battle broke a good many such bonds, new ties have been forming—as the boys say, new couples are getting married. If married people could always live as congenial and content as two soldiers sleeping under the same blanket, there would be more happiness in the world.

An example of the kind of foraging done by the Federals during this part of the march is given by another member of McPherson's corps, this man unnamed:

The first place we stopped at was a fine two-story white house.... The people had gone visiting. We got a large tin can, holding perhaps twenty-five gallons, full of lard, some cornmeal, meat, and a jug of molasses....

At another place we got sugar ... loads of it. Then we came to a plantation where they raised hams and shoulders, and the proprietor kindly mounted into the upper regions of his smokehouse and passed down nearly a wagon load of the needful....

"I suppose," said he, "you will leave me, will you not, a part of these for my own use?"

... He looked discouraged when informed that the presumption of our military law was that he had buried his share before we came around, and what was in sight belonged to us.

While he was passing down the meat some of our boys got his

oxen and yoked them up to his wagon, and so he furnished us with transportation also. . . .

On other plantations a common practice was followed: The livestock was shot and the fences were torn down to provide fuel for barbecue fires. Many of the soldiers did not stop with foraging for food but also plundered valuables. Some were seen wearing necklaces, broaches, and bracelets; others had silver knives and forks peeping from heavy pockets.

A female citizen later lamented in a letter that she lost a prized sidesaddle to "one of those fancy yellow girls, an especial pet of one of the officers." The same citizen said also that the Yankees, in their search for concealed treasure, dug up a newly buried baby "no less than three different times."

While the Federals were marching from Raymond to Jackson, a new Confederate leader arrived in Jackson by rail from Tullahoma, Tennessee: General Joseph E. Johnston, head of the Department of the West. President Davis had ordered Johnston, who was General Pemberton's immediate superior, to give his personal attention to the defense of Vicksburg. At this time Pemberton was headquartered near that city; Johnston remained in Jackson.

A Virginian who graduated from West Point, Joe Johnston won his first distinction fighting the Seminole Indians in Florida, where he suffered two wounds and acquired thirty bullet holes in his clothing. He added to his record for gallantry in the war with Mexico, during which he was wounded no less than five times. Resigning the service in 1861 to become a senior commander in the Confederate army, he helped Pierre G. T. Beauregard to rout the Federals at First Bull Run. Head of the troops in northern Virginia when the Union's George B. McClellan advanced upon Richmond by way of the Peninsula in 1862, Johnston—who had an amazing proneness for stopping enemy missiles—was twice wounded in the Battle of Fair Oaks, or Seven Pines, first taking a musket ball in the shoulder, then a shell fragment in the chest. He was succeeded by Robert E. Lee. Upon his recovery six months later, Johnston was assigned to the Department of the West.

A private from Tennessee who got the chance to observe the general closely gives this description of him:

Fancy, if you please, a man about fifty years old [he was fifty-six], rather small of stature but firmly built, an open countenance with a keen restless eye that seemed to read your inmost thoughts. In his dress he was a perfect dandy. He ever wore the finest clothes that could be obtained, carrying out, in dress and the paraphernalia of the soldier, the plan adopted by the War Department at Richmond, never omitting anything, even to the trappings of his horse, bridle and saddle. His hat was decorated with a star and feather, his coat with every star and embellishment, and he wore a bright new sash, big gauntlets, and silver spurs. He was the very picture of a general.

Johnston wasn't at his best when he reached Jackson, having risen from a sickbed to obey President Davis's order. But he began at once to send telegraphic dispatches to Pemberton. That agitated general was at the same time receiving dispatches also from Davis in Richmond.
    Says Vicksburg's chief engineer, Samuel Lockett:

I saw, or heard read, most of these dispatches. They were very conflicting in their tenor, and neither those of Mr. Davis nor those of General Johnston exactly comported with General Pemberton's views. He then made the capital mistake of trying to harmonize instructions from his superiors diametrically opposed to each other, and at the same time to bring them into accord with his own judgment, which was adverse to the plans of both.

    Mr. Davis's idea was to hold Vicksburg at all hazard, and not to endanger it by getting too far from it. Johnston's plan was to cut loose from Vicksburg altogether, manoeuvre so as to avoid a general engagement with Grant until the Confederate forces could be concentrated, and then beat him.

    Pemberton wished to take a strong position on the line of the Big Black [the river that came down past Vicksburg, ten miles to the east, on its way to join the Mississippi at Grand Gulf] and wait for an attack, believing that it would be successfully resisted, and that then the tables could be turned upon Grant in a very bad position, without any base of supplies, and without a well-protected line of retreat.

    As I have said, none of these plans was carried out, but a sort of compromise or compound of all of these. . . .

7

TO VICKSBURG'S REAR AT LAST

*O*N *THE morning of May 14, 1863, Grant's forces approached Jackson on two roads, the Clinton road from the west and the Raymond road from the southwest. McPherson's corps was on the left, Sherman's on the right.*

Confederate General Johnston, in personal command at Jackson, decided he could do very little with the few thousand toops that made up the garrison:

A brigade was sent forward to meet each corps to delay the enemy's approach by skirmishing with the heads of the two columns. The resistance offered in this way so impeded the progress of the Federal troops as to give ample time for the evacuation of the place and the removal of such military property as we had the means of transporting.

The unit of McPherson's corps to which Sergeant Oldroyd belonged, after being so badly shot up at Raymond, made the march to Jackson in a safe position in the corps' rear. Oldroyd relates in his diary:

When within five miles of the city we heard heavy firing. It has rained hard today, and we have had both a wet and muddy time, pushing at the heavy artillery and provision wagons accompanying us when they stuck in the mud. The rain came down in perfect torrents! What a sight! Ambulances creeping along at the side of the track—artillery toiling in the deep ruts, while generals with their aides and orderlies splashed mud and water in every direction in passing. We were all wet to the skin, but plodded on patiently....

When within a few miles of Jackson, the news reached us that Sherman had slipped around to the right and captured the place [actually, the leading units of McPherson's corps had closed in on

Union troops closing in on Jackson

the left at the same time], and the shout that went up from the men on the receipt of that news was invigorating . . . in the midst of trouble. I think they could have been heard in Jackson. . . .

. . . If my own regiment has not had a chance today to cover itself with glory, it has with mud.

General Grant explains:

Our loss in this engagement was: McPherson, 37 killed, 228 wounded; Sherman, 4 killed and 21 wounded and missing. The enemy lost 845 killed, wounded and captured. Seventeen guns fell into our hands, and the enemy [before leaving the city to head northward on the Canton road] destroyed by fire their storehouses containing a large amount of commissary stores.

Young Fred Grant, traveling with the army, and much of the time looking out for himself, reached the heart of Jackson ahead of his father. The boy enjoyed a thrilling moment:

I saw a mounted officer with a Union flag advancing toward the Capitol. I followed him into the building and entered the Governor's room, which had been hastily abandoned. Returning to the street, I saw the officer in the act of raising the Union flag over the building.

Father and his staff, advancing at the head of the army [the men of which were cheering lustily], soon reached the State House, where I joined them, and went with them to the Bowen House, the best hotel in Jackson, where we took the room in which General Joseph E. Johnston had slept the night before.

General Grant was not yet settled in. After meeting with his corps commanders, he left the hotel on a tour of inspection. He tells of one of his stops:

Sherman and I went together into a manufactory which had not ceased work on account of the battle nor for the entrance of Yankee troops. Our presence did not seem to attract the attention of either the manager or the operatives, most of whom were girls.

We looked on for a while to see the tent cloth which they were making roll out of the looms with "C.S.A." woven in each bolt. There was an immense amount of cotton, in bales, stacked outside.

Finally I told Sherman I thought they had done work enough. The operatives were told they could leave and take with them what cloth they could carry. In a few minutes, cotton and factory were in a blaze.

Grant ordered the destruction of other public property, including the city's foundries, machine shops, arsenals, and warehouses. At first there was widespread looting of private property, not only by Union stragglers but by bands of blacks and poor whites. But soon the city was placed under martial law.

A Union newspaper correspondent paused in his rounds to write: "Yankee soldiers are patrolling the streets. . . . Negroes are grinning from the sidewalks; citizens look silently and sullenly at us from behind screens and closed window-blinds."

Those citizens who ventured out, another correspondent noted, "are very loud in their denunciations of Pemberton and declare that he has sold the State of Mississippi to the enemy."

As disclosed by Charles Dana, the man from Washington:

The very evening of the day that we reached Jackson, Grant learned that Lieutenant-General Pemberton had been ordered by General Joe Johnston to come out of Vicksburg and attack our rear. Grant immediately faced the bulk of his army about to meet the enemy, leaving Sherman in Jackson to tear up the railroads and destroy all the public property there that could be of use to the Confederates. I remained with Sherman to see the work of destruction.

Says a diarist with the troops that marched westward with Grant:

After we left Jackson [on the morning of May 15], and as we were passing a farmhouse by the side of the road, a woman stood by the gate who wanted to see General Grant. She said that some of our boys had taken her cow, and she thought that if she could only see General Grant he would make them give it up.

The general and his staff were just riding up, and he was pointed out to her, but she would not believe that it was him, he was dressed so plainly. A staff officer was riding behind the rest, and as he was finely clad, she called to him, thinking he was the general and that we were fooling her.

The officer rode up and pointed ahead to the general, saying, "That man there in the middle."

Then she believed, but he had passed.

Back in Jackson, about this time, Charles Dana was reading a telegram, signed by Secretary of War Edwin Stanton, that had just arrived from Washington. Dana explains:

General Grant had been much troubled by the delay Mc-Clernand had caused at New Carthage, but he had felt reluctant to remove him as he had been assigned to his command by the President. My reports to the Secretary on the situation had convinced him that Grant ought to have perfect independence in the matter, so he telegraphed me as follows:

". . . General Grant has full and absolute authority to enforce his own commands and to remove any person who by ignorance in action or any cause interferes with or delays his operations. He has the full confidence of the Government, is expected to enforce his authority, and will be firmly and heartily supported, but he will be responsible for any failure to exert his powers. You may communicate this to him."

Dana planned to show the telegram to Grant the next time he caught up with him. In Jackson Dana took to watching groups of Sherman's soldiers with torches ignite great quantities of baled cotton: "I was greatly astonished to see how slowly it burned."

Sherman takes up:

I kept my troops busy in tearing up railroad tracks, etc., but early on the morning of the 16th received notice from General Grant that a battle was imminent. . . .

Just as I was leaving Jackson, a very fat man came to see me to inquire if his hotel, a large frame building . . . were doomed to be burned. I told him we had no intention to burn it. . . .

He professed to be a law-abiding Union man, and I . . . said that this fact was manifest from the sign of his hotel, which was the "Confederate Hotel," the sign "United States" being faintly painted out, and "Confederate" painted over it!

. . . I had not the least purpose, however, of burning it, but, just as we were leaving the town, it burst out in flames and was burned to the ground. I never found out exactly who set it on fire.

Grant's next battle was fought before Sherman reached the scene. Confederate preparations are described by Samuel Lockett:

Pemberton moved out from Edward's Depot [on the railroad about fifteen miles east of Vicksburg] in obedience to a dispatch from General Johnston, ordering him to attack in the rear a force which he supposed General Johnston was going to engage in front. Instead of this, he encountered Grant's victorious army returning, exultant and eager for more prizes, from the capture of Jackson.

Pemberton's army, which was making a retrograde movement at the time [marching temporarily from south to north, at right angles to Grant's approach from the east], was put into line of battle by being faced to the right, with infantry, artillery, baggage, and ordnance wagons just as they were.

Pemberton had some 23,000 men, having left about 10,000 in the Vicksburg defenses. His northern flank, where Major General Carter L. Stevenson commanded, was advantageously posted atop a crescent-shaped ridge about seventy-five feet high on the Sid Champion plantation. Pemberton's line extended about three miles to the right, or the south.

Grant had a total of 32,000 men available for the battle. He himself was with General McPherson at "Champion's Hill," the Union right, and he took personal charge of that part of the attack. Four divisions of McClernand's corps made up the left of the Union line, that part to the south and facing Pemberton's right.

It was the morning of May 16. After two or three hours of skirmishing as the lines formed, the gunfire began to swell just before noon.

Among the soldiers of McPherson's corps who moved forward to

Champion's Hill at this time was a corporal from Iowa, Samuel H. M. Byers:

We approached the field in that overpowering Mississippi sun. Our brigade was soon in line, on the edge of a meadow, or open field, sloping [up] toward the woods where the enemy were concealed and steadily firing upon us. We were in the most trying position of soldiers . . . being fired on without permission to return the shots. We were standing two files deep, bearing as patiently as we could, not a heavy but a steady fire from infantry, while an occasional cannon ball tore up the turf in front or behind us.

A good many men were falling, and the wounded were being borne to the rear of the brigade, close to an old well whose wooden curb seemed to offer the only protection from bullets on the exposed line.

"Colonel, move your men a little by the left flank," said a quiet though commanding voice.

On looking round, I saw immediately behind us Grant, the commander-in-chief, mounted on a beautiful bay mare and followed by perhaps half a dozen of his staff. For some reason he dismounted, and most of his officers were sent off, bearing orders, probably to other quarters of the field.

The Battle of Champion's Hill

It was Grant under fire. The rattling musketry increased on our front; and grew louder, too, on the left flank. Grant had led his horse to the left and thus kept near the company to which I belonged. He now stood leaning complacently against his favorite steed, smoking—as seemed habitual with him—the stump of a cigar. His was the only horse near the line, and must, naturally, have attracted some of the enemy's fire.

What if he should be killed, I thought to myself, and the army be left without its commander? In front of us was an enemy.... For days we had been away from our base of supplies and marching inside the enemy's lines. What if Grant should be killed and we be defeated here—in such a place and at such a time? I am sure everyone who recognized him wished him away; but there he stood—clear, calm, and immovable.

I was close enough to see his features. Earnest they were, but sign of inward movement there was none.... Whatever there may have been in his feelings there was no effort to conceal; there was no pretense, no trick; whatever that face was, it was natural.

A man close by me had the bones of his leg shattered by a ball and was being helped to the rear. His cries of pain attracted the attention of Grant, and I noticed the ... sympathizing shades that crossed his quiet face as the bleeding soldier seemed to look toward him for help....

That Grant was fearless in battle would be hard to say. If he possessed true bravery, he also possessed fear. Brave men are not fearless men.... He was eminently and above all things a cool man, and that, I take it, was ... the first great key to his success. He was not made hilarious by victory, nor was he depressed by defeat.... He recognized simple duty, and his worst enemies envied the ardor with which that duty was performed. He was called a born soldier, but was, in fact, nothing of the kind. He was simply a man of correct methods and a fixed will....

We had not waited many minutes at the meadow when an orderly dashed up to Grant and handed him a communication. Then followed an order to move rapidly to the left and into the road. The fire grew heavier, and the air seemed too hot to be borne.

"Forward!" came a second order, all along the line. "Forward! Double quick!"

Everybody shouted "double quick" as the noise was becoming terrific.

We had forgotten to fix bayonets . . . and again the screaming was, "Fix bayonets! Fix bayonets!"

. . . A moment more and we were at the top of the ascent and among thinner wood and larger trees. The enemy had fallen back a few rods, forming a solid line parallel with our own. And now commenced, in good earnest, the fighting of the day.

Confederate General Pemberton, finding Stevenson's grip on the hill in jeopardy, sent a courier galloping down the lines to the right to order John Bowen's division to come up. Bowen's two brigades had been listening to the mounting uproar on the hill and speculating on what it portended. Little was occurring in their front, for McClernand had failed to get his four divisions moving, though ordered by Grant to do so.

With Francis Cockrell's brigade of Bowen's division was Corporal Ephraim Anderson, last heard from during the fighting at Grand Gulf, on the Mississippi. Anderson says that Pemberton's order quickly came down the brigade's command structure to his own battalion commander, Colonel Finley L. Hubbell:

By a blast of the bugle the command was rallied, and the men came up and formed in quick time. The order, "Forward, double-quick!" was given, and the colonel dashed off at the head of the column at a gallop; the men followed in full run.

Moving rapidly on for the distance of half a mile, we passed General Pemberton and staff standing in the road, almost in the edge of the action. His manner seemed to be somewhat excited. He and his staff were vainly endeavoring to rally some stragglers. . . .

Calling out to Colonel Hubbell, "What command?" and receiving a prompt reply, he told him to hurry on and join the brigade, as it would be in action in a few minutes. . . .

The battalion still moved forward at a double-quick, and soon passed [a] house . . . upon the road, very nearly within the line of the engagement. In the yard was a group of ladies who cheered the men on and were singing "Dixie." At sight of this, a novel appearance on the battlefield, the boys shouted zealously, and I could not refrain from hallooing just once, expressive of my admiration for the perfect abandon with which these fair creatures gave their hearts to the cause. . . .

About two hundred yards from the house we came upon . . . the center of Stevenson's division, which had now given way en masse, while the Federals were advancing with triumphant cheers.... At this point we came upon the brigade, which was formed for action....

Cockrell rode down the lines. In one hand he held the reins and a large magnolia flower, while with the other he waved his sword and gave the order to charge.

With a shout of defiance, and with gleaming bayonets and banners pointing to the front, the gray line leaped forward, and, moving at quick-time across the field, dislodged the enemy with a heavy volley and pressed on....

The fighting now became desperate and bloody. The ground in dispute was a succession of high hills and deep hollows, heavily wooded.... Our lines advanced steadily, though obstinately opposed, and within half a mile we recaptured the artillery lost by Stevenson's division, and captured one of the enemy's batteries.

The battle here raged fearfully—one unbroken, deafening roar of musketry was all that could be heard.... The ground was fought over three times, and, as the wave of battle rolled to and fro, the scene became bloody and terrific.

In the words of a Union enlisted man, J. B. Harris of the Thirty-fourth Indiana:

After losing one-third of the regiment in killed and wounded and being out of ammunition, [we] were ordered to fall back....

While on the retreat we came across General Logan, who shouted... "What regiment is that?"

... Hearing that it was the 34th Indiana, he said that Indiana should not be disgraced, and we must stop right there. Of course we stopped, and as our adjutant came riding up the general said, "Adjutant, get your men together."

"General, the rebels are awful thick up there," replied the adjutant.

"Damn it! That's the place to kill them—where they are thick," shouted the general.

On another part of the field, the Union regiment to which Samuel Byers belonged was not only fleeing but was under hot pursuit:

"Stop! Halt! Surrender!" cried a hundred rebels.... But there was no stopping and no surrender. We ran.... It was terribly hot, a hot afternoon under a Mississippi sun, and an enemy on flank and rear, shouting and firing. The grass, the stones, the bushes, seemed melting under the shower of bullets that was following us to the rear.

We tried to halt, and tried to form. It was no use. Again we ran, and harder, and farther, and faster. We passed over the very spot where . . . we left Grant leaning on his bay mare and smoking his cigar. Thank God he was gone! The dead were still there, and the wounded called pitiably to us to halt and help them as we ran. . . . The enemy pursued, closer and closer, and we scarcely dared look back. . . .

Grant had seen it all, and in less time than I can tell it a line of cannon had been thrown across our path, which, as soon as we had passed, belched grapeshot and canister into the faces of our pursuers. They stopped, they turned, and they, too, ran, and left their dead side by side with our own. Our lines, protected by the batteries, rallied and followed. . . .

The fighting continued, with fluctuating fortunes, for about four hours. Then, according to an unnamed Union participant, the advantage went to Grant:

The enemy was beaten back and compelled to seek the cover of the forest in his rear. Following up . . . without waiting to re-form, the soldiers of the Western army fixed their bayonets and charged into the woods after them. The rebels . . . thought only of escape. In this terrible charge men were slaughtered without mercy. The ground was literally covered with the dead and dying. The enemy scattered in every direction and rushed through the fields to reach the column now moving to the west along the Vicksburg road.

Charles Dana, having arrived from Jackson after watching Sherman's work of destruction, had spent the afternoon just behind the lines. Now he and John Rawlins, Grant's most valued staff member, paid a horseback visit to the field. The Confederates were at this time covering their retreat with artillery fire. Dana relates:

When we reached Logan's command we found him greatly excited. He declared the day was lost, and that he would soon be swept from his position. I contested the point with him.

"Why, general," I said, "we have gained the day."

He could not see it.

"Don't you hear the cannon over there?" he answered. "They

will be down on us right away! In an hour I will have twenty thousand men to fight."

... This was simply a curious idiosyncrasy of Logan's. In the beginning of a fight he was one of the bravest men that could be, saw no danger, went right on fighting until the battle was over. Then, after the battle was won, his mind gained an immovable conviction that it was lost.... It was merely an intellectual peculiarity. It did not in the least impair his value as a soldier or commanding officer. He never made any mistakes on account of it.

On leaving Logan, Rawlins and I were joined by several officers, and we continued our ride over the field. On the hill where the thickest of the fight had taken place we stopped, and were looking around at the dead and dying men lying all about us, when suddenly a man, perhaps forty-five or fifty years old, who had a Confederate uniform on, lifted himself up on his elbow and said:

"For God's sake, gentlemen, is there a Mason among you?"

"Yes," said Rawlins, "I am a Mason."

He got off his horse and kneeled by the dying man, who gave him some letters out of his pocket. When he came back Rawlins had tears on his cheeks. The man, he told us, wanted to convey some souvenir ... to his wife, who was in Alabama. Rawlins ... sometime afterward ... succeeded in sending it to the woman.

Many of the battlefield's dead lay in grotesque positions, some horribly torn and crimson-hued, others with scarcely a mark. A strange picture involving a dead horse and rider was sighted by enlisted man Alonzo L. Brown of a regiment from Minnesota:

The animal lay on the side of a sharp little slope so that the right leg of the rider was under its body while the other was extended naturally, with the foot in the stirrup. He held the bridle rein in his right hand, and with eyes wide open, as if looking to the front, sat upright in the saddle as naturally as if still alive. His features looked like marble; and he was apparently not over seventeen years of age.

Again in the words of Union Corporal Byers:

Grant passed along the lines, after the fight, as we stood in the narrow roads, waiting to pursue the enemy.... Every hat was in the air, and the men cheered till they were hoarse; but, speechless and almost without a bow, he pushed on past, like an embarrassed man hurrying to get away from some defeat. Once he stopped near the colors, and, without addressing himself to anyone in particular, said: "Well done!"

According to the anonymous Union participant quoted earlier:

We pursued the enemy until nearly dark, when we entered the little village known as Edward's Station, just as the enemy was leaving it. . . . We discovered, on the left, a large building in flames, and on the right a smaller one from which, just then, issued a series of magnificent explosions. The former contained commissary stores, and the latter shell and ammunition—five carloads—brought down from Vicksburg. . . . In their hasty exit from Edward's Station the rebels could not take this ammunition with them.

Safe at last in the growing darkness, the Confederates continued their retreat. "The midnight hour was near at hand," says one soldier, "when the men sank heavily to rest behind the breastworks which protected the bridge over the Big Black." Other units were ordered by Pemberton to continue on across the bridge, and these men trudged along the road toward Vicksburg until their strength gave out between one and two in the morning.

The Federals had bivouacked as soon as the pursuit was stopped, and their fires dotted the fields from Edward's Station back toward Champion's Hill. Says Charles Dana:

I remained out late that night conversing with the officers who had been in the battle, and think it must have been about eleven o'clock when I got to Grant's headquarters, where I was to sleep. Two or three officers who had been out with me went with me into the little cottage which Grant had taken possession of.

We found a wounded man there, a tall and fine-looking man, a Confederate. He stood up suddenly and said:

"Kill me! Will someone kill me? I am in such anguish that it will be mercy to do it—I have got to die. Kill me—don't let me suffer!"

We sent for a surgeon, who examined his case but said it was hopeless. He had been shot through the head so that it had cut off the optic nerve of both eyes. He never could possibly see again. Before morning he died.

Grant's casualties at the Battle of Champion's Hill came to about 2,400. Pemberton lost about 3,800. In addition, an entire division, cut off from

Pemberton's army during the retreat, had been obliged to swing south and east and head for a junction with Joe Johnston in the Jackson area.

All of Sherman's troops had now left Jackson and were moving up with Grant. During his forced march along the route of the Jackson-Vicksburg railroad, Sherman gained a remarkable souvenir. He explains:

Just beyond Bolton there was a small hewn-log house, standing back in a yard, in which was a well. At this, some of our soldiers were drawing water. I rode in to get a drink, and, seeing a book on the ground, asked some soldier to hand it to me. It was a volume of the Constitution of the United States, and on the title page was written the name of Jefferson Davis. On inquiry of a Negro, I learned that the place belonged to the . . . President of the Southern Confederation [then living in Richmond].

His brother Joe Davis's plantation [the property upon which Joe had settled after abandoning his previously mentioned plantation on the Mississippi River below Vicksburg] was not far off. One of my staff officers went there, with a few soldiers, and took a pair of carriage horses, without my knowledge. . . . He found Joe Davis at home, an old man, attended by a young and affectionate niece. But they were overwhelmed with grief to see their country overrun and swarming with Federal troops.

Grant gave Pemberton little rest. In the words of an unnamed Confederate officer with the troops stationed in the defensive works on the east bank of the Big Black:

Early in the morning, eyes weary and bloodshot were opened to respond to new alarm. A heavy reconnaissance approached and was driven back. We lay quietly in the trenches, munching hardtack and uncooked corn-beef, until ten o'clock, when the grand charge was made. Our entrenchments were thrown up in the soft soil of the bottom land, shaped like a horseshoe . . . and covering two bridges which constituted our only line of retreat. [One was the regular bridge; the other had been improvised over a steamboat lying in the center of the river.]

The fight opened briskly, far away to our left, confined to muskets and Enfield rifles, and no attack made in our front. We were standing by our arms, idly waiting for something to do, when we were thunderstruck at the receipt of an order to "retreat; we are flanked!"

Mounting the parapet, I could see through my glass the place where a Mississippi regiment had been stationed, swarming with blue-coats, and hordes besides pouring over our defenses. We had been flanked, or, rather, our center pierced; were enfiladed both ways, and no alternative remained but to get away from there as fast as possible. In a jumbled crowd we rushed for the bridges.

Before the crossing was completed, details of Confederates set fire to the bridges in order to stop the Federals, who were charging with flaunting colors and bared bayonets, their lines ringing with shouts and cheers.

Grant says that many of the Confederates tried to escape by swimming the river. Some succeeded and some were drowned in the attempt. Eighteen guns were captured and 1,751 prisoners. Our loss was 39 killed, 237 wounded and 3 missing.

Among the wounded was twelve-year-old Fred Grant. He tells how it happened:

Following the retreating Confederates to the Big Black, I was watching some of them swim the river when a sharpshooter on the opposite bank fired at me and hit me in the leg. The wound was slight, but very painful.

Colonel Lagow came dashing up and asked what was the matter. I promptly said, "I am killed."

The colonel presumed to doubt my word, and said, "Move your toes," which I did with success. He then recommended our hasty retreat.

In the words of Confederate officer Samuel Lockett, who helped to destroy the bridges:

After the stampede . . . orders were issued for the army to fall back to Vicksburg, Major General Stevenson being placed in command of the retreating forces. General Pemberton rode on himself to Bovina, a small railroad station about two and a half miles from the river. I was the only staff officer with him. He was very much depressed by the events of the last two days, and for some time after mounting his horse rode in silence. He finally said:

"Just thirty years ago I began my military career by receiving my appointment to a cadetship at the U.S. Military Academy; and today—the same date—that career is ended in disaster and disgrace."

I strove to encourage him, urging that things were not so bad as they seemed to be; that we still had two excellent divisions . . .

which had not been engaged and were, therefore, fresh and not demoralized; that they could occupy our lines at Vicksburg . . .; that the rest of the troops could be put at first . . . in reserve, until they had steadied themselves; that Vicksburg was strong and could not be carried by assault; and that Mr. Davis had telegraphed to him "to hold Vicksburg at all hazard," adding that "if besieged he would be relieved." To all of which General Pemberton replied that my youth and hopes were the parents of my judgment. . . .

We finally reached Bovina, where the general halted, and at my earnest instance wrote an order directing me to return to Vicksburg in all possible haste to put the place in a good state of defense.

On this Sunday morning, May 17, the people of Vicksburg were uncertain as to what was happening to their army. Some were still expecting Pemberton to beat Grant.

Mary Loughborough and a friend took to the street in an effort to learn some reliable news:

After walking a square or two, we met an officer who told us . . . it had been rumored that General Pemberton had been repulsed—that many citizens had gone out to attend to the wounded. . . .

Still, as the bell of the Methodist Church rang out clear and loud, my friend and I decided to enter, and were glad that we did so, for we heard words of cheer and comfort in this time of trouble. The speaker . . . was a plain man of simple, fervent words. . . . After the blessing, he requested the ladies to meet and make arrangements for lint and bandages for the wounded.

As we returned home . . . in all the pleasant air and sunshine of the day, an anxious gloom seemed to hang over the faces of men: a sorrowful waiting for tidings that all knew now would tell of disaster. There seemed no life in the city. Sullen and expectant seemed the men, tearful and hopeful the women—prayerful and hopeful, I might add. . . .

And so, in all the dejected uncertainty, the stir of horsemen and wheels began. . . . Now and then a worn and dusty soldier would be seen passing with his blanket and canteen. Soon, straggler after straggler came by, then groups of soldiers worn and dusty with the long march.

"What can be the matter?" we all cried, as the streets and

pavements became full of these worn and tired-looking men. . . .

"Where are you going?" we asked.

No one seemed disposed to answer the question. An embarrassed, pained look came over some of the faces that were raised to us. Others seemed only to feel the weariness of the long march.

Again we asked: "Where on earth are you going?"

At last one man looked up in a half-surly manner and answered: "We are running."

"From whom?" exclaimed one of the young girls. . . .

"The Feds, to be sure," said another [man]. . . .

"Oh, shame on you!" cried the ladies. . . .

"It's all Pem's fault," said an awkward, long-limbed, weary-looking man. . . .

"Shame on you all!" cried some of the ladies across the street, becoming excited.

I could not but feel sorry for the poor worn fellows, who did seem indeed heartily ashamed of themselves.

Some of the other women continued to complain, asking the soldiers and one another, "Whom shall we look to now for protection?"

These few troops, of course, were but the leading figures of a great ingression. Says Dora Miller, the lawyer's bride:

About three o'clock the rush began. I shall never forget that woeful sight of a beaten, demoralized army that came rushing back—humanity in the last throes of endurance. Wan, hollow-eyed, ragged, footsore, bloody—the men limped along, unarmed but followed by siege-guns, ambulances, gun-carriages, and wagons in aimless confusion. At twilight two or three bands on the courthouse hill and other points began playing "Dixie," "Bonnie Blue Flag," and so on; and drums began to beat all about; I suppose they were rallying the scattered army.

Another eyewitness claims that the rush into the city was accompanied by frequent condemnations of General Pemberton:

Many of the troops declared their willingness to desert rather than serve under him again. The stillness of the Sabbath night was broken in upon, and an uproar in which the blasphemous oaths of the soldier and the cry of the child, mingled, formed a scene which the pen cannot depict. . . .

There were many gentlewomen and tender children torn from their homes by the advance of a ruthless foe, and compelled to fly to our lines for protection; and mixed up with them in one vast crowd were the gallant men who had left Vicksburg . . . in all the pride and confidence of a just cause, and [were] returning to it a demoralized mob.

On the street where Mary Loughborough lived, the scene at this time was a little more encouraging:

At dark the fresh troops from Warrenton marched by, going out to the intrenchments in the rear of the city about two miles. . . . The ladies waved their handkerchiefs, cheering them and crying:

"These are the troops that have not run. You'll stand by us and protect us, won't you? You won't *retreat* and bring the Federals behind you."

And the men, who were fresh and lively, swung their hats and promised to die for the ladies—never to run—never to retreat; while the poor fellows on the pavement, sitting on their blankets—lying on the ground—leaning against trees or anything to rest their wearied bodies, looked on silent and dejected. They were not to blame, these poor, weary fellows. If they were unsuccessful, it is what many a man had been before them. . . .

"There has been many a life lost today," said a soldier to me. . . .

"Ah! truly, yes," I said; for the ambulances had been passing with wounded and dead; and one came slowly by with officers riding near it, bearing the dead body of General [Lloyd] Tilghman, the blood dripping slowly from it. . . .

What a sad evening we spent—continually hearing of friends and acquaintances left dead on the field, or mortally wounded and being brought in ambulances to the hospital. We almost feared to retire that night. No one seemed to know whether the Federal army was advancing or not. Some told us that they were many miles away, and others that they were quite near. How did we know but in the night we might be awakened by the tumult of their arrival!

At this time Grant's troops were still on the eastern bank of the Big Black, about ten miles from Vicksburg. Bridges to replace the burned ones were being built by the engineers. Trees, planks, cotton bales, and regular pontoon materials were being employed. Sherman's corps, having brought up a pontoon train, finished first. Sherman recounts:

The whole scene was lit up with fires of pitch-pine. General Grant joined me there, and we sat on a log, looking at the passage of the troops by the light of those fires. The bridge swayed to and fro under the passing feet, and made a fine war picture.

Sergeant Oldroyd, of McPherson's corps, was one of those who used another of the bridges the next morning:

As we crossed the river and marched up the bank, a brass band stood playing national airs. O, how proud we felt as we marched . . . up to the muzzles of the abandoned guns that had been planted to stay our progress. Every man felt the combined Confederate army could not keep us out of Vicksburg.

It was a grand sight, the long lines of infantry . . . winding their way up the bluffs, with flags flying in the breeze and the morning sun glancing upon the guns as they lay across the shoulders of the boys. Cheer after cheer went up.

This is supposed to be the last halting place before we knock for admittance at our goal—the boasted Gibraltar of the West.

In spite of his limited vantage point, Oldroyd was aware of how the entire army was disposed:

McClernand is on the left, McPherson in the center, and Sherman on the right. In this position the three great corps will move to Vicksburg by different roads.

It was now eighteen days since the Federals had crossed the Mississippi River at Bruinsburg. Colonel William Vilas, of the Twenty-third Wisconsin, sums up:

One hundred and eighty miles of marching done; five battles and many skirmishes fought; an enemy . . . excelling in total numbers, so skillfully beaten in detail that in no engagement was his [full] strength available; many guns captured and thousands of the enemy destroyed or taken.

Vilas goes on to boast that this was all done by an army that had been issued only five days' rations and had had to depend on "pickings" for the rest. He marvels:

And what a transformation! So shortly before, that army was still completing months of weary toil, distress, disappointment, amid Southern scoffing and Northern disheartenment, marching in the Louisiana swamps, gazing at the lofty, unassailable, hopeless fortress over the river, which now, presto! so suddenly lay within its clutch.

Grant was eager to close in:

I moved along the Vicksburg road in advance of the troops and as soon as possible joined Sherman. My first anxiety was to

Skirmishing near Vicksburg

secure a base of supplies on the Yazoo River above Vicksburg. Sherman's line of march led him to the very point on Walnut Hills occupied by the enemy the December before when he was repulsed.

Sherman was equally anxious with myself. Our impatience led us to move in advance of the column and well up with the advanced skirmishers.... The bullets of the enemy whistled by thick and fast for a short time. In a few minutes Sherman had the pleasure of looking down from the spot coveted so much by him the December before....

He turned to me, saying that up to this minute he had felt no positive assurance of success. This, however, he said was the end of one of the greatest campaigns in history.... Vicksburg was not yet captured, and there was no telling what might happen ... but whether captured or not, this was a complete and successful campaign.

8

THE SIEGE

*I*T WAS now *May 18, 1863. Twenty-nine-year-old Major Joseph Stockton of the Seventy-second Illinois Regiment, co-founder of a prosperous freight-hauling business in Chicago before the war, recorded in his diary:*

Reached our long-looked-for destination at last, the rear of Vicksburg. We arrived about dusk a mile outside of the rebel fortifications.... The 72d Illinois was thrown out as advance guard ... and myself as officer of the guard. Although completely worn out, I did not dare to sleep, but kept moving from point to point.... A large fire was burning in Vicksburg, but we could not discover what it was.

This conflagration was explained the next day in the diary of one of the city's residents, Emma Balfour, forty-five-year-old wife of Dr. William T. Balfour:

Last night we saw a grand and awful spectacle. The darkness was lit up by burning houses all along our lines. They were burnt that our firing [upon the Union army] would not be obscured. It was sad to see. Many of them we knew to be handsome residences put up in the last few years as country residences—two of them very large and handsome houses. But the stern necessity of war has caused their destruction.

The morning of May 19 found Grant's entire army exuding cheer and confidence. Wrote Sergeant Oldroyd:

This day beholds a cordon of steel, with rivets of brave hearts, surrounding Vicksburg.... We have now come here to compel them to surrender, and we are prepared to do it either by charge or by siege.... They have fought well to keep their homes free from invasion, and surely deserve praise for their brave return to battle after so many defeats.

Our army encircles the city from the river above to the river below.... The three corps have taken respective positions as follows: Sherman's Fifteenth occupies the right of the line, resting on the river above; General McClernand's Thirteenth touches the river below, while McPherson's Seventeenth stands in the center....

In taking our position we did a great deal of skirmishing.... The long lines of rebel earthworks following the zig-zag courses of the hills ... bristle with defiance to the invaders.

According to Vicksburg engineer Samuel Lockett:

The main works ... had, for the most part, exterior ditches from six to ten feet deep, with rampart, parapet, banquette for infantry, and embrasures and platforms for artillery ... with 102 guns ready for service.... Some portions of our front were protected by abatis of fallen trees and entanglements of telegraph wire....

The troops were ... in position as I had recommended. General C. L. Stevenson's division extended from the Warrenton road on our extreme right to the railroad [from Jackson]; General John H. Forney's division occupied the center, from the railroad to the Graveyard road; General M. L. Smith's division filling up the space between the Graveyard road and the river on our left. General John S. Bowen's Missourians and [General T. N.] Waul's Texas Legion were held in reserve.

Lockett says also that "the river batteries were still strong and intact." This was important because Admiral Porter had brought his fleet back up the Mississippi to join those vessels he had left at Vicksburg and was now deploying his gunboats and mortar schooners so as to menace the city in front while Grant pressed it from the rear.

The people of Vicksburg had no choice but to prepare for the ordeals of total war. Business was largely suspended, with the few surviving stores charging exorbitant prices for their goods. One of the city's newspapers had already been burned out by Federal shellfire, but the Citizen *planned to keep publishing, at least on a part-time basis.*

Suddenly many more people saw the need to have a cave handy. "Negroes who understood their business," says Mary Loughborough, "hired themselves out to dig them, at from thirty to fifty dollars, according to their size."

Mary found some consolation in the fact that the city's rear defenses were about two miles out, though she wasn't too sure they would keep Grant's eager army in check. She tells how the defenses were tested on the afternoon of May 19:

At three o'clock... the artillery boomed from the intrench-ments, roar after roar, followed by the rattle of musketry. The Federal forces were making their first attack. Looking out from the back veranda, we could plainly see the smoke before the re-port of the guns reached us. Our anxiety was great....

The discharges of musketry were irregular. Yet, to us who were thinking of the dear ones exposed to this frequent firing, the restless forebodings and unhappiness caused by the distant din of battle pained us indeed.... At every report our hearts beat quicker. The excitement was intense in the city. Groups of people stood on every available position where a view could be obtained of the distant hills, where the jets of white smoke constantly passed out from among the trees.

Some of our friends proposed going for a better view up on the balcony around the cupola of the court house. The view from there was most extensive and beautiful. Hill after hill arose in the distance, enclosing the city in the form of a crescent. Immediately in the center... the firing seemed more continuous, while to the left and running northerly, the rattle and roar would be sudden, sharp, and vigorous, then ceasing for some time.

The hills around near the city, and indeed every place that seemed commanding and secure, was covered with anxious spectators—many of them ladies—fearing the result of the after-noon's conflict.

To the extreme left and north ... the warfare became general, while toward the center the firing became less rapid.... It was amid the clump of trees on the far distant hillside that the Federal batteries could be discerned by the frequent puffings of smoke from the guns.

Turning to the river, we could see a gunboat that had the temerity to come down as near the town as possible, and lay just out of reach of the Confederate batteries, with steam up. Two more lay about half a mile above.... Below the city a gunboat had come up... on the Louisiana side, striving to engage the lower batteries of the town—firing about every fifteen minutes.

While we were looking at the river, we saw two large yawls start out from shore [on the Vicksburg side], with two larger boats tied to them, and full of men. We learned that they were . . . Federal prisoners that had been held in the town, and today paroled and sent over to the Federal encampment, so that the resources of the garrison might be husbanded as much as possible and the necessity of sustaining them avoided.

The idea made me serious. We might look forward truly now to perhaps real suffering. Yet I did not regret my resolution to remain, and would have left the town more reluctantly today than ever before, for we felt that now, indeed, the whole country was unsafe, and that our only hope of safety lay in Vicksburg.

The little boats, with their prisoners, had gained the opposite shore, and we could see the liberated men walking along the river bank. . . .

In looking again with a glass in the rear of the city, we could see the Southern soldiers working at their guns. . . . The Federal troops were too distant to discern.

Some ambulances were coming into the city, probably bringing the wounded from the field. We saw an officer coming in with his head bound up and his arm in a sling, his servant walking by his side leading his horse. . . .

Looking again toward the river, the gunboat near the lower batteries kept its old position, slowly firing at the lower part of the city. And far over on the other shore, walking rapidly, I observed the figures of the freed prisoners near the canal, and fast becoming indistinct, even with the aid of a glass.

So twilight began falling over the scene—hushing . . . the noise and uproar of the battlefield—falling softly and silently upon the river . . . bringing only the heaven above us . . . distinctly to our eyes.

Grant's troops, states Samuel Lockett, "were repulsed with great loss [about 950 killed, wounded, captured or missing], leaving five stand of colors close to our lines and the ground being strewn with their dead and wounded." Lockett goes on to explain that the Federals had been met by troops which had not been in any of the recent disastrous engagements, and were not in the least demoralized. These men stood to their arms like true soldiers, and helped to restore the morale of our army.

That night two of Admiral Porter's gunboats took turns at bombarding the city from below. At dawn a division of mortar vessels opened from the far side of the De Soto peninsula, "adding to the tremendous din their hoarse bellowing, accompanied with the fearful screams and tremendous concussions of their huge, exploding missiles." It was Confederate Sergeant Willie H. Tunnard, of the Third Louisiana Infantry, upon whom the great shells made this impression.

Tunnard was Northern born but had been raised in New Orleans, returning to the North, however, to attend college, where he showed a talent for journalism. Now twenty-six years old, Tunnard was dedicated to the Confederacy and saw the war as having a glorious side. He took deep pride in his regiment:

Its gallant men bore their banner triumphantly through the sulphureous canopy and thunder-voices of deadly conflicts, making, by their heroic deeds and undaunted bravery, an imperishable record on the scroll of time.

The sergeant says of the scene in Vicksburg on the day after the Union assault:

Fair ladies, in all the vigor and loveliness of youth, hurried with light tread along the torn up pavements, fearless of the storm of iron and lead penetrating every portion of the city.... They flitted about the hospitals ... to relieve the sufferings of those who so gallantly defended their hearthstones.

By this time the sporadic shelling of Vicksburg from Porter's gunboats and mortar schooners was being augmented by occasional shells from the Union artillery in the city's rear.

Two or three of the army's shells landed near the house where Mary Loughborough and her two-year-old daughter were guests: "This was our first shock, and a severe one." Mary was surprised to note that some of the household's black servants "kept on with their work as if feeling a perfect contempt for the shells."

Mary continues:

In the evening we were terrified and much excited by the loud rush and scream of mortar shells. We ran to the small cave near the house, and were in it during the night....

The caves were plainly becoming a necessity, as some persons had been killed on the street by fragments of shells. The room that I had so lately slept in had been struck by a fragment of shell the first night, and a large hole made in the ceiling.

I shall never forget my extreme fear during the night, and my utter hopelessness of ever seeing the morning light. Terror stricken, we remained crouched in the cave, while shell after shell followed each other in quick succession. I endeavored by constant prayer to prepare myself for the sudden death I was almost certain awaited me.

My heart stood still as we would hear the reports from the guns and the rushing and fearful sound of the shell as it came toward us. As it neared, the noise became more deafening; the air was full of the rushing sound; pains darted through my temples; my ears were full of the confusing noise; and, as it exploded, the report flashed through my head like an electric shock, leaving me in a quiet state of terror . . . cowering in a corner, holding my child to my heart. . . .

As singly they fell short or beyond the cave, I was aroused by a feeling of thankfulness that was of short duration. Again and again the terrible fright came over us in that night. I saw one fall in the road [outside] the mouth of the cave, like a flame of fire, making the earth tremble. . . .

Morning found us more dead than alive, with blanched faces and trembling lips. We were not reassured on hearing, from a man who took refuge [with us] in the cave, that a mortar shell in falling would not consider the thickness of the earth above us a circumstance. Some of the ladies, more courageous by daylight, asked him what he was in there for, if that was the case. He was silenced for an hour, when he left.

As the day wore on and we were still preserved . . . we were somewhat encouraged.

As during previous bombardments of the city, the shells were a lot more frightening than they were destructive of life and property. Serious hits did occur, however. One of the houses struck late in the day was that of Dr. William W. Lord, rector of Christ Church and chaplain of the First Mississippi Brigade (though a native of New York). Conditions had moderated enough in the early part of the day for the family to eat in their dining room, with the windows open and the smell of roses wafting in.

Before sunset [says Lida Lord, who was a small girl at the time], a bombshell burst in the very center of that pretty dining-room, blowing out the roof and one side, crushing the well-spread teatable like an eggshell, and making a great yawning hole in the floor, into which disappeared supper, china, furniture, and the safe [i.e., food chest] containing our entire stock of butter and eggs.

On the Union side, the two days of shooting at the city, such a trial to the Confederates, was considered to be only incidental to more important work. According to General Grant:

The 20th and 21st were spent in strengthening our position and in making roads in rear of the army, from Yazoo River or Chickasaw Bayou. Most of the army had now been for three weeks with only five days' rations issued by the commissary. They ... began to feel the want of bread.

... In passing around to the left of the line on the 21st, a soldier, recognizing me, said in rather a low voice, but yet so that I heard him, "Hardtack."

In a moment the cry was taken up all along the line, "Hardtack! Hardtack!"

I told the men nearest to me that we had been engaged ever since the arrival of the troops in building a road over which to supply them with everything they needed. The cry was instantly changed to cheers.

By the night of the 21st all the troops had full rations issued to them. The bread and coffee were highly appreciated.

One need of the soldiers, as Sergeant Oldroyd pointed out in his diary, was as yet only a hope:

We are ragged and dirty, for we have had no change of clothes for over a month. But we have the promise of new suits soon. If we were to enter Vicksburg tomorrow, some of our nice young fellows would feel ashamed to march before the young ladies there.

We can see the court house in the city with a Confederate flag floating over it. What fun it will be to take that down and hoist in its stead the old stars and stripes. Then yonder is the Mississippi River again. We want to jump into that once more and have a good bath.

Even as he put his troops on full rations the evening of May 21, Grant ordered them to prepare for a new assault on the Confederate works the next morning. He explains his reasoning:

Johnston was in my rear, only fifty miles away ... and I knew he was being reinforced. There was danger of his coming to the

Mortars firing in the night

assistance of Pemberton. . . . The immediate capture of Vicksburg would save [Washington the need of] sending me the reinforcements which were so much wanted elsewhere, and would set free the army under me to drive Johnston from the state. But the first consideration of all was—the troops believed they could carry the works in their front, and would not have worked so patiently in the trenches [afterward] if they had not been allowed to try.

The upcoming assault was the chief topic of conversation around the army's evening campfires. In the camp of the Seventy-second Illinois, however, another topic soon took precedence.

As related in the diary of Major Joseph Stockton:

Quite a number of officers were sitting together just before dark eating their supper ... when the bugler of the regiment, who was sitting near, was shot through the heart and killed instantly. No one could tell where the shot came from. He was just raising his spoon to his mouth when he fell over dead.

We buried him ... performing a soldier's burial. ... A number of the officers and men had service over the dead, and we all sang a hymn.

Who knows who may be living tomorrow night.

Even as Major Stockton, along with thousands of others around the great semicircle of campfires, meditated upon their chances for survival, the first rumblings of the assault's preliminary bombardment were heard.

In the words of a correspondent for the Chicago Tribune:

During the night ... the gunboats and mortars lying in front of Vicksburg kept up a continual fire and dropped their fiery messengers right and left without distinction. ... Several buildings were set on fire by the exploding shells and lighted up the darkness, revealing strange shapes and wonderful outlines standing out in relief against the dark sky.

Admiral Porter states that he bombarded not only the city but those sections of the defense works within his range, paying particular attention to "places where troops might be resting during the night."

In the morning, the Tribune *correspondent goes on to say, the army's cannonading began: "From every hilltop in front of the enemy's works ... the fiery tempest raged fearfully." With his glasses, the correspondent could see the effect: "Guns were dismounted, embrasures torn up, parapets destroyed, and caissons exploded. It was a fearful demonstration."*

Union Sergeant Oldroyd adds that "nothing could be heard at the time but the thundering of great guns." All this obliged the Confederates to keep their heads down and restricted their ability to reply.

The assault had been scheduled to begin at ten o'clock. During the tumultuous waiting period, according to another Union soldier, "Officers, outwardly calm, moved aimlessly about, anxiously consulting their timepieces. Aides from brigade headquarters came and went."

At the same time, says Sergeant Oldroyd:

The boys ... were busy divesting themselves of watches, rings, pictures and other keepsakes, which were being placed in the custody of the cooks, who were not expected to go into action. ... The instructions left with the keepsakes were varied. For instance:

"This watch I want you to send to my father if I never return."
"... If I do not get back, just send these little trifles home, will
you?"

... This was done while we awaited orders, which at last came in
earnest, and in obedience to them we moved up and took our
place. ... The air was so thick with the smoke of cannon that we
could hardly see a hundred yards before us.

*Among the thousands of Confederates who were peering cautiously over
their parapets at this time was Corporal Ephraim Anderson:*
The enemy could be seen massing his forces in the edge of the
woods, some four hundred yards distant, and it was the impression he was preparing for a charge; and in a short time a shout
went up from his ranks, that extended round as far as we could
see or hear on either side. The dark masses then rolled forward to
the onslaught. They were in two lines, within supporting distance,
and advanced in a very gallant manner.

The artillery opened upon the lines as they approached, and
the infantry joined in as soon as they were within range. The
action immediately became severe and bloody; the destruction
among the Federal ranks was fearful, yet they still advanced. The
roll of musketry along our lines was deafening, and the peal on
peal of the artillery reverberated and thundered throughout the
length and breadth of the fortifications.

General Grant explains that
portions of each of the three corps succeeded in getting up to the
very parapets of the enemy and in planting their battle flags upon
them; but at no place were we able to enter.

General McClernand reported that he had gained the enemy's
intrenchments at several points and wanted reinforcements. I occupied a position from which I believed I could see as well as he
what took place in his front, and I did not see the success he
reported. But his request for reinforcements being repeated I
could not ignore it, and sent him [a] division of the 17th corps.
Sherman and McPherson were both ordered to renew their assaults as a diversion in favor of McClernand.

This last attack only served to increase our casualties without
giving any benefit whatever.

*At sunset the Federals, who had suffered more than 3,000 in killed,
wounded, captured or missing, as compared with less than 500 casualties*

James B. McPherson

on the Confederate side, began withdrawing to the security of their entrenchments. Hastened on their way by Confederate artillery fire, they left behind hundreds of the dead and wounded and a great scattering of muskets, cartridge boxes, canteens, and other equipage. Numbers of the wounded, too weak to rise but not altogether helpless, could be seen crawling after their vanishing comrades.

General Sherman says that he, Grant, and McPherson discussed McClernand with "great feeling and severe criticism" for making this defeat worse than it should have been.

Again in the words of Confederate Corporal Anderson:

That night the Federals were actively engaged in fortifying, and daylight exhibited works on several advantageous positions, at the distance of from two to three hundred yards. Their skirmishers were nearer and sheltered in holes dug during the night, which entirely concealed them, and from which they fired throughout the day.

This work went on with all the dead and some of the wounded of May 22 still lying between the lines. The next day, Sunday, May 24, was passed with an equal inattention to this problem. Wrote Union Sergeant Oldroyd:

How little like the Sabbath day it seems. Cannon are still sending their messengers of death into the enemy's lines, as on week days, and the minnie balls sing the same song, while the shovel throws up as much dirt as on any other day. What a relief it would be if, by common consent, both armies should cease firing today.

It is our regiment's turn to watch at the front, so before daylight we moved up and took our position. We placed our muskets across the rifle pits, pointing towards the fort, and then lay down and ran our eyes over the gun, with finger on trigger, ready to fire at anything we might see moving.

For hours not a movement was seen, till finally an old half-starved mule meandered too close to our lines, when off went a hundred or more muskets, and down fell the poor mule. This little incident, for a few minutes, broke the monotony.

A coat and hat were elevated on a stick above our rifle pits, and in an instant they were riddled with bullets from the enemy. The rebels were a little excited at the ruse, and probably thought, after their firing, there must be one less Yankee in our camp. In their eagerness a few of them raised their heads a little above their breastworks, when a hundred bullets flew at them from our side. They all dropped instantly, and we could not tell whether they were hit or not. . . .

A shell from an enemy's gun dropped into our camp rather unexpectedly and bursted near a group, wounding several, but only slightly, though the doctor thinks one of the wounded will not be able to sit down comfortably for a few days. I suppose, then, he can go on picket, or walk around and enjoy the country.

During these past two days, Confederate Corporal Anderson and his regiment had been overlooking one of the spots where the fighting of May 22 had been especially fierce:

It is truly horrible to relate that some of the enemy's wounded lay in sight and died for want of attention. One poor fellow, in full view of our regiment, about seventy-five yards from the works, although never heard to call out, yet was seen repeatedly raising both his arms and legs for nearly two days, when he became still—was dead, most probably from want of timely and proper attention. . . .

A number that were near our lines were taken from the field during the night following the charge and sent to our hospitals, where they received the same care and attention that was bestowed upon our own wounded.

On the evening of the twenty-fifth ... General Pemberton asked for a short armistice, that the enemy might bury his dead, which had now become very offensive.

Some of the Confederates who had been noting the growing swarms of flies and breathing the putrid odors were moved to jest wryly that General Grant, unable to overcome them by assault, was trying to "stink them out."
Anderson continues:

A few hours' cessation of hostilities ensued, and the enemy came forward with shovels and spades and covered most of the bodies where they lay, by simply throwing a bank of dirt over them. I observed two men carried back into their lines that still had life in them.

All the soldiers came out of their works and hiding-places, and gave us a good opportunity to look at them. Many gibes and cuts were exchanged between the lines, in which the Confederates seemed to hold their own. One of the Confederates hallooed out something to a Federal ... which he did not like, and received the very laconic reply, "Go to hell," when the Reb retorted that "hell was so full of blue-bellies, there was no room for white men."

I saw a young soldier of our command meet a brother, on half-way ground, from the Federal lines, where they sat upon a log and conversed with one another.

Union Sergeant Oldroyd says that many of the Federals and Confederates "mingled together in various sports, apparently with much enjoyment."

Here a group of four played cards—two Yanks and two Rebs. There, others were jumping, while everywhere blue and gray mingled in conversation over the scenes which had transpired since our visit to the neighborhood.

I talked with a very sensible rebel, who said he was satisfied we should not only take Vicksburg but drive the forces of the South all over their territory, at last compelling them to surrender. Still, he said, he had gone into the fight, and was resolved not to back out. He said they had great hope of dissension in the North, to such an extent as might strengthen their cause.

There have been grounds for this hope, I am sorry to say, and such dissensions in the North must prolong the war, if our "peace party" should succeed in materially obstructing the war measures of the government.

From the remarks of some of the rebels, I judged that their supply of provisions was getting low, and that they had no source from which to draw more. We gave them from our own rations some fat meat, crackers, coffee, and so forth.

"On this occasion," states Confederate officer Samuel Lockett,
I met General Sherman for the first time. Naturally, the officers of both armies took advantage of the truce to use their eyes to the best possible advantage. I was on the Jackson road redan, which had been terribly pounded and was the object of constant attention from a battery of heavy guns in its immediate front. The Federals were running [a trench] toward it in a zigzag... and were already in uncomfortable proximity to it.

While standing on the parapet of this work a Federal orderly came up to me and said that General Sherman wished to speak to me. Following the orderly, I reached a group of officers standing some two hundred yards in front of our line. One of these came forward, introduced himself as General Sherman, and said:

"I saw that you were an officer by your insignia of rank, and have asked you to meet me to put into your hands some letters intrusted to me by Northern friends of some of your officers and men. I thought this would be a good opportunity to deliver this mail before it got too old."

To this I replied: "Yes, General, it would have been very old indeed if you had kept it until you brought it into Vicksburg yourself."

"So you think, then," said the general, "I am a very slow mail route?"

"Well, rather," was the reply, "when you have to travel by regular approaches, parallels, and zigzags."

"Yes," he said, "that is a slow way of getting into a place, but it is a very sure way, and I was determined to deliver those letters sooner or later."

The general then invited me to take a seat with him on an old log nearby, and thus the rest of the time of the truce was spent in pleasant conversation. In the course of it the general remarked:

"You have an admirable position for defense here, and you have taken excellent advantage of the ground."

"Yes, General," I replied, "but it is equally as well adapted to offensive operations, and your engineers have not been slow to discover it."

To this General Sherman assented. Intentionally or not, his civility certainly prevented me from seeing many other points in our front that I, as chief engineer, was very anxious to examine.

The truce ended with a few final jibes among those who hadn't warmed to each other, but with a widespread shaking of hands and many friendly warnings to "take care" among those who had.

"The hours of peace," says Confederate Sergeant Willie Tunnard, had scarcely expired ere those who had so lately intermingled in friendly intercourse were once again engaged in the deadly struggle. Heavy mortars, artillery of every calibre, and small-arms, once more with thunder tones awakened the slumbering echoes of the hills surrounding the heroic city of Vicksburg.

Both the Confederate troops and the citizens of Vicksburg had been encouraged by the victory of May 22. Hope was now entertained that the garrison would be able to hold out until rescued by Joe Johnston or perhaps even by a force from the Confederate states west of the Mississippi.

Emma Balfour, the doctor's wife, who lived near the house General Pemberton was using as his headquarters and who considered herself to be "a great favorite" of his, told her diary on May 26:

General Pemberton was here yesterday. He seems very hopeful. Says we can hold the place sixty days and even more by living on very short rations.

The next day Emma wrote:

Nothing from the outside world yet. All day and all night the shells from the mortars are falling around us, and all day from the guns around the fortifications. No rest for our poor soldiers who have to stay down in the trenches all day in the hot sun. It is a most discouraging sort of warfare. The enemy shoot from muskets and Parrott guns all day. If a head, even a hand, appears above the breastworks it is fired on. . . .

I have stayed at home every night except two. I could not stand the mosquitoes and the crowd in the caves. Most people spend their time entirely in them, for there is no safety anywhere else. Indeed, there is no safety there. Several accidents have occurred. In one cave nearly a whole family were killed or crippled. . . .

Last night I thought we would have to go somewhere, but at last worn out with watching we retired and slept as if we were in safety. Now and then when a shell exploded nearer than usual, or the house shook more than usual, we would listen for a while and then sleep again.

The doctor says he begins to realize now that we can get used to anything—to think of one's sleeping with these twelve and thirteen inch shells... falling and exploding all around, now and then tearing a house to pieces, and knowing that yours may be the next, seems strange; but so we are constituted....

I sent out buttermilk every day to General [Stephen] Lee and staff; and yes, today when Joe [a slave] came for it I told him to go over and give my compliments to General Grant and ask him to send me some newspapers and to tell him not to shoot those shells so near here, that they might break some of my flower pots.

Joe took it all in earnest and ... he said he would tell [General Lee] what I said, but he did not believe he would send him over to those Yankees.

Up until the battle of May 22, Mary Loughborough and her child had been sharing the cave of the family with whom they were living. But then Mary's husband, a captain in the front lines (referred to as "M." in Mary's narrations), sent a friend to see that they were provided with a cave of their own. It was quickly finished, and Mary moved in:

We had neighbors on both sides of us; and it would have been an amusing sight to a spectator to witness the domestic scenes presented [outside] by the number of servants preparing the meals under the high bank containing the caves.

Cave life in Vicksburg

Our dining, breakfasting, and supper hours were quite irregular. When the shells were falling fast, the servants came in for safety and our meals waited for completion some little time. Again they would fall slowly, with the lapse of many minutes between, and out would start the cooks to their work.

Some families had light bread made in large quantities, and subsisted on it with milk—provided their cows were not killed from one milking time to another—without any more cooking until called on to replenish. Though most of us lived on corn bread and bacon, served three times a day, the only luxury of the meal consisting in its warmth, I had some flour, and frequently had some hard, tough biscuit made from it, there being no soda or yeast to be procured. At this time we could also procure beef.

A gentleman friend was kind enough to offer me his camp bed, a narrow spring mattress, which fitted within the contracted cave very comfortably. Another had his tent-fly stretched over the mouth of our residence to shield us from the sun. And thus I was the recipient of many favors, and under obligations to many gentlemen of the army for delicate and kind attentions. . . .

And so I went regularly to work, keeping house under ground. Our new habitation was an evacuation . . . branching six feet from the entrance, forming a cave in the shape of a T. In one of the wings my bed fitted. The other I used as a kind of a dressing room. . . . Our quarters were close indeed; yet I was more comfortable than I expected I could have been made under the earth in that fashion.

We were safe at least from fragments of shell—and they were flying in all directions; though no one seemed to think our cave any protection should a mortar shell happen to fall directly on top of the ground above us. We had our roof arched and braced, the supports of the bracing taking up much room in our confined quarters. The earth was about five feet thick above, and seemed hard and compact; yet poor M., every time he came in [from the front lines] examined it, fearing, amid some of the shock it sustained, that it might crack and fall upon us.

Mary was hardly settled before she herself was led into greater doubts about her security. During an afternoon bombardment she heard some women screaming "amid the rush and explosion of the shells."

The servant boy, George, after starting and coming back once or twice . . . at last gathered courage to go to the ravine near us from whence the cries proceeded, and found that a Negro man had been buried alive within a cave, he being alone at that time. Workmen were instantly set to deliver him, if possible; but when found, the unfortunate man had evidently been dead some little time. His wife and relations were distressed beyond measure, and filled the air with their cries and groans. . . .

That night, after my little one had been laid in bed, I sat at the mouth of the cave, with the servants drawn around me, watching the brilliant display of fireworks the mortar boats were making— the passage of the shell as it travelled through the heavens looking like a swiftly moving star. As it fell, it approached the earth so rapidly that it seemed to leave behind a track of fire. . . .

The incendiary shells were still more beautiful in appearance. As they exploded in the air, the burning matter and balls fell like large, clear blue-and-amber stars, scattering hither and thither.

"Miss Mary," said one of the more timid servants, "do they want to kill us all dead? Will they keep doing this until we all die?"

I said most heartily, "I hope not!"

The servants we had with us seemed to possess more courage than is usually attributed to Negroes. They seldom hesitated to cross the street for water at any time. The "boy" slept at the entrance of the cave with a pistol I had given him, telling me I need not be "afeared—dat anyone dat come dar would have to go over his body first."

He never refused to carry out any little article to M. on the battlefield. I laughed heartily at a dilemma he was placed in one day: The mule that he had mounted to ride out to the battlefield took him to a dangerous locality, where the shells were flying thickly, and then, suddenly stopping through fright, obstinately refused to stir. It was in vain that George kicked and beat him—go he would not. So, clenching his hand, he hit him severely in the head several times, jumped down, ran home [i.e., back to the cave] and left him. The mule stood a few minutes rigidly, then, looking round and seeing George at some distance from him, turned and followed quite demurely.

Each day, as the couriers came into the city [from the front lines] M. would write me little notes, asking after our welfare. . . . I, in return, would write to him of our safety, but was always careful in speaking of the danger to which we were exposed. I thought poor M. had enough to try him, without suffering anxiety for us; so I made light of my fears. . . . In his letters he charged me particularly to be careful of the provisions—that no one could tell what our necessities might be.

By this time General Grant had turned his full attention to pressing his siege works:

The experience of the 22d convinced officers and men that this was best, and they went to work on the defenses and approaches with a will. With the navy holding the river, the investment of Vicksburg was complete. As long as we could hold our position the enemy was limited in supplies of food, men and munitions of war to what they had on hand. These could not last....

My line was more than fifteen miles long, extending from Haynes' Bluff [on the Yazoo River]... to Warrenton. The line of the enemy was about seven. In addition to this, having an enemy at Canton and Jackson, in our rear, who was being constantly reinforced, we required a second line of defense facing the other way. I had not troops enough under my command to man these. General Halleck [in Washington] appreciated the situation, and ... forwarded reinforcements with all possible dispatch....

The labor of building the batteries and intrenching was largely

Scene just behind Grant's front lines

done by the pioneers, assisted by Negroes who came within our lines and who were paid for their work. But details from the troops had often to be made.

Says an unnamed Union soldier:

Every man in the investing line became an army engineer day and night. The soldiers worked at digging narrow, zigzag approaches to the rebel works. Entrenchments, rifle pits, and dirt caves were made in every conceivable direction. When entrenchments were safe and finished, still others yet farther in advance were made, as if by magic, in a single night. Other zigzag underground saps and mines were made for explosion under forts. Every day the regiments, foot by foot, yard by yard, approached nearer the strongly armed rebel works. The soldiers got so they bored like gophers and beavers, with a spade in one hand and a gun in the other.

Grant explains another aspect of the siege:

As soon as the news of the arrival of the Union army behind Vicksburg reached the North, floods of visitors began to pour in. Some came to gratify curiosity; some to see sons and brothers. . . . Members of the Christian and Sanitary Associations came to minister to the wants of the sick and the wounded.

Often those coming to see a son or brother would bring a

Federal troops in front-line entrenchment

dozen or two of poultry. They did not know how little the gift would be appreciated. Many of the soldiers had lived so much on chickens, ducks and turkeys without bread during the march that the sight of poultry . . . almost took away their appetite. But the intention was good.

Among the earliest arrivals was the Governor of Illinois, with most of the State officers. I naturally wanted to show them what there was of most interest. In Sherman's front the ground was the most broken and most wooded, and more was to be seen without exposure [to the enemy's fire]. I therefore took them to Sherman's headquarters and presented them. . . .

There was a little knot around Sherman and another around me, and I heard Sherman repeating, in the most animated manner, what he had said to me when we first looked down from Walnut Hills upon the land below on the 18th of May, adding:

"Grant is entitled to every bit of the credit for the campaign. I opposed it. I wrote him a letter about it."

But for this speech it is not likely that Sherman's opposition would have ever been heard of. His untiring energy and great efficiency during the campaign entitle him to a full share of all the credit. . . . He could not have done more if the plan had been his own.

Among the volunteer nurses, or "sanitary agents," who arrived from the North was Iowa's Annie Wittenmyer:

I came down the river with a heavy lot of supplies at the beginning of the siege. I sent an order to the quartermaster for an ambulance. Instead of sending the ambulance he sent me a fine silver-mounted easy carriage captured at Jackson. . . .

I drove out in company with Mrs. General [William M.] Stone to the nearest hospital one day. We had gone through the tents and attended to the business that had brought us, and were standing beside the carriage, when a shell from Vicksburg burst near us, scattering fragments all around us. To me the shock was terrific. I could feel my flesh crawl . . . and every hair on my head seemed to stand upright.

"Are you so near the enemy's guns?" I questioned [one of the surgeons].

"Oh, yes; all the hospitals are under fire. A shell burst in this hospital a few days ago, killing one man and wounding three others."

"It's horrible that sick men must be placed under fire. Why don't the authorities remove the sick and wounded to a safe distance?" I spoke with some spirit.

"You forget," said the surgeon, "that General Johnston's army is near, and that we are forced to draw in our lines. We would rather take the risk of a random shell than to risk being between two contending armies during a battle."

This was quite another view of the matter, and now I was brought face to face with the facts of the situation. If I visited the hospitals I must do it under fire.... I went back to the sanitary boat at the Yazoo Landing in a very thoughtful mood.... That night was spent in prayer. The next morning I arose with a courage born of faith. I seemed immortal; not a bullet had been moulded that could hit me.

I went out to my work without fear. My carriage was struck time and again, and bullets whizzed past me, but never a feeling of fear crept into my heart. I was "under the shadow of His wings, and He covered me with His feathers."

Mrs. General Stone ... camped with her father out on the bluffs. She invited me to leave the sluggish river with its miasma and come up and stay with her.... She had a beautiful tent put up beside her own; and as the lizards were very abundant, the feet of our cots were put in jars of water ... to keep them off of our beds. We could hear their little feet scratching as they raced after each other over the tents....

Night and day the battle went on. The shells with their burning fuses would sail up into mid-air like stars of the first magnitude and burst into a shower of sparks and fragments, setting the heavens ablaze with their scintillation and jarring the foundations of the earth with the thunder of their explosions. We became so accustomed to the horrid sounds of war that the absence or abatement of it would awaken us out of our sleep.

It wasn't long before Mrs. Wittenmyer had another personal experience with one of the enemy's daytime shells. She was in her carriage with her driver and her assistants at the time:

Coming in from a weary round, a day's work of unusual peril and hardship, we reached a point in the road sheltered from the enemy by a clump of trees. Though at no great distance from the Confederate guns, it seemed more secure because we were out of sight of the frowning batteries.

Suddenly there was a crash in the timber, and we knew and

heard no more. We were all so stunned that we did not know that a shell, crushing through the tops of the trees, had struck the ground in the middle of the roadway not forty feet behind our carriage. If it had come a moment sooner, we would all have been scattered in fragments to the four winds. . . .

The horses fell to the earth, the driver seemed dazed for a time, the carriage was covered with the dirt thrown out—for an ox might have been buried in the pit. . . . Fortunately . . . no one was killed or hurt. . . .

George, the driver, a soldier detailed for that service . . . was about the worst frightened person I ever saw. That evening he said: "I wish you would release me and ask for someone else. I'd rather be with my regiment behind the fortifications than driving around this way all the time."

"You'll feel better about it in the morning, George—you will get over the shock. . . . But think about it; and if in the morning you would rather go back to your regiment, I will have the change made."

The next morning George was all right, and he continued to drive for me.

Early in the siege, Mrs. Wittenmyer became accustomed to a sight that was a source of both admiration and apprehension to the Union troops:

Nearly every day . . . General Grant rode around the fiery line of the besieged city on his little black horse; and his son Fred, about thirteen years old [he would turn thirteen on May 30], who acted as his orderly, followed about fifty yards in the rear. It was a wild ride over the rough, roadless fields and bluffs in the rear of our batteries, where the enemy's guns were ploughing the ground. . . .

Almost every day as I drove about the lines, at some point or other I would see General Grant and his brave little orderly riding at full speed in the face of the long lines of the enemy's batteries, and within range of their murderous fire. But most of all to be feared was the surer fire of the Confederate sharpshooters. . . .

There was great anxiety for General Grant. . . . Personally he was beloved by officers and men, but there were deeper reasons. His life was so important to the Union cause that his death would have been the greatest calamity that the army could have suffered. Officers and civilians warned and entreated him, but as far as I could see he made no change in his course.

Fred Grant shared his father's dangers; and although he was

one of the nicest boys I ever saw, few knew his real merits and bravery. Like his distinguished father, he was free from bombast and was quiet and reserved, so his heroic services during the siege were not paraded before the public. . . .

It was fortunate that his devoted mother was not there at that time to see his danger as he went out under the guns daily. Her anxiety would have been unbearable.

Another who often rode with General Grant on his trips along the lines was the observer from Washington, Charles Dana. After his seven or eight weeks with the army, Dana had formed some firm opinions of Grant's corps commanders. His favorite was Sherman:

He began his siege works with great energy and admirable skill. Everything I saw of Sherman . . . increased my admiration for him. He was a very brilliant man and an excellent commander of a corps. Sherman's information was great, and he was a clever talker. He always liked to have people about who could keep up with his conversation. Besides, he was genial and unaffected. . . .

McPherson was an engineer officer of fine natural ability and extraordinary acquirements . . . and was held in high estimation by Grant and his professional brethren. . . . He was a man without any pretensions, and always had a pleasant handshake for you.

It is a little remarkable that the three chief figures in this great Vicksburg campaign—Grant, Sherman, and McPherson—were all born in Ohio. The utmost cordiality and confidence existed between these three men. . . . There was no jealousy or bickering, and in their unpretending simplicity they were as alike as three peas. No country was ever more faithfully, unselfishly served than was ours in the Vicksburg campaign by these three Ohio officers.

Dana goes on to discuss McClernand of Illinois, next to Grant the ranking officer in the army:

He was very inefficient and slow in pushing his siege operations. Grant had resolved on the 23d to relieve McClernand for his false dispatch of the day before stating that he held two of the enemy's forts, but he changed his mind, concluding that it would be better on the whole to leave him in his command till the siege was concluded.

From the time that I had joined Grant's army at Milliken's Bend . . . I had been observing McClernand narrowly myself. My own judgment of him by this time was that he had not the qualities necessary for a commander even of a regiment. In the first place, he was not a military man; he was a politician and a member of Congress. . . .

McClernand was merely a smart man, quick, very active-minded, but his judgment was not solid, and he looked after himself a good deal. Mr. Lincoln also looked out carefully for McClernand because he was an Illinois Democrat with a considerable following among the people. . . . As long as he adhered to the war [i.e., supported Lincoln and his policies] he carried his Illinois constituency with him.

And chiefly for this reason, doubtless, Lincoln made it a point to take special care of him. In doing this the President really served the greater good of the cause. But from the circumstance of Lincoln's supposed friendship, McClernand had more consequence in the army than he deserved.

Toward the end of May, General Grant, wishing to keep a sharp eye on his rear against the possibility of an attack by Joe Johnston, dispatched one of his aides, Colonel James Wilson, to McClernand with an order directing him to send some troops to the crossings of the Big Black River.

McClernand scowled as he read the order. "I'll be God-damned if I'll do it. I'm tired of being dictated to. I won't stand it any longer. And you can go back and tell General Grant."

Colonel Wilson promptly took exception to McClernand's disrespect for his commanding general, and an argument developed, with Wilson at last clenching his fists and offering battle.

McClernand cooled off, decided to obey the order, and said, "I was simply expressing my intense vehemence on the subject matter, sir, and I beg your pardon."

Wilson reported the affair to Grant, who found McClernand's apology amusing. Next time Grant heard one of his aides explode with profanity, he said, "He's not swearing—he's just expressing his intense vehemence on the subject matter."

9

A SEASON OF TUMULT AND TERROR

*F*OR A *brief time on May 27 the Federals shifted the emphasis of their attack to Vicksburg's northern waterfront. That morning Dr. Richard R. Hall, an assistant surgeon on board the ironclad gunboat Cincinnati, stationed up the river, said in a letter addressed to his family at home, "Today we are ordered to run down to Vicksburg." Hall explained that the chief aim of the mission, which was to be supported by several other vessels, was "to destroy a masked battery that holds General Sherman in check." Exuding confidence, the doctor added, "We will do it for him."*

According to Confederate Sergeant Willie Tunnard:

About 11 o'clock A.M. the gunboats approached our batteries, both from above and below, while all around the lines a tremendous, rapid cannonading began. The roar of artillery was terrific in its volume of sound. The *Cincinnati*, one of the finest ironclads in the enemy's fleet, boldly approached our upper batteries.

Says Admiral Porter, who was above the city on the deck of the Black Hawk, *which had replaced the* Benton *as his flagship:*

As the vessel [commanded by Lieutenant George M. Bache] rounded to and opened her broadside, the battery on the bluff opened on her stern with its heaviest guns. The first shot... passed through the magazine and then through the bottom, causing the *Cincinnati* to fill rapidly. Then the starboard tiller was shot away, the enemy firing rapidly and with great accuracy. Eight-inch and ten-inch shot went clear through the bulwarks of hay and logs, and plunging shots from the heights went through the deck and did much damage.

The vessel could not return this fire, and, putting on steam, crept along the shore, upriver, making against the current not

Sherman's right flank on the riverfront north of Vicksburg

more than three miles an hour. The *Cincinnati* was soon in a sinking condition, and her gallant commander ran her into the bank. . . . A hawser was taken on shore and made fast to a tree, but, unfortunately, it was not properly secured, and, giving way, allowed the vessel to slide off into deep water.

All this time the enemy continued to pour in a destructive fire. Bache would not haul down his flag, but nailed it to the stump of his flagpole, which had been shot away.

As the vessel was now sinking the order was given for all who could to swim to the shore, which was not far off. The boats had all been shot to pieces and were of no use. There were but three fathoms of water where the *Cincinnati* went down, and her colors and smokepipes remained in sight. Fifteen men were drowned in attempting to reach the bank, and [earlier] twenty[-five] . . . were killed or wounded.

Again in the words of Confederate Sergeant Tunnard:
This combat was witnessed by hundred of ladies who ascended on the summits of the most prominent hills in Vicksburg. There were loud cheers, the waving of handkerchiefs, amid general exultation, as the vessel went down. . . .

The *Black Hawk*

This disastrous termination of the gunboat fight seemed to satisfy the enemy in front, and they were quiet during the remainder of the day.... A large number of articles from the sunken boat were picked up in the river, including hay, clothing, whisky, a medical chest, letters, photographs, etc.

To add to the Confederate elation over the sinking of the Cincinnati, *that night a courier from the outside managed to slip through the Union lines with 18,000 much-needed percussion caps, or musket detonators.*

The man was also a fount of rumorous news. He said that Robert E. Lee had marched to the gates of Washington (when, in actuality, Lee was in Virginia, not yet having launched the invasion of the North that would lead to Gettysburg); that Joe Johnston had raised 40,000 men at Canton and Jackson (when he really had only about half that number); and that General Braxton Bragg's army was on its way from Tennessee (when the general was actually sending only a detachment). But the courier was believed on all counts.

Vicksburg diarist Emma Balfour, the doctor's wife, says that she and the doctor learned the courier's story in the morning:

This, the first piece of news from the outside world we have had in ten days, was glorious.... The doctor invited Colonel [Edward] Higgins and some of the battery officers and General Pemberton and a few others to come up to lunch, and such a thanksgiving for this good news and the sinking of the boat the day before! So we made merry over it. General Pemberton said that the Yankees, if they could look in, would not think that we minded the siege very much.

Most of the city's civilians, as diarist Balfour pointed out in an earlier entry, were staying close to their caves. She herself had the remarkable courage to try to live as normally as possible in her house. In between these extremes were a few people who remained in their houses but often retired to their cellars. One of the last group was Dora Miller, wife of the Unionist lawyer, who wrote in her diary on May 28:

We are utterly cut off from the world, surrounded by a circle of fire. Would it be wise like the scorpion to sting ourselves to death? The fiery shower of shells goes on day and night. H.'s occupation, of course, is gone, his office closed. Every man has to carry a pass in his pocket. People do nothing but eat what they can get, sleep when they can, and dodge the shells.

There are three intervals when the shelling stops, either for the guns to cool or for the gunners' meals, I suppose—about eight in the morning, the same in the evening, and at noon. In that time we have both to prepare and eat ours. Clothing cannot be washed or anything else done. . . .

The cellar is so damp and musty the bedding has to be carried out and laid in the sun every day, with the forecast that it may be demolished at any moment. The confinement is dreadful. To sit and listen as if waiting for death in a horrible manner would drive me insane. I don't know what others do, but we read when I am not scribbling in this. H. borrowed somewhere a lot of Dickens's novels, and we reread them by the dim light in the cellar.

When the shelling abates, H. goes to walk about a little or get the *Daily Citizen,* which is still issuing a tiny sheet at twenty-five and fifty cents a copy. It is, of course, but a rehash of speculations which amuses a half hour.

Today he heard while out that expert swimmers are crossing the Mississippi on logs at night to bring and carry news to Johnston.

I am so tired of corn bread, which I never liked, that I eat it with tears in my eyes. We are lucky to get a quart of milk daily from a family near who have a cow they hourly expect to be killed. I send five dollars to market each morning, and it buys a small piece of mule meat. Rice and milk is my main food; I can't eat the mule meat. We boil the rice and eat it cold with milk for supper. Martha [the couple's black cook] runs the gantlet to buy the meat and milk once a day in perfect terror.

The shells seem to have many different names. I hear the soldiers say, "That's a mortar shell. There goes a Parrott. That's a rifle shell." They are all equally terrible.

A pair of chimney-swallows have built in the parlor chimney. The concussion of the house often sends down parts of their nest, which they patiently pick up and reascend with.

Emma Balfour and her physician husband found the night of Saturday, May 30, to be particularly trying. Their house was threatened first by missiles from the river. Then, as Emma explains, "the guns all along the lines opened, and the Parrott shells flew as thick as hail around us!"

We had gone upstairs determined to rest, lying down but not sleeping, but when these commenced to come it was not safe upstairs. So we came down in the dining room and lay down upon the bed there, but soon found that would not do, as they came from the southeast as well as the east and might strike the house. Still . . . we remained there until a shell struck in the garden against a tree, and at the same time we heard the servants all up and making exclamations. We got up thoroughly worn out and disheartened, and after looking to see the damage went into the parlor and lay on the sofas there until morning, feeling that at any moment a mortar shell might crash through the roof. . . .

The general impression is that they fire at the city . . . thinking that they will wear out the women and children and sick, and General Pemberton will be obliged to surrender the place on that account; but they little know the spirit of the Vicksburg women and children if they expect this. Rather than let them know they are causing us any suffering I would be content to suffer martyrdom!

The morning after her tiring ordeal, the indomitable Emma went to church. Indeed, the service was held largely because she and another courageous woman had petitioned the Reverend Dr. Lord to ring his bell and attempt to draw a crowd. Fortunately, there wasn't much firing that morning, and thirty people turned out. Says Emma:

I walked there and back—but I was glad to do so for the sake of worshipping once more. The church has been considerably injured and was so filled with bricks, mortar and glass that it was difficult to find a place to sit. Next Saturday I intend sending out another petition.

"Last night," wrote Emma on June 2, "was one long to be remembered in the annals of our little city."

In addition to the usual shelling from the bombs and Parrott guns, there was a terrible fire in town. Nearly the whole of the block from Brown and Johnston to Crutcher's Store burned, only two houses left. It is the third fire that has taken place in that neighborhood and it is doubtless the work of an incendiary. . . .

It was an awful and strange sight. As I sat at my window, I saw the mortars from the west passing entirely over the house and the Parrott shells from the east passing by, crossing each other, and this terrible fire raging in the center.

Many people blamed Union agents for this disaster in the city's business district, but it seems to have been the work of a group of citizens outraged by merchants engaged in profiteering.

During the past week, cave-dweller Mary Loughborough had been undergoing repeated shocks and trials:

One morning after breakfast the shells began falling so thickly around us that they seemed aimed at the particular spot on which our cave was located. Two or three fell immediately in the rear of it . . . and the fragments went singing over the top. . . .

I at length became so much alarmed—as the cave trembled excessively—for our safety that I determined, rather than be buried alive, to stand out from under the earth; so, taking my child in my arms and calling the servants, we ran to a refuge near the roots of a large fig tree. . . .

As we stood trembling there—for the shells were falling all around us—some of my gentlemen friends came up to reassure me, telling me that the tree would protect us and that the range would probably be changed in a short time. While they spoke, a shell . . . fell screaming and hissing immediately before the mouth of our cave . . . sending up a huge column of smoke and earth, and jarring the ground most sensibly where we stood. . . .

Long it was before the range was changed and the frightful missiles fell beyond us—long before I could resolve to return to our sadly threatened home. I found on my return that the walls were seamed here and there with cracks, but the earth had remained firm above us. . . .

The [ensuing] night was so warm and the cave so close that I tried to sit out at the entrance, George saying he would keep watch and tell when they were falling toward us. Soon the report of the guns would be heard, and George, standing on the hillock of loose earth near the cave, looked intently upward; while I, with suspended breath, would listen anxiously as he cried, "Here she comes! Going over!" Then again, "Coming—falling—falling right dis way!"

Then I would spring to my feet, and for a moment hesitate about the protection of the cave. Suddenly, as the rushing descent was heard, I would beat a precipitate retreat into it, followed by the servants.

That night I could scarcely sleep, the explosions were so loud and frequent. Before we retired, George had been lying without the door. I had arisen about twelve o'clock and stood looking at the different courses of light marking the passage of the shells, when I noticed that George was not in his usual place at the entrance.

On looking out, I saw that he was sleeping soundly some little distance off, and many fragments of shell falling near him. I aroused him, telling him to come to the entrance for safety. He had scarcely started when a huge piece of shell came whizzing along, which fortunately George dodged in time; and it fell in the very spot where he had so lately slept.

Fearing to retire, I sat in the moonlight at the entrance, the square of light that lay in the doorway causing our little bed, with the sleeping child, to be set out in relief against the dark wall of the cave.

Heretofore the only missiles Mary had to worry about came from the river, but now the Parrott shells from the Union lines in the rear began to seek her out. One afternoon she was sitting in her cave enjoying a period of relative quiet when she heard a telltale sound:

I was reading in safety, I imagined, when the unmistakable whirring of Parrott shells told us that the battery we so much feared had opened from the intrenchments. I ran to the entrance to call the servants in; and immediately after they entered, a shell struck the earth a few feet from the entrance, burying itself without exploding.

I ran to the little dressing room, and could hear them striking around us on all sides. I crouched closely against the wall, for I did not know at what moment one might strike within the cave. A man came in much frightened, and asked to remain until the danger was over. The servants stood in the little niche by the bed, and the man took refuge in the small ell where I was stationed.

He had been there but a short time, standing in front of me, and near the wall, when a Parrott shell came whirling in at the entrance and fell in the center of the cave before us all, lying there smoking. Our eyes were fastened upon it, while we expected every moment the terrific explosion would ensue. I pressed my child closer to my heart and drew nearer the wall. Our fate seemed almost certain.

The poor man who had sought refuge within was most exposed of all. With a sudden impulse, I seized a large double blanket that lay near and gave it to him for the purpose of shielding him from the fragments.

And thus we remained for a moment, with our eyes fixed in terror on the missile of death, when George, the servant boy, rushed forward, seized the shell, and threw it into the street, running swiftly in the opposite direction.

Fortunately the fuse had become nearly extinguished, and the shell fell harmless—remaining near the mouth of the cave as a trophy of the fearlessness of the servant and our remarkable escape.

Very thankful was I for our preservation, which was the theme of conversation for a day among our cave neighbors. The incident of the blanket was also related; and all laughed heartily at my supposition that the blanket could be any protection from the heavy fragments of shells.

Nor was this all. I had occasion to go to the mouth of the cave one evening to speak to George; and there, with an enlightened audience of servants from the surrounding caves collected near him, George was going through a grave pantomime of the whole affair.

George first mimed the white man who had taken refuge in the cave. Pressing himself back against the wheel of a wagon that represented the cave's wall, he showed the man as cringing and shaking, his hands thrown up and his eyes wild—a portrayal that delighted the all-black audience.

Then, Mary goes on to explain, George's whole manner changed:

He put on the bravest port imaginable, pushing his hat, with an independent air, on the side of his head; and, assuming a don't-carish look, he sauntered forward to a large piece of shell that lay conveniently near, caught it with both hands, gave it a careless swing and throw far different from the reality, turned on his heels, walked back to the wagon with the peculiar swinging step of a proud Negro; then, leaning his arm on the wheel, carelessly surveyed his audience with a look that plainly said, "What do you think o' dat, niggers?"

The benefited group immediately began laughing and applauding . . . in which they were soon joined by George himself.

Soon after, I received a note from M. imploring me to be careful and remain within the cave constantly. I could see that he was restless and troubled in regard to the new peril from the battlefield. . . .

Even the very animals seemed to share the general fear of a sudden and frightful death. The dogs would be seen in the midst of the noise to gallop up the street, and then to return, as if fear had maddened them. On hearing the descent of a shell, they would dart aside—then, as it exploded, sit down and howl in the most pitiful manner.

There were many walking the street, apparently without homes. George carried on a continual warfare with them as they came about the fire where our meals were cooking. . . .

The horses . . . fastened to the trees . . . would frequently strain the halter to its full length, rearing high in the air with a loud snort of terror, as a shell would explode near. I could hear them, in the night, cry out in the midst of the uproar, ending in a low, plaintive whinny of fear.

The poor creatures subsisted entirely on cane tops and mulberry leaves. Many of the mules and horses had been driven outside of the lines, by order of General Pemberton, for subsistence. . . .

Sitting in the cave one evening I heard the most heart-rending screams and moans. I was told that a mother had taken a child into a cave about a hundred yards from us; and having laid it on its little bed, as the poor woman believed, in safety, she took her seat near the entrance of the cave. A mortar shell came rushing through the air and fell with much force, entering the earth above the sleeping child—cutting through into the cave—oh! most horrible sight to the mother—crushing in the upper part of the little sleeping head and taking away the young innocent life. . . .

I sat near the square of moonlight, silent and sorrowful, hearing the sobs and cries—hearing the moans of a mother for her dead child—the child that a few moments since lived to caress and love.

How very sad this life in Vicksburg! How little security can we feel. . . . I could not sit quietly within, hearing of so much grief; and, leaving my seat, I paced backward and forward before the low entrance of my house.

The court-house bell tolled twelve; and though the shells fell, slowly, still around the spot where the young life had gone out, yet friends were going to and from the place. . . .

The moans of pain came slowly and more indistinct, until all was silent. . . .

The fresh air told of the coming morning. The guns were still. Peace for a short time reigned in the troubled city. . . . My eyes grew heavy, and I once more sought my bed.

It was about June 1 when Mary received another note sent by "M." from the battlefield.

He was very much troubled in regard to our safety in the city—fearing that sometime a mortar shell might fall on our cave, or that the constant jarring of the earth . . . might cause it to seam and fall upon us. Therefore he had decided to have a home made for me near the battlefield—where he was stationed—one that would be entirely out of reach of the mortar shells [from the river].

I was positively shocked at the idea—going to the battlefield! Where ball and shell fell without intermission. Was M. in earnest? I could scarcely believe it.

A friend came soon after and told me that I would find my home on the battlefield far more pleasant and safe than the one in town . . . that on the battlefield the missiles were of far less weight and . . . far less dangerous. . . .

I was delighted at the prospect of a change in our mouldy lives, and . . . I was sitting near the entrance, about five o'clock, thinking of the pleasant change . . . that tomorrow would bring, when the bombardment commenced more furiously than usual, the shells falling thickly around us, causing vast columns of earth to fly upward, mingled with smoke.

As usual, I was uncertain whether to remain within or run out. . . . In my anxiety I was startled by the shouts of the servants and a most fearful jar and rocking of the earth, followed by a deafening explosion, such as I had never heard before. The cave filled instantly with powder smoke and dust.

I stood with a tingling, prickling sensation in my head, hands and feet, and with a confused brain. Yet alive! . . . Child, servants, all here, and saved!

. . . I stepped out, to find a group of persons before my cave, looking anxiously for me; and lying all around, freshly torn rose bushes, arborvitae trees, large clods of earth, splinters, pieces of plank, wood, etc. A mortar shell had struck the corner of the cave . . . breaking large masses from the side of the hill . . . sweeping all, like an avalanche, down near the entrance of my good refuge. . . .

That evening some friends sat with me. One took up my guitar and played some pretty little airs for us. Yet the noise of the shells threw a discord among the harmonies. . . . How could we sing and laugh amid our suffering fellow beings—amid . . . this sad news of a Vicksburg day:

A little Negro child, playing in the yard, had found a shell; in rolling and turning it, had innocently pounded the fuse. The terrible explosion followed, showing, as the white cloud of smoke floated away, the mangled remains of a life that to the mother's heart had possessed all of beauty and joy.

A young girl, becoming weary in the confinement of the cave, hastily ran to the house in the interval that elapsed between the slowly falling shells. On returning, an explosion sounded near her—one wild scream and she ran into her mother's presence, sinking like a wounded dove, the life blood flowing over the light summer dress in crimson ripples from a death wound in her side. . . .

A fragment had also struck and broken the arm of a little boy playing near the mouth of his mother's cave. This was one day's account. . . .

The next evening, about four o'clock, M.'s dear face appeared. He told us that he had heard of all the danger through which we had passed, and was extremely anxious to have us out of reach of the mortar shells and near him. . . . He urged me to be ready in the shortest time possible; so I hastened our arrangements, and we soon were in the ambulance, driving with great speed toward the rifle pits. . . .

The road we were travelling was graded out through the hills; and on every side we could see, thickly strewn among the earthy cliffs, the never-to-be-lost-sight-of caves—large caves and little caves....

Driving on rapidly, we reached the suburbs of the city, where the road became shady and pleasant—still with caves at every large road excavation....

Suddenly a turn of the drive brought in sight two large forts on the hills above us; and passing down a ravine near one of these, the ambulance stopped. Here we saw two or three of the little shell-and-bomb-proof houses in the earth, covered with logs and turf.

We were hastily taken out and started for our home, when I heard a cutting of the air ... above my head; and the balls dropped thickly around me, bringing leaves and small twigs from the trees with them.

I felt a sudden rush to my heart; but the soldiers were camped near, and many stood curiously watching the effect of the sudden fall of metal around me. I would not for the world have shown fear. So, braced by my pride, I walked with a firm and steady

Mary Loughborough's cave near the front lines

pace, notwithstanding the treacherous suggestions of my heart . . . "Run, run!"

M., fearing every moment that I might fall by his side, hurried me anxiously along. Within a short distance was the adjutant's office, where we took refuge until the firing became less heavy. . . . The "office" was a square excavation made in the side of the hill, covered over with logs and earth. . . .

At sundown there was a cessation in the rapid fall of balls and shells, and we again started for our home. I was taken up a little footpath . . . under a careless, graceful arch of wild grapevines, whose swinging branches were drawn aside; and a low, long room, cut into the hillside and shaded by the growth of forest trees around, was presented to my view as our future home. . . . I took possession delightedly. . . .

The next morning at four o'clock I was awakened by a perfect tumult in the air. The explosion of shrapnel and the rattling of shrapnel-balls around us reminded me that my dangers and cares were not yet over. . . . I was almost deafened by the noise and explosions. I lay and thought of the poor soldiers down below in the ravine, with only their tents over their heads. . . .

In even greater danger than these behind-the-lines troops were those at the front. As explained by Confederate Corporal Ephraim Anderson:

The enemy continued to prosecute the siege vigorously. From night to night and from day to day a series of works was presented. Secure and strong lines of fortifications appeared. Redoubts, manned by well-practiced sharpshooters, were thrown out to the front. Parapets blazing with artillery crowned every knoll and practicable elevation around, and oblique lines of intrenchments, finally running into parallels, enabled the untiring foe to work his way slowly but steadily forward.

The work of strengthening the fortifications, on both sides, was hourly going on. . . . Vague and false rumors daily circulated within our lines . . . generally about Johnston, who was reported to have concentrated quite a large force in Grant's rear, and to be moving to our relief. . . . Some of the troops were already becoming dissatisfied and demoralized. In many of the commands this feeling did not exist to any extent, and no adverse fortune could have induced in them an anxiety to surrender . . . except in the very last extremity. . . .

It soon became evident that there was not an abundant supply of rations.... We were somewhat surprised, one day, to see among the provisions sent up that the only supply in the way of bread was made of peas.... This "pea bread" ... was made of ... "cow peas," which is, rather, a small bean, cultivated quite extensively as provender for animals....

There was a good supply of this pea in the commissariat at Vicksburg, and the idea grew out of the fertile brain of some official that, if reduced to the form of meal, it would make an admirable substitute for bread.... But the nature of it was such that it never got done, and the longer it was cooked the harder it became on the outside, which was natural, but, at the same time, it grew relatively softer on the inside, and, upon breaking it, you were sure to find raw pea meal in the center....

The Federals found out by some means, through deserters I suppose, that we were eating pea bread, and hallooed over for several nights afterwards, enquiring how long the pea bread would hold out; if it was not about time to lower our colors; and asking us to come over and take a good cup of coffee and eat a biscuit with them. Some of the boys replied that they need not be uneasy about [our] rations, as we had plenty of mules to fall back upon.

Life in the front lines was a curious mixture of friendly banter and deadly dueling. An example of the serious work is provided by an entry Union Major Joseph Stockton made in his diary on June 3:
I was much interested today in watching a number of Indians that belong to the 14th Wisconsin acting as sharpshooters.... These Indians had fixed their heads with leaves in such a way that you could not tell them. They would creep on their bellies a little distance, then keep quiet, then move ahead until they could get the position they were after, which was generally a log, behind which they could lie without very much exposure. They silenced the rebel cannon in front [of our position] almost entirely.

Two days later, Stockton wrote:
Siege life can be made monotonous or otherwise, as you wish. A visit to the outworks is always interesting, and to see the devices the men use in trying to get a Reb to put his head above their works is very amusing. Holding their caps on the end of their guns or fixing a coat so that the arm can be seen, and the Reb, thinking it is a Yank, blazes away ... while our boys go for him [with shooting of their own].

The Confederates, of course, employed similar tricks. Says Union Corporal Samuel Byers:

One day I and two of my companions fired for an hour at a rebel who kept forever hopping up and down behind the sand bags and calling constantly, "Try again, will you, Mr. Yankee?"

Finally the figure mounted up in full view, when we discovered we were cheaply sold, as the daring rebel was a stuffed suit of old clothes on a pole, while the mockery came from the real rebel, safe behind the sand bags.

Another one, more reckless however, placed himself in the open embrasure of a low earthwork for a moment and shouted "Fire!" In an instant he lay stretched dead in the embrasure. An effort was made by his comrades to pull away his body, but shots were constantly fired into the opening at everyone daring to show himself for an instant.

They tried to pull the body away with poles, but in vain. The firing increased almost to the dignity of an action, and finally a battery joined in the conflict over the poor corpse which, darkness hiding the combatants, they were at last able to secure.

. . . Owing to the risks run on his behalf . . . the poor man was possibly not dead after all, but sadly wounded and lying there under the hot sun dying—with help so near and yet so powerless to save.

But incidents, though as dangerous, touching the ludicrous also occurred. . . . A young Federal sergeant foolishly insisted on exposing himself to the fire of the enemy by creeping over the earthwork and surveying the lines with an opera glass borrowed, during his raids, from some planter's house. The captain had repeatedly and vainly warned him against his recklessness, till one sunny morning, while engaged in his usual observations with glass to eye, a bullet fired from an unlooked-for quarter smashed the glass in his hand. Our boys, seeing he was not killed . . . gave three cheers for the rebel who fired the shot. It was a close shave, but our sergeant was cured of reckless curiosity.

The siege had now settled into a more or less routine operation, and General Grant, undergoing a kind of letdown after the sharp challenges of the past seven or eight weeks, seems to have succumbed to one of his more serious sessions with the bottle. It began during the afternoon of June 5, though under just what circumstances is not known.

About 1 A.M. in the morning on June 6, Grant's assistant adjutant general and good friend, John Rawlins, sat by a candle in his tent and wrote the general a letter that began: "The great solicitude I feel for the safety of this army leads me to mention, what I had hoped never again to do, the subject of your drinking." Rawlins went on to say that he had found Grant, that very evening, "where the wine bottle has just been emptied, in company with those who drink and urge you to do likewise."

Rawlins hadn't actually seen Grant drinking, but the general had apparently conducted some military business before retiring, for Rawlins added that "the lack of your usual promptness and decision, and clearness in expressing yourself in writing, conduces to confirm my suspicion."

Years later Rawlins was to say of the letter: "Its admonitions were heeded and all went well." But the admonitions, it appears, were not heeded at once. That morning after breakfast, Grant and Charles Dana rode to Haynes' Bluff and boarded a small army steamer for a twenty-five-mile trip up the Yazoo River to Satartia, site of a Federal outpost commanded by Brigadier General Nathan Kimball. Grant had heard that some of Joe Johnston's Confederates were threatening the station, and he told Dana he wanted to meet with Kimball and discuss the situation.

Dana relates:

Grant was ill and went to bed soon after he started. We had gone up the river to within two miles of Satartia when we met two gunboats coming down. Seeing the general's flag, the officers in charge of the gunboats came aboard our steamer and asked where the general was going. I told them to Satartia.

"Why," said they, "it will not be safe. Kimball . . . has retreated from there, and is sending all his supplies to Haynes' Bluff. The enemy is probably in the town now."

I told them Grant was sick and asleep, and that I did not want to waken him. They insisted that it was unsafe to go on, and that I would better call the general. Finally I did so, but he was too sick to decide.

"I will leave it with you," he said.

I immediately said we would go back to Haynes' Bluff, which we did.

The next morning [still on the steamer] Grant came out to breakfast fresh as a rose, clean shirt and all, quite himself.

"Well, Mr. Dana," he said, "I suppose we are at Satartia now."

"No, general," I said, "we are at Haynes' Bluff." And I told him what had happened.

Another version of this trip is given by a newspaper correspondent, Sylvanus Cadwallader of the Chicago Times, who claims to have been pres-

ent and who says flatly that Grant was drunk. Furthermore, asserts the newsman, Grant got hold of another bottle that morning and started all over again, acting so irresponsibly both on the steamer and when he went ashore that he had to be followed, cajoled, threatened, and even taken firmly in hand (by Cadwallader) in order to be kept from disgracing himself beyond salvation. At last, says the newsman, the general was talked into entering an army ambulance for a quiet return to his Vicksburg headquarters.

Cadwallader's story was to raise a controversy among historians, some accepting it and others calling it a fabrication. It gets some strong support from Dana's account of Grant's "sickness," which is mysterious to say the least. The general seems to have been more stupefied than sick. If he really was so seriously sick that he couldn't even make a simple decision regarding his safety, his complete recovery by the next morning was nothing less than miraculous.

As it turned out, Joe Johnston did not move upon Satartia. The alarm was a false one. However, explains Grant,

On the 7th of June our little force of colored and white troops across the Mississippi, at Milliken's Bend, were attacked by about 3,000 men from Richard Taylor's trans-Mississippi command. With the aid of the gunboats they were speedily repelled. . . . This was the first important engagement of the war in which colored troops were under fire.

Charles Dana elaborates:

General E. S. Dennis, who saw the battle, told me that it was the hardest fought engagement he had ever seen. It was fought mainly hand to hand. After it was over, many men were found dead with bayonet stabs, and others with their skulls broken open by butts of muskets.

"It is impossible," said General Dennis, "for men to show greater gallantry than the Negro troops in that fight."

The bravery of the blacks at Milliken's Bend completely revolutionized the sentiment of the army with regard to the employment of Negro troops. I heard prominent officers, who formerly in private had sneered at the idea of the Negroes fighting, express themselves, after that, as heartily in favor of it.

Among the Confederates, however, the feeling was very different. All the reports that came to us showed that both citizens and soldiers on the Confederate side manifested great dismay at the idea of our arming Negroes. They said that such a policy was certain to be followed by insurrection with all its horrors.

Although the presence of Joe Johnston on the east and the rumors of invasion ... from the west compelled constant attention, the real work behind Vicksburg was always that of the siege. No amount of outside alarm loosened Grant's hold on the rebel stronghold. The siege went on steadily and effectively.

By this time Grant had about 75,000 troops, nearly 30,000 reinforcements having come down the Mississippi. Dana says that a special show was made of 5,000 men under Major General Francis J. Herron who arrived at Young's Point on June 11:

They were debarked and marched across the peninsula [opposite Vicksburg], care being taken ... that the Confederate garrison ... should see the whole march. The troops were then ferried across the Mississippi, and took a position south of Vicksburg....

Just as our reinforcements arrived we began to receive encouraging reports from within Vicksburg. Deserters said that the garrison was worn out and hungry. Besides, the defense had for several days been conducted with extraordinary feebleness, which Grant thought was due to the deficiency of ammunition or to exhaustion and depression in the garrison, or to their retirement to an inner line of defense.... The deserters also said that fully one third of the garrison were in the hospital, and that officers, as well as men, had begun to despair of relief from Johnston.

These reports from within the town, as well as the progress of the siege and the arrival of reinforcements, pointed so strongly to a speedy surrender of the place that I asked Mr. Stanton in my dispatch of June 14th [to Washington] to please inform me by telegram ... [where] he wished me to go ... after the fall of Vicksburg....

The next day after this letter, however, the enemy laid aside its long-standing inactivity and opened violently with both artillery and musketry. Two mortars which the Confederates got into operation that day ... particularly interested our generals.

I ... [went] with a party of some twenty officers ... to the brow of a hill on McPherson's front to watch this battery with our field glasses. From where we were we could study the whole operation. We saw the shell start from the mortar, sail slowly through the air toward us, fall to the ground and explode, digging out a hole which looked like a crater.... One of these craters ... must have been nine feet in diameter.

Confederate shell exploding in Union lines

As you watched a shell coming you could not tell whether it would fall a thousand feet away or by your side. Yet nobody budged. The men sat there on their horses, their reins loose, studying and discussing the work of the batteries, apparently indifferent to the danger. It was very interesting as a study of human steadiness.

By the middle of June our lines were so near the enemy's on Sherman's and McPherson's front that General Grant began to consider the project of another general assault.... But the chief difficulty in the way was the backwardness of McClernand. His trenches were mere rifle pits, three or four feet wide, and would allow neither the passage of artillery nor the assemblage of any considerable number of troops. His batteries were, with scarcely an exception, in a position they apparently had held when the siege was opened.

This obstacle to success was soon removed. On the 18th of June, McClernand was relieved and General [Edward O. C.] Ord was put into his place.

The immediate occasion of McClernand's removal was a congratulatory address to the Thirteenth Corps which he had fulminated in May, and which first reached the besieging army in a copy of the Missouri *Democrat*. In this extraordinary address McClernand claimed for himself most of the glory of the campaign, reaffirmed that on May 22d he had held two rebel forts for several hours, and imputed to other officers and troops failure to support him in their possession, which must have resulted in the capture of the town, etc.

Though this congratulatory address [which violated procedures established by the War Department] was the occasion of McClernand's removal, the real causes of it dated farther back. These causes . . . were his repeated disobedience of important orders, his general unfortunate mental disposition, and his palpable incompetence for the duties of his position.

I learned in private conversation that in General Grant's judgment it was necessary that McClernand should be removed for the reason, above all, that his bad relations with [the] other corps commanders . . . rendered it impossible that the chief command of the army should devolve upon him, as it would have done were General Grant disabled, without some pernicious consequence to the Union cause.

The aide from headquarters who delivered the bad news, in the form of a dispatch, to McClernand's tent was Colonel James Wilson, the same aide who had come close to striking the general on the occasion of his profane disrespect for Grant.

McClernand read the order, then said, "I see I am relieved."

Wilson responded, "By God, sir, we are both relieved!" And he spun on his heel and strode from the tent.

10

GRANT CATCHES HIS RABBIT

*V*ICKSBURG'S DORA MILLER, *still dividing her time between her cellar and her upstairs rooms (the hours being dictated by the Union shellfire), informed her diary on June 18:*

Today the *Citizen* is printed on wallpaper, therefore has grown a little in size. It says, "But a few days more and Johnston will be here...."

On June 21, Dora wrote:

I had gone upstairs today, during the interregnum, to enjoy a rest on my bed and read the reliable items in the *Citizen* when a shell burst right outside the window in front of me. Pieces flew in, striking all around me, tearing down masses of plaster that came tumbling over me.

When H. rushed in I was crawling out of the plaster, digging it out of my eyes and hair. When he picked up a piece as large as a saucer beside my pillow, I realized my narrow escape.

The window frame began to smoke, and we saw the house was on fire. H. ran for a hatchet and I for water, and we put it out.

Another [shell] came crashing near, and I snatched up my comb and brush and ran down here. It has taken all the afternoon to get the plaster out of my hair, for my hands were rather shaky.

Living in a house, Dora was spared one worry that came to many of the cave-dwellers. Lida Lord, one of the four children of the Reverend Dr. and Margaret Lord, was to say later:

We were ... in hourly dread of snakes. The vines and thickets were full of them, and a large rattlesnake was found one morning under a mattress on which some of us had slept all night.

Lida adds that the family's ears "were always strained to catch the first sound of Johnston's guns. Every extra-heavy cannonading [heard from the direction of the battlefield] was a message of hope. . . ."

To Mary Loughborough, in her new shelter just behind her husband's zone of duty, none of the cannonadings were ever anything more than nerve-racking:

We were in the first line of hills back of the heights that were fortified; and, of course, we felt the full force of the very energetic firing that was constantly kept up; and, being so near, many [shells] that passed over the first line of hills would fall directly around us.

Mary noted that amid all the noise and human suffering, "the birds sang as sweetly, and flew as gayly from tree to tree, as if there were peace and plenty in the land."

One morning George made an important discovery—a . . . stump of sassafras, very near the cave, with large roots extending in every direction, affording us an inexhaustible vein of tea. . . . We had been drinking water with our meals. . . . Coffee and tea had long since been among the things that *were*. . . . We, however, were more fortunate than many of the officers, having access to an excellent cistern near us; while many of our friends used muddy water, or river water, which, being conveyed so great a distance, became extremely warm and disagreeable. . . .

The men in the rifle pits were on half rations. . . . They sat cramped up all day in the pits—their rations cooked in the valley and brought to them—scarcely daring to change their positions and stand erect, for the Federal sharpshooters were watching for the heads. . . . Frequently a Parrott shell would penetrate the intrenchments, and, exploding, cause frightful wounds, and death most frequently.

"Ah!" said M. one day, "it is to the noble men in the rifle pits that Vicksburg will owe aught of honor she may gain in this siege. I revere them as I see them undergoing every privation with courage and patience. . . ."

They amused themselves, while lying in the pits, by cutting out little trinkets from the wood of the parapet and the Minié balls that fell around them. Major Fry, from Texas, excelled in skill and ready invention. . . . He sent me one day an armchair that he had cut from a Minié ball—the most minute affair of the kind I ever saw, yet perfectly symmetrical. . . .

It was astonishing how the young officers kept up their spirits, frequently singing quartets and glees amid the pattering of Minié balls; and I often heard gay peals of laughter from headquarters, as the officers that had spent the day, and perhaps the night previous, in the rifle pits would collect to make out reports.

[One] evening a gentleman visited us and, among other songs, sang words to the air of the "Mocking Bird" which [went as follows]:

> "... Listen to the Parrott shells—
> Listen to the Parrott shells;
> The Parrott shells are whistling through the air....
> Listen to the Minié balls—
> Listen to the Minié balls;
> The Minié balls are singing in the air."

Songs of every description [were] composed in honor of narrow escapes, unlucky incidents, brave deeds, etc. Songs humorous, pathetic, and tragic....

I heard, one night, a soldier down the ravine singing one of the weird, melodious hymns that Negroes often sing; and, amid the firing and crashing of projectiles, it floated up to me in soft, musical undertones that were fascinating in the extreme: the wailing of the earthly unrest—the longing for the glorious home... of ... brilliant happiness!

... I was sewing one day, near one side of the cave ... when I suddenly remembered some little article I wished in another part of the room. Crossing to procure it, I was returning when a Minié ball came whizzing through the opening, passed my chair, and fell beyond it. Had I been still sitting, I should have stopped it....

One old, gray-headed, cheerful-hearted soldier, whom I had talked with often, was passing through the ravine for water, immediately opposite our cave. A Minié ball struck him in the lower part of the leg. He coolly stooped down, tied his handkerchief around it, and passed on....

A soldier named Henry had noticed my little girl often, bringing her flowers at one time, an apple at another, and again a young mocking bird, and had attached her to him by these little kindnesses. Frequently, on seeing him pass, she would call his name and clap her hands gleefully, as he rode the general's handsome horse for water, causing him to prance past the cave for her amusement.

She called my attention to him one morning, saying, "O mamma, look at Henny's horse how he plays!"

... Soon after, he rode the horse for water; and I saw him return and fasten it to a tree. Afterward I saw him come down the hill opposite, with an unexploded shrapnel shell in his hand. In a few moments I heard a quick explosion in the ravine, followed by a cry—a sudden, agonized cry.

I ran to the entrance, and saw a courier, whom I had noticed frequently passing by, roll slowly over into the rivulet of the ravine and lie motionless. . . .

Henry—oh, poor Henry!—holding out his mangled arms— the hands torn and hanging from the bleeding, ghastly wrists—a fearful wound in his head—the blood pouring from his wounds.

... Gasping, wild, he staggered around, crying piteously, "Where are you, boys? O boys, where are you? Oh, I am hurt! I am hurt! Boys, come to me! Come to me! God have mercy! Almighty God, have mercy!"

My little girl clung to my dress, saying, "O mamma, poor Henny's killed! Now he'll die, mamma. Oh, poor Henny!"

I carried her away from the painful sight.

A crowd of soldiers had gathered at once; and, as Mary goes on to say:

In a few moments the litters pass by, going toward the hospital, the blood streaming from that of Henry, who still moaned and cried "for the boys to come to him" and "for God to pity him."

... The other [litter] bore the still, motionless body of the young courier. . . .

It seems that the two men had been trying to take out the screw from the unexploded shell for the purpose of securing the powder. In turning it, the fuse had become ignited, communicating the fire to the powder, and the fatal explosion ensued.

Henry had been struck in the head by a fragment—his hands torn from his arms. One or two fragments had also lodged in his body. The courier had been struck in two places in his head, and a number of balls had entered his body. Poor soldier! His mother lived in Yazoo City, and he was her only son. . . . He lived until the sun went down, speaking no word, making no moan. . . . Henry died also that night, still unconscious of the sorrowful comrades around his bed—still calling on God to pity him.

These men died in one of the hospitals the necessities of the siege had brought into existence. "There were two classes of hospitals in Vicksburg," explains a Confederate officer, "those for the sick, and those for the wounded." In the former, the officer goes on to say,

very few wounded were admitted, so that, although much suffering was depicted upon the countenances of the poor inmates, yet were the scenes not so heartrending as those exhibited by a visit to the hospitals containing the wounded.

In the latter could be seen men with both legs off; some with an eye out; others without arms; and again some who could once boast of manly beauty and personal attractions rendered hideous by the loss of the nose or a portion of the face, so as to be unrecognizable by their nearest and dearest kindred....

One more picture and the tableau is complete—the burial of the dead.... Trenches fifty feet long and three feet wide were dug to receive the bodies of the brave men and officers. They usually contained about eight bodies. It was seldom a coffin could be procured, and the brave defender of his country had to be wrapped in his blanket, and... the... earth... hastily heaped above his mortal remains.

The field hospitals on the Union side were by this time well organized, having received much attention from the civilians of the Sanitary and Christian commissions. One of these volunteers, Mrs. Jane Hoge, an associate manager of the Northwestern Branch of the Sanitary Commission, with headquarters in Chicago, had just come down the Mississippi, and on her first visit to the hospitals she rejoiced to find them "so clean, comfortable and well supplied." She describes one as being situated

Jane Hoge

on a clearing on a pleasant green bluff, with sufficient trees for shade. There were three long rows of new hospital tents abreast, with accommodations for several hundred men, provided with comfortable cots, mattresses, soft pillows, clean sheets and pillow-slips—even mosquito bars admirably arranged on uprights. The refreshing air that rustled through the tents kept the atmosphere pure, and fanned the patients with their welcome breezes. . . .

From these tents I passed to a hospital in an adjoining house, filled with badly wounded men from the assaults of the 19th and 22d of May. As I entered, a group of soldiers was gathered around a cot near the door. All fell back to give place to me.

There lay a young man, apparently twenty-five years of age, with a fine Saxon face. . . . He was white and silent, seemingly insensible. Beads of water stood on his face, and his breathing was not perceptible. . . . He had been fearfully mangled, had just had a severe convulsion, subdued by chloroform, and the surgeon had decided he could live but a few hours.

Involuntarily I passed my hand across his clammy brow and exclaimed, "Poor fellow!"

With a suddenness that startled the group, the great blue eyes, as if touched by a spring, opened widely; and with a clear, low voice, he said, "Madam, there are no poor fellows here. We are all soldiers."

"Excuse me, I should have said brave fellow!"

"Not that, either. I only did my duty."

Despite the surgeon's prediction, this soldier was to survive, though in a badly crippled condition.

Mrs. Hoge continues:

In the hospital in which I found this noble fellow, I met a nine-year-old hero, minus two fingers. His hand was covered with bloody bandages. . . . I stroked his almost infantile head and asked what was the matter.

Straightening himself with an important air, he replied, "I'm a drummer boy, and had my fingers shot off yesterday."

"What will you do now?"

Looking up . . . he answered, "Drum on, I s'pose. I've been tryin' it, and can drum as well without 'em as with 'em."

Mrs. Hoge goes on to reveal that she herself was a person of courage:

The crowning interest of my Vicksburg trip was my visit to the rifle pits, where I stood beside the brave men holding them, looked through the loopholes of the earthworks, and, like every other civilian, imagined I barely escaped with my life as I heard the whizzing Miniés speeding a few inches above my head....

The intense excitement of the position, the manly, cheerful bearing of the men amid their hardships, the screaming of shells through the trees, the booming of the heavy mortars, ever and anon throwing their huge balls into the city, and the picturesque panorama of the army, with its white tents nestling in the ravines, obliterated all sense of personal danger ... and made even the stifling heat of the rifle pits endurable.

The soldiers talked of the rebels as prisoners they were guarding, and treated suggestions as to Johnston's junction with Pemberton with scornful derision, saying, "the boys in the rear could whip Johnston without those in the front knowing it, and the boys in the front could take Vicksburg without disturbing those in the rear."

After leaving the topmost ledge of rifle pits, I descended to the second line [a short way behind], where the sound of singing reached me. I turned in the direction from whence it came, and a few steps brought me to a litter of boughs, on which lay a [wounded] gray-haired veteran ... with a comrade on either side. They did not perceive me, but sang on to the closing line of the [first] verse:

"Come, humble sinner, in whose breast
    A thousand thoughts revolve;
Come with thy sins and fears oppressed
    And make this last resolve."

I joined in the second verse:

"I'll go to Jesus, though my sins
    Have like a mountain rose;
I know His courts I'll enter in,
    Whatever may oppose."

In an instant each man turned, and would have stopped, but I sang on ... and they continued.

At the close of the hymn, one exclaimed, "Why, ma'am, where did you come from? Did you drop from heaven into these rifle pits? You are the first lady we have seen here."

... I answered, "I have come from your friends at home to see and comfort you and bring words of love and gratitude..., I dare not go home without seeing and hearing you, else would I be scorned by all the loyal women."

"Do they think so much of us as that?" he asked. "Why, boys, we can fight another year on that, can't we?"

"Yes! Yes!" they cried. . . .

A crowd of eager listeners had gathered from their hiding places. . . . The gray-haired soldier drew from his breast pocket a daguerreotype and said, "Here are my wife and daughters. . . ." Then each man drew forth the inevitable daguerreotype and held it up for me to look at. . . . There were aged mothers and sober matrons, bright-eyed maidens and laughing cherubs. . . mute memorials of home. . . .

I had much work for the day, and prepared to leave. I said, "Brave men, farewell. When I go home . . . I'll tell them that eyes that never weep for their own suffering overflow at the name of wife and mother and at the pictures of wife and children. They will feel more than ever that such men must conquer and that enough cannot be done for them."

"God bless you! God bless you!" burst from the assembled crowd.

"Three cheers for the women at home!" cried one.

They were given with a will, and echoed through the rifle pits. Hard, honest hands were grasped, and I turned away to visit other regiments.

In a valley not far behind the rifle pits, the overly dramatic Mrs. Hoge entered the encampment of an infantry regiment from Illinois:

Its ranks had been fearfully thinned by the terrible assaults of the 19th and 22d of May. . . . I knew many of the men personally, and as they gathered round me and inquired after home and friends, I could but look in sadness for familiar faces to be seen no more on earth.

I said, "Boys, I was present when your colors were presented to you by the Board of Trade. I heard your colonel pledge himself that you would bring them home or cover them with blood and glory. Where are they, after your many battles?"

With great alacrity, the man in charge of them ran into an adjoining tent and brought them forth, carefully wrapped in an oil-silk covering. He drew it off and flung the folds to the breeze. . . .

"What does this mean? So soiled and faded and rent and tattered I should not know them."

The man that held them said, "Why, ma'am, 'twas the smoke and balls that did that."

"Ah, so it must have been! You have covered them with glory! How about the blood?"

A painful silence followed, and then a low voice said, "Four men were shot down holding them—two are dead and two in the hospital."

"Verily, you have redeemed your pledge. . . ."

After a tearful farewell to this noble regiment, I stepped into the ambulance that was waiting to convey me to the hospital. The brave fellows crowded around me with last messages for their friends up North. As we parted, three cheers arose for the Sanitary Commission and the women at home.

In spite of Mrs. Hoge's depictions, the Federal soldiers were not developing into a race of unblemished heroes, as was well understood by the Confederate civilians who had chosen to remain in their homes behind Grant's lines. Though foraging was now strictly forbidden, under threat of the sternest punishment, some of the Federals had begun to hunger again for fresh fowl. One day, says Union Sergeant Osborn Oldroyd,

two soldiers of the 13th corps were arrested and brought before General A. J. Smith at his headquarters in a fine grove of stately poplars, where the general was informed by the guard that the men had been caught in the act of stealing chickens.

The gallant general appeared to be revolving the heinousness of the charge as he looked aloft among the poplars, and presently the guard inquired what should be done with the men, when the general, after another glance upward, turning to the guard, replied:

"O, damn 'em, let 'em go. There ain't any tree here high enough to hang 'em on."

The steady forward progress of the Federal digging in the front lines continued to be accompanied by sniping and skirmishing. On the night of June 22, according to Confederate Corporal Ephraim Anderson, two Southern regiments

charged a Federal breastwork about fifty yards in their front, which had been thrown up the night before and contained a regiment of the enemy. They succeeded in dislodging this force at the point of the bayonet, and captured a number of prisoners with very slight loss. The work was filled up, and the spades and shovels of the enemy were taken.

As the work of filling the excavation began, Anderson adds, the Confederates had a good laugh at the expense of the Federal officer in charge of the regiment they had bested:

Seeing that he was either to be captured or run the gantlet in getting away, he laid down among the dead in the ditch, expecting to remain "perdue" until our force retired, and then his escape would be secured. In this conclusion, however, he had not taken into account that the ditch might be filled. A few spadesful of earth had the salutary effect of bringing him to, and the dead ... rose up and walked, declaring he was not ready to be buried ... and, notwithstanding his ingenious conceit, became a prisoner.

Digging with particular industry during this period of the siege were the Federals assigned to the zigzag saps, or trenches, ending in mines, or tunnels, directly beneath points in the enemy's defensive system chosen to be blown up. It was hoped that at least one of the breaches thus made could be exploited by the infantry, charging immediately after the blast.

Foremost among these breaching operations was that aimed at the Third Louisiana redan, a strong fortification covering the main Jackson road and lying in Union General McPherson's sector. The chief engineer in charge of the operation was Brevet Brigadier Andrew Hickenlooper, who relates:

The general plan of conducting the work with flying sap by night and deepening and widening by day was pushed forward with the utmost energy until June 22, when the head of the sap reached the outer ditch surrounding the fort. A few days previous an order had been issued for all men in the corps having a practical knowledge of coal mining to report to [my headquarters]. Out of those reporting, thirty-six of the strongest and most experienced were selected and divided into two shifts for day and night duty, and each shift was divided into three reliefs.

On the night of the 22d, these men, properly equipped with drills, short-handled picks, shovels, etc. . . . commenced the mining operations by driving a gallery, four feet in width by five feet in height, in at right angles to the face of the parapet of the fort. Each relief worked an hour at a time, two picking, two shoveling, and two handing back the grain-sacks filled with earth, which were deposited in the ditch until they could be carried back.

The main gallery was carried in 45 feet, and then a smaller gallery extended in on the same line 15 feet, while from the end of the main gallery two others were run out on either side at angles of 45 degrees for a distance of 15 feet. The soil through which this gallery was driven was a reddish clay of remarkable tenacity, easily cut and requiring but little bracing.

So rapidly was this work executed that on the morning of the 25th the miners commenced depositing the powder, 800 pounds at the extreme end of the main gallery and 700 pounds at the end of each of the lateral galleries, making a total of 2200 pounds. From each of these deposits there were laid two strands of safety fuse ... this duplication being made to cover the possible contingency of one failing to burn with the desired regularity and speed. These six strands were cut to exactly the same length. ...

The Confederate garrison, surmising the object in view, were active in their efforts to thwart the purpose of the Union forces by throwing hand grenades and rolling shells with lighted fuses over their parapet down into the trench in front of the fort. They also countermined in hopes of tapping the gallery. So near were they to the attainment of this object that during the last day the miners could distinctly hear the conversation and orders given in the countermine.

The powder [had been] brought up in barrels and kept in the main sap at a safe distance from the enemy's hand grenades and shells, and there opened and placed in grain-sacks, each one of which contained about 25 pounds. These were taken upon the backs of the miners, who made the run over the exposed ground during the intervals between the explosions of the enemy's shells; and so well timed were these movements that, although it required nearly one hundred trips with the dangerous loads, all were landed in the mine without a single accident.

The commanding general [Grant] having been advised on the day previous that the work would be completed before 3 P.M. of the 25th, general orders were issued directing each corps commander to order up the reserves and fully man the trenches, and immediately following the explosion to open with both artillery and musketry along the entire ... investing line; under cover of which the assaulting columns ... preceded by ten picked men from the pioneer corps under charge of [myself], were to move forward and take possession of the fort.

For an hour or two previous to the time of the explosion the scene from "Battery Hickenlooper," where General Grant and his subordinate commanders had taken their positions, was one of the most remarkable ever witnessed. As far as the eye could reach

The fort is blown up

to the right and left could be seen the long winding columns of blue moving to their assigned positions. . . .

Gradually as the hour of 3 approached, the booming of artillery and incessant rattle of musketry, which had been going on day and night for thirty days . . . subsided, and a deathlike and oppressive stillness pervaded the whole command. Every eye was riveted upon that huge redoubt standing high above the adjoining works.

"At length all was in readiness," says Union newspaper correspondent James C. Fitzpatrick:

The fuse train was fired, and it went fizzing and popping through the zigzag line of trenches, until for a moment it vanished. Its disappearance was quickly succeeded by the explosion. . . . So terrible a spectacle is seldom witnessed. Dust, dirt, smoke, gabions, stockades, timber, gun-carriages, logs—in fact, everything connected with the fort—rose hundreds of feet into the air, as if vomited forth from a volcano. Some who were close spectators even say that they saw the bodies of the poor wretches who a moment before had lined the ramparts of the work.

"Six of our counterminers," laments Vicksburg engineer Samuel Lockett, "were buried by this explosion."

Again in the words of Union engineer Hickenlooper:

Fire along the entire [Union] line instantly opened with great fury, and amidst the din and roar of 150 cannon and the rattle of 50,000 muskets the charging column moved forward to the assault. But little difficulty was experienced in entering the crater, but the moment the assaulting forces attempted to mount the artificial parapet which had been formed by the falling debris about midway across the fort, completely commanded by the Confederate artillery and infantry in the rear, they were met by a withering fire so severe that to show a head above the crest was certain death.

Two lines [of Federals] were formed on the slope of this parapet, the front line raising their muskets over their heads and firing at random over the crest while the rear rank were engaged in reloading. But soon the Confederates began throwing shortfused shells over the parapet, which, rolling down into the crater crowded with the soldiers of the assaulting column, caused the most fearful destruction of life ever witnessed under like circum-

The battle at the crater

stances. The groans of the dying and shrieks of the wounded became fearful.

The Federals reeled backward, but only until they were outside the range of the deadly missiles. From this new line they continued the fight on into the night. The troops farther back could see their flags by the light of the bursting shells. Their courage, however, was unavailing. The attempt to breach the Confederate line had failed.

Though the main Federal effort of this day had centered upon the mine, Vicksburg had not escaped its usual bombardment. Dora Miller reported in her diary:

A horrible day. The most horrible yet to me, because I've lost my nerve. We were all in the cellar when a shell came tearing through the roof, burst upstairs, tore up that room; and the pieces coming through both floors down into the cellar, one of them tore open the leg of H.'s pantaloons. This was tangible proof the cellar was no place of protection from them.

On the heels of this came Mr. J. to tell us that young Mrs. P. had had her thighbone crushed. When Martha went for the milk, she came back horror-stricken to tell us the black girl there had her arm taken off by a shell.

For the first time I quailed.... Every night I had lain down expecting death, and every morning rose to the same prospect, without being unnerved. It was for H. I trembled. But now I first seemed to realize that something worse than death might come: I might be crippled, and not killed. Life without all one's powers and limbs was a thought that broke down my courage.

I said to H., "You must get me out of this horrible place. I cannot stay. I know I shall be crippled."

Now the regret comes that I lost control, because H. is worried and has lost his composure because my coolness has broken down.

The once proud and prosperous city of Vicksburg was by this time in a pathetic condition. Confederate Sergeant Willie Tunnard says it had the appearance "of being visited with a terrible scourge."

Signs wrenched from their fastenings; houses dilapidated and in ruins, rent and torn by shot and shell; the streets barricaded with earthworks and defended by artillery over which lonely sentinels kept guard. The avenues were almost deserted, save by hunger-pinched, starving and wounded soldiers, or guards lying on the banquettes, indifferent to the screaming and exploding shells. The stores, the few that were open, looked like the ghost of more prosperous times, with their empty shelves and scant stock of goods, held at ruinous prices. . . .

Palatial residences were crumbling into ruins, the walks torn up by mortar shells, the flower beds . . . trodden down, the shrubbery neglected. No fair hands were there to trim their wanton growth. . . . Fences were torn down and houses pulled to pieces for firewood. Even the enclosures around the remains of the revered dead were destroyed, while wagons were parked around the graveyard, horses tramping down the graves, and men using the tombstones as convenient tables for their scanty meals. . . .

Dogs howled through the streets at night; cats screamed forth their hideous cries; an army of rats, seeking food, would scamper around your very feet and across the streets and over the pavements. Lice and filth covered the bodies of the soldiers. Delicate women and little children, with pale, careworn and hunger-pinched features, peered at the passer-by with wistful eyes from the caves in the hillsides.

Add to all these horrors . . . the deep-toned thunder of mortars and heavy guns . . . the fearful detonation of the explosions shaking heaven and earth . . . and you may form some conception of the condition of the city. . . .

At the breastworks were the tried heroes. . . . The brave men, growing daily weaker under their increasing labors and starvation, began to complain at the long delayed succor, so frequently announced as near at hand. They would not stop to reason on the subject.... Even with such a leader as General Joe Johnston, it required time... to organize an army sufficiently powerful to successfully attack the enemy, securely posted within strong intrenchments.

Already six weeks of unceasing battle had passed away—six weeks of such fighting as the world had seldom witnessed.... The Spartan band of Southern heroes held their position... regardless of... the overwhelming forces of the Federals. With the demon of famine gnawing at their heartstrings, they still daily shouted their defiance to the assailants, and their rifles were as actively handled, as skillfully aimed, as if nearly half their number were not disabled and many sleeping peacefully beneath the green turf....

The undaunted soul would ask: Ought we not to succeed? Are all these horrors, sufferings and fearful sacrifices to bring forth no fruit?

Growing numbers of troops were coming to believe the worst. General Pemberton received a letter signed "Many Soldiers" that gave him full credit for conducting a good defense but deplored the fact that their rations were "not enough scarcely to keep soul and body together, much less to stand the hardships we are called upon to stand.... If you can't feed us, you had better surrender us, horrible as the idea is...."

On the Federal side, however, the siege was not being pressed with enough vigor to finish Pemberton. Charles Dana explains:

Little advancement was made... after McPherson sprang his first mine on the 25th of June.... Several things conspired to produce inactivity and a sort of listlessness among the various commands—the heat of the weather, the unexpected length of the siege, the endurance of the defense, the absence of any thorough organization of the engineer department, and, above all, the well-grounded general belief of our officers and men that the town must presently fall through starvation, without any special effort or sacrifice....

While apathy grew in our ranks, the Confederates displayed more activity than ever. On the morning of June 27th they sprang a countermine on Sherman's front which destroyed the mines

Sherman's engineers had nearly finished and threw the head of his sap into general confusion. . . .

The operations west of the Mississippi became more threatening, too. Our scouts brought in word that [Generals Sterling] Price and Kirby Smith were about to attempt to provision Vicksburg by way of Milliken's Bend. There were rumors also that some two thousand or more skiffs had been prepared within the town, by which it was thought the garrison might escape.

Some of Grant's Eastern critics had grown restless again, but their complaints died on their lips, for a great crisis developed in their own territory: Robert E. Lee invaded Pennsylvania. With several Northern cities in a condition bordering on panic, the war in the West was nearly forgotten.

As June drew to a close, the chief contention in the Vicksburg lines was between the teams of sappers and miners. In the words of Samuel Lockett:

It was very difficult to determine distances under ground, where we could hear the enemy's sappers picking, picking, picking, so very distinctly that it hardly seemed possible for them to be more than a few feet distant, when in reality they were many yards away.

On the 29th of June the enemy had [again] succeeded in getting close up to the parapet of the Third Louisiana redan. We rolled some of their unexploded 13-inch shells down upon them and annoyed them so much as to force them to stop operations. At night they protected themselves against this method of attack by erecting a screen in front of their sap. This screen was made of heavy timbers, which even the shells could not move.

I finally determined to try the effect of a barrel of powder. One containing 125 pounds was obtained, a time-fuse set to fifteen seconds was placed in the bunghole, was touched off by myself by a live coal, and the barrel was rolled over the parapet by two of our sappers. The barrel went true to its destination and exploded with terrific force. Timbers, gabions, and fascines were hurled into the air in all directions, and the sappers once more were compelled to retire. They renewed their operations, however.

Confederate Corporal Ephraim Anderson, whose regiment was a part of these activities, takes up:

Countermining was resorted to upon our part. . . . A detail of six Negroes was set to work.... Two white men were also with them.... The Negroes were relieved as often as the white men, and it was well understood that nothing short of a miracle would save a single member of this party, unless our countermining was successful....

At twelve o'clock on the first of July, our regiment retired to its position when off duty, a little over a hundred yards back in the hollow. The Sixth Missouri was placed on duty in our stead. We had just stacked arms and entered the holes; some had taken their boots off, others their pants, as it was very warm, and were arranging to be comfortable for a time, when the ground heaved as if by an earthquake....

No sound immediately accompanied this motion.... But in an instant more the terrific thunder of the explosion reached us.... Immense columns of earth and shattered fragments ascended into the air and darkened the heavens.... Simultaneously, the concentrated fire of more than fifty pieces of artillery opened upon this devoted position....

Rushing to get my gun, the first man I observed was [Lieutenant Thompson] Alford, waving his sword and commanding the men to fall into line. The regiment was quickly formed and rapidly hastened to the scene. We were met by Cockrell [the regiment's top commander], who was not very far from the parapet when the explosion occurred, and, with many others, was blown up. He fell some distance down the hill, and miraculously escaped without any fatal injury.... He was very much excited, and greeted ... the regiment in a loud and animated tone: "Forward, my brave old Second Missouri, and prepare to die!"

Before reaching the lines, we encountered many fearful evidences of the frightful and terrible character of the affair—men being borne back by the infirmary corps whose faces and hands presented a charred, blackened and swollen appearance, truly shocking and most horrible.

Upon arriving at the ruins, the sight presented to our view was frightful. Men were lying round in every direction, of whom some had been maimed and mangled and were still living, while others were dead.... Those that were blown beyond the immediate circle of the explosion ... were being gathered up....

Many were covered and buried beneath the falling earth and wreck, and men were already engaged in digging for the bodies, to save if possible those in whom life might not yet be extinct. This labor was performed under a heavy fire, and was rewarded in finding a few living, who were immediately borne off on litters. . . .

Sergeant Willie Tunnard, another eyewitness, states that the critical victims, both of the explosion and of the storm of Federal fire, were cared for just behind the lines:

Surgeons with sleeves rolled up to their elbows—hands, arms, and shirts red with human gore—hastened hither and thither, or were using their keen-edged instruments in amputating some shattered limbs, extracting balls and fragments of shells from the lacerated bodies, or probing some ghastly wound. . . .

Again in the words of Corporal Anderson:

Above, around and amidst this scene of woe and death, the enemy's balls and shells whizzed and flashed in wild riot and with fatal destruction. Our position was immediately in rear of the ruins. The shelling was severe—fearful. Under any ordinary circumstances the post would have been considered untenable; but now it must be maintained, for every moment it was thought the artillery would cease and a charge be made.

Actually, no charge had been planned, the Federals remembering too well their experience of June 25.

Anderson continues:

We were kept in position here for two hours. . . . The artillery at last ceased firing for a while, but [a] destructive little mortar . . . continued to play upon us with serious effect. About forty men of the regiment were struck by it, and more of them were killed than wounded. . . .

Those who were at work exhuming the bodies could find no trace . . . of the mining detail. They were buried too deep for exhumation, except one Negro who was blown over into the Federal lines and miraculously escaped without any fatal injury. . . .

At dark the work of repairing the parapet began. . . . During the night, while the work of repairing was going on, General Pemberton . . . visited the parapet. I have heard General Pemberton accused of being a traitor and of selling Vicksburg. It is scarcely possible. Looking upon that careworn and deeply concerned countenance, and beholding the expression of anxious solicitude upon his face as he surveyed the work that was going on around him by the dim light, his loyalty to his pledges and honor cannot for a moment be doubted.

Around the Union campfires that night, much was made of the remarkable experience of the young black miner, Abraham, who had been blown out of the bowels of the Confederate lines and had landed virtually unhurt near a group of Federals. Asked by one of the astonished soldiers how high he had gone up, the youth replied, "Dunno, massa, but t'ink 'bout t'ree mile."

Abraham was promptly sketched by an artist for Harper's Weekly, *a watching officer adding to the youth's delight by giving him fifty cents for posing. Abraham was then taken to General Logan's headquarters, where he became a paid servant. His response to those who questioned him about his experience was that "somethin' busted" and blew him out of the Confederacy "plumb into de Union."*

While keeping a lonely vigil during the night hours that followed the big explosion, a Yankee picket called out to his counterpart on the Confederate side, "We are coming over to see you on the Fourth of July for dinner!" He was answered that the visit had better be made early in the day, since everything was usually eaten up by dinnertime.

July 2 began with the usual roar of guns, explosion of shells, and tremblings of the earth. In Vicksburg, J. M. Swords, publisher of the Citizen, *ignored the tumult and wrote a defiant item:*

The great Ulysses—the Yankee Generalissimo surnamed Grant—has expressed his intention of dining in Vicksburg on . . . the Fourth of July. . . . Ulysses must get into the city before he dines in it. The way to cook a rabbit is "first catch the rabbit."

Attitudes of defiance, however, were no longer the rule among the beleaguered people. Says Mary Loughborough:

We were now swiftly nearing the end of our siege life. The rations had nearly all been given out. For the last few days I had been sick. Still I tried to overcome the languid feeling of utter prostration. My little one had swung in her hammock, reduced in strength, with a low fever flushing in her face. M. was all anxiety, I could plainly see.

A soldier brought up . . . a little jaybird as a plaything for the child. After playing with it for a short time, she turned wearily away.

"Miss Mary," said the servant, "she's hungry. Let me make her some soup from the bird."

At first I refused. The poor little plaything should not die. Then, as I thought of the child, I half consented.

With the utmost haste, Cinth disappeared; and the next time she appeared it was with a cup of soup and a little plate, on which lay the white meat of the poor little bird.

As explained by Confederate officer Samuel Lockett:
We had been from the beginning short of ammunition, and continued so throughout, in spite of the daring exploits of Lamar Fontaine, Captain E. J. Sanders, and Courier Walker, who floated down the river on logs and brought, respectively, 18,000, 20,000, and 200,000 caps.

We were short of provisions, so that our men had been on quarter rations... had eaten mule meat and rats and young shoots of cane....

Dora Miller states that during the final days of the siege her servant Martha found rats "hanging dressed in the market," and that "the officer at the battery told me he had eaten one."
Willie Tunnard was surprised to find that rat flesh, when fried, had a flavor "fully equal to that of squirrels."
Samuel Lockett resumes:
We were so short-handed that no man within the lines had ever been off duty more than a small part of each day.... Every general officer and colonel ... reported his men as physically exhausted and unfit for any duty but simply standing in the trenches and firing. Our lines were badly battered, many of our guns were dismounted, and the Federal forces were within less than a minute of our defenses, so that a single dash could have precipitated them upon us in overwhelming numbers.

All of these facts were brought out in [a] council of war on the night of the 2d of July.... General Pemberton said he had lost all hopes of being relieved by General Johnston. He had considered every possible plan of relieving ourselves, and to his mind there were but two alternatives—either to surrender while we still had ammunition enough left to give us the right to demand terms, or to sell our lives as dearly as possible in what he knew must be a hopeless effort to cut our way through the Federal lines.

He then asked each officer present to give his vote on the question *surrender or not?* Beginning with the junior officer present, all voted to surrender but two ... and these had no reasons to offer. After all had voted, General Pemberton said:

"Well, gentlemen, I have heard your votes and I agree with your almost unanimous decision, though my own preference would be to put myself at the head of my troops and make a desperate effort to cut our way through the enemy. That is my only hope of saving myself from shame and disgrace. Far better would it be for me to die at the head of my army, even in a vain effort to force the enemy's lines, than to surrender it and live and meet the obloquy which I know will be heaped upon me. But my duty is to sacrifice myself to save the army which has so nobly done its duty to defend Vicksburg. I therefore concur with you and shall offer to surrender."

The next morning, under a bright blue sky and a sun already too warm for comfort, the Confederates raised several flags of truce near the center of their lines. Within the range of visibility, all firing stopped.

Mary Loughborough's cave was in this area, and she found the sudden calm, after the weeks of tumult, "absolutely oppressive." She wasn't sure what was going on, but she soon saw General John Bowen, accompanied by an aide and a courier bearing another white flag, ride past her cave on his way toward the Union lines:

M. came by and asked me if I would like to walk out; so I put on my bonnet and sallied forth beyond the terrace for the first time since I entered. On the hill above us the earth was literally covered with fragments of shell.... The grass seemed deadened, the ground ploughed into furrows in many places.... I could now see how very near to the rifle pits my cave lay....

In about two hours, General Bowen returned. No one knew, or seemed to know, why a truce had been made; but all believed that a treaty of surrender was pending. Nothing was talked about among the officers but the all-engrossing theme.

Bowen had set up a meeting between Pemberton and Grant, to take place that afternoon. Hostilities now ceased all along the great semicircle of fortifications.

Says an unnamed Confederate soldier:

For forty-seven days we had been fighting, and hardly caught a glimpse of each other, save hurriedly and beneath the black smoke of a charge or the rush of a retreat. Now the two armies stood up and gazed at each other with wondering eyes.

Winding around the crests of hills—in ditches and parallels hitherto undreamed of by us—one long line [of Federals] after another started into view, looking like huge blue snakes coiling around the ill-fated city. They were amazed at the paucity of our

Meeting of Grant and Pemberton near Confederate lines

numbers; we were astonished at the vastness of theirs.... Their parallels, in many places, had been pushed to within twenty feet of us.

In Grant's words:
    At three o'clock Pemberton appeared at the point suggested in my verbal message, accompanied by the same officers who had borne his letter of the morning. Generals Ord, McPherson, Logan and A. J. Smith and several officers of my staff accompanied me. Our place of meeting was on a hillside within a few hundred feet of the rebel lines. Nearby stood a stunted oak tree, which was made historical by the event.

Even while the officers conferred, something equally momentous, but involving bloodshed instead of words, was happening at Gettysburg, Pennsylvania. Confederate General George E. Pickett was making his abortive charge against the Federals on Cemetery Ridge.
    The meeting of Grant and Pemberton resulted in no immediate agreement on terms, since Pemberton responded with a sharp refusal to Grant's demand that he surrender unconditionally. Both parties soon returned to their lines. But hostilities were not resumed, with Admiral Porter and his vessels also holding their fire, much to the relief of the people in the city.

Negotiations between Grant and Pemberton were continued by letter through the night, with Pemberton winning his main point, that his men be paroled rather than sent to Northern prisons. He was refused some minor requests. At last, early in the morning on July 4, the Confederate commander sent Grant a short note of submission.

Relates Fred Grant, who was at his father's headquarters when the note arrived:

He opened it, gave a sigh of relief, and said calmly, "Vicksburg has surrendered." I was thus the first to hear officially announced the news of the fall of the Gibraltar of America, and I ran out to spread the glad tidings. Officers rapidly assembled, and there was a general rejoicing.

Even Grant became a bit more animated than usual. His great campaign, with all its crucial decisions and calculated gambles, was now a complete success, with the total cost, by Civil War standards, having been low: less than 10,000 in killed, wounded, captured, and missing. Already Grant was in the process of sending that part of his army facing east, headed by Sherman, to drive Joe Johnston from the area. And Port Hudson, Louisiana, the one remaining post in Confederate hands, was now certain to fall to General Banks. The Father of Waters would again go "unvexed to the sea," with Union traffic re-established and with the Confederacy neatly cut in two.

Up to this time many of the Confederate soldiers in the Vicksburg lines had been uncertain as to what was going on. According to Sergeant Tunnard, whose regiment was one of the few that had retained much of its original fighting spirit:

Early in the day it became known that negotiations were pending for the surrender of the Southern stronghold. A perfect storm of indignation burst forth among the troops. What? Surrender? And that, too, on the 4th of July, above all other days! Impossible! Alas, it became too true! The following order was early promulgated:

"... At 10 o'clock A.M. today, each brigade will be marched out in front of its respective position, stacking arms. It will then return and bivouac in rear of the trenches. ... So soon as this order is received you will cause white flags to be displayed along your lines."

As the white flags began to flutter above the Confederate parapets, a number of cannoneers near the Union center began to fire unshotted

*charges in celebration, but Grant soon put a stop to this, complaining that
the sector's commanding officer should have known better "than to allow
any triumphing over conquered countrymen."*

*When the surrender ceremony began at ten o'clock, many among the
thousands of watching Federals were melancholy rather than jubilant. In
the words of one:*

Brave men had been conquered and humbled.... They
marched out of their intrenchments in regiments on the grassy
declivity, stacked their arms, hung their colors in the center, laid
off their knapsacks, belts, cartridge-boxes, etc....

I watched the whole proceeding, and ... my eyes grew dim
with unshed tears as I saw the cheeks of bronzed and brave Confederates wet as they looked upon the colors which they were
leaving.

The men went through the scene with downcast look, never
uttering a word. The officers spoke the necessary words of command in a low tone, much like what we hear at funerals.

*The disarmed Confederates soon marched to the rear of their trenches,
where they were to bivouac, and Federal guards were posted along the
miles of battered parapets to see that no escapes were attempted before the
paroles were arranged.*

Again as seen by Confederate Sergeant Tunnard:

... No word of exultation was uttered to irritate the feelings of
the prisoners. On the contrary, every sentinel who came upon
post brought haversacks filled with provisions.

*Mary Loughborough says that her husband returned from the surrender
ceremony with the announcement that it had gone much better than he had
expected. While the two were talking, Mary spied one of the friends she had
made during the past weeks:*

The old gray-headed soldier, in passing on the hill near the
cave, stopped and, touching his hat, said, "It's a sad day this,
madam. I little thought we'd come to it.... I hope you'll yet be
happy, madam, after all the trouble you've seen."

To which I mentally responded, "Amen."

*In Vicksburg that morning, Dora Miller and her husband, both Unionist
in their sympathies, were anticipating a good show. Dora relates:*

Breakfast dispatched, we went on the upper gallery. What I
expected to see was files of soldiers marching in, but it was very

different. The street was deserted save by a few people carrying home bedding from their caves.

But General Grant was even then riding into the city, a column of troops behind him. Young Fred was present, also mounted, and presumably wearing his father's sash and sword in honor of the occasion. Fred explains that Grant headed for a meeting with General Pemberton:

His reception . . . was most frigid. With a group of Confederate officers, Pemberton was seated on the porch of a large house, but when father expressed a desire for a glass of water, he was allowed to go to hunt for it in the kitchen. This surly reception to the man who would not allow his men to celebrate their victory was deeply resented by the members of General Grant's staff, but father was satisfied with his success in capturing Vicksburg, and manifested no resentment.

Meanwhile, an advance unit of Federals, preceded by a proud color guard and a band playing patriotic airs, was on its way to the courthouse. As related by De Bow Keim, correspondent for the New York Herald:

As might be expected . . . no demonstrations of satisfaction . . . were made along the line of march [except by a few blacks who viewed the Federals as their liberators]; but on the contrary, houses were closed, the citizens within doors, and the city was wrapped in gloom. . . .

Upon arriving at the Court House, the troops were drawn up in line facing the building. This done, the ceremony of possession was completed by the display of the flags of the Forty-fifth Illinois Infantry and of the headquarters of the Seventeenth Corps, from the dome of the Court House.

Upon the appearance of the flags the troops cheered vociferously, making the city ring to its very suburbs with shouts of the votaries of liberty.

Still on their upper gallery, Dora Miller and her husband saw the flags unfurl in the light breeze. Said he, drawing a long breath of satisfaction, "Now I feel once more at home in mine own country!"

About this same time, Margaret Lord, wife of the Reverend Dr. Lord, was feeling a different emotion. Embittered by the surrender, she reached her home from her cave to find a group of Federal soldiers on her back porch. She remonstrated at this invasion of "the privacy of a lady's home." Responded one of the soldiers, casting an eye over two or three places where

the boards had been shattered by shells: "Do you call this a lady's home?
You ought to keep it in better order."

Cases of looting soon developed in various parts of the city, this mainly
by Union stragglers, army followers, and a few local blacks overreacting to
their sudden release from bondage. But if there was shabby work, there was
also generosity, for many a Federal soldier dipped into his haversack to
share his rations with a hungry Confederate soldier or civilian.

The Federals were naturally interested in seeing every part of the city
that had so long denied them admittance. The caves, most of them already
empty of people but still partly furnished, were a particular attraction. It
was the houses, however, that drew the special attention of an unnamed
correspondent for the New York Tribune:

Nearly every gate in the city is adorned with unexploded
thirteen-inch shells placed atop of each post. The porches and
piazzas ... are also adorned with curious collections of shot and
shells that have fallen in the yards. . . . It is said that there are some
houses in the city that have escaped unscathed, but in my rambles
through the streets I could not find them.

I entered perhaps twenty buildings in all, and found frightful-
looking holes in the walls and floors of every one. The house
occupied by General Pemberton as his headquarters has a hole ...
a mule could crawl through without difficulty.

The publisher of the Vicksburg *Citizen* invited me into his
residence, and interspersed his remarks while showing me around
with frequent cautions not to tread here and there for fear a
shattered piece of its flooring would let me through into the cellar.

The publisher soon had other visitors, these not invited. A group of Feder-
als who understood printing invaded his shop, where they found the type
for the one-page issue of July 2 still in its chase. Noting the item challeng-
ing Grant to "first catch the rabbit," they added a few lines of type of their
own and began striking off copies. The special lines declared:

Two days bring about great changes. The banner of the Union
floats over Vicksburg. General Grant has "caught the rabbit." ...
The *Citizen* lives to see it. For the last time it appears on
wallpaper ... and is, excepting this note, from the types as we
found them. It will be valuable hereafter as a curiosity.

By this time a great commotion was developing along Vicksburg's
waterfront. Admiral Porter's entire fleet, plus dozens of other Federal

Army of occupation passing the courthouse

steamers, were gathering there, many of them tooting their whistles and some firing thunderous salutes.

"Truly it was a fine spectacle," says Union sympathizer Dora Miller, *"to see that fleet . . . anchor in the teeth of the batteries so lately vomiting fire."*

The vessels were greeted by a great crowd of blacks, and even many whites began hurrying toward the wharves. Dora goes on:

Presently Mr. J. passed and called, "Aren't you coming? There's provisions on those boats—coffee and flour!"

. . . The townsfolk continued to dash through the streets with their arms full, canned goods predominating. Towards five, Mr. J. passed again. "Keep on the lookout," he said, "the army of occupation is coming." And in a few minutes the head of the column appeared.

What a contrast to the suffering creatures we had seen were these stalwart, well-fed men, so splendidly set up and accoutred! Sleek horses, polished arms, bright plumes—this was the pride and panoply of war. Civilization, discipline, and order seemed to enter with the measured tramp of those marching columns; and the heart turned with throbs of added pity to the worn men in gray who were being blindly dashed against this embodiment of modern power.

In the words of Admiral Porter, who was on the deck of his flagship, the Black Hawk, *now lying alongside a Vicksburg wharf:*

We discerned a dust in the distance, and in a few moments General Grant, at the head of nearly all his generals with their staffs, rode up to the gangway and, dismounting, came on board. That was a happy meeting—a great handshaking and general congratulation.

I opened all my wine lockers, which contained only Catawba on this occasion. It disappeared down the parched throats . . . [and] exhilarated that crowd as weak wine never did before.

There was one man there who preserved the same quiet demeanor he always bore, whether in adversity or in victory, and that was General Grant. No one, to see him sitting there with that calm exterior amid all the jollity . . . would ever have taken him for the great general who had accomplished one of the most stupendous military feats on record. There was a quiet satisfaction on his face that could not be concealed, but he behaved on that occasion as if nothing of importance had occurred.

General Grant was the only one in that assemblage who did not touch the simple wine offered him. He contented himself with a cigar. . . .

Accompanied by two or three of his subordinates, Grant soon left the admiral's ship and remounted his horse. Making his way through crowds of smiling blacks, and nodding to white citizens who eyed him curiously, unaware of his identity, he rode back up the dusty road through the city. He passed numerous empty caves and an occasional battered house that was already being cleared of debris and undergoing makeshift repairs.

At the courthouse, which had escaped with only light damage, Grant drew up to lift his glance to the Stars and Stripes, which hung from a pole jutting almost straight out between two columns of the cupola. Moving on, he passed scattered groups of soldiers, some of them standing and some lounging on grassy banks, the uniforms a mingling of blue and gray. Many of these recent foemen were conversing in the friendliest manner possible.

In the eastern suburbs, the general rode through the great semicircle of defenses, now dead silent and manned by only a few bored Union sentries.

Finally reaching his headquarters in the woods, Grant dismounted and settled into a camp chair. Resting in the shade felt good. For the time being, there was little for him to do but to write a few dispatches.

The main dispatch of the occasion was already on its way to Washington. Grant was to say later:

This news, with the victory at Gettysburg won the same day, lifted a great load of anxiety from the minds of the President, his Cabinet, and the loyal people all over the North. The fate of the Confederacy was sealed when Vicksburg fell. Much hard fighting was to be done afterward, and many precious lives were to be sacrificed; but the morale was with the supporters of the Union ever after.

EPILOGUE

A NOTEWORTHY SIDELIGHT of the Vicksburg story is that the Fourth of July was not celebrated in the city for the next eighty-one years. It took the military fervors of the victory period of World War II to get the patriotic fireworks popping again. Except perhaps for a few ancient whites and blacks who were very young in 1863, the survivors of the siege were gone. Some had been dust for many years.

General Grant, as is well known, followed his Vicksburg success by winning again at Chattanooga and then leading the Army of the Potomac against Richmond, finally forcing Lee to surrender at Appomattox. Grant was less successful as President of the United States, his administration being rocked by political and financial scandals. But he left office with his personal integrity intact, and he added to his heroic stature by writing his memoirs while fatally and painfully ill with cancer of the throat. Grant said toward the end that he figured that he and his book would be finished about the same time. He won the race by only a few days, dying at the age of sixty-three. His last wish was that the book would bring his family financial security. It did, nearly half a million dollars' worth, becoming the best seller of the century.

Young Fred Grant went on to attend West Point and serve in the army for a decade, during which time he took part in the campaign against the Indians of the Western frontier. In 1889, President Benjamin Harrison made him minister to Austria-Hungary, a post he held for four years, afterward serving as a police commissioner in New York City. In 1898 Fred re-entered the army to take part in the war with Spain. Thereafter remaining on active duty and achieving the rank of major general, he died in New York City in 1912.

John Pemberton, even though Jefferson Davis stuck by him, received all the condemnation from the Southern people that he expected. Some made a complete Benedict Arnold of him, claiming he had secured the promise of a million dollars from Washington if he delivered Vicksburg to Grant. The terms of Pemberton's parole released him to Richmond, and he was soon eligible to return to duty. But no job befitting his rank was found for him. At last he volunteered to fight as a common soldier, but Davis instead made him a lieutenant colonel of artillery in the Eastern theater, in which capacity he finished the war.

With money sent from Philadelphia by his well-to-do mother, Pemberton bought a war-ravaged farm near Warrenton, Virginia, where he settled with his wife and children. A heroic effort to restore the farm and make it pay was unsuccessful. Pemberton found his solace in the company of his family and in the reading of books at his fireside, among them the ancient classics, Shakespeare, Charles Dickens, and Mark Twain.

One evening Pemberton's youngest daughter, becoming impatient with his absorption in Virgil and his neglect of her, said, "Come on, Mama, let's go to bed and leave Papa with his Virgins."

Toward the end of 1875, with his health beginning to fail, Pemberton sold the farm at a loss and returned to his ancestral roots in Pennsylvania. He got some financial assistance in 1879 through a special act of Congress that reinstated the citizenship he had relinquished in 1861 and restored to him "such property as might be lawfully his."

Pemberton died in 1881, at the age of sixty-six. He was buried under a simple marker in his mother's plot in Philadelphia. No public tributes marked his passing. None could have been expected in the North, and the South chose to remain as silent.

William Tecumseh Sherman and Joseph E. Johnston did not end their roles as foemen when Sherman pushed Johnston from the Vicksburg area. In May, 1864, as Sherman began his invasion of the Deep South from Chattanooga, it was Johnston who tried to stop him. Johnston was driven southward to Atlanta, where Jefferson Davis replaced him with John Hood, the fighting general who had already lost a leg and the use of an arm to the Confederate cause.

Sherman wrested Atlanta from Hood and burned it. Then, burning and pillaging as he went, he marched to Savannah and the sea. Next he took his ravaging columns northward through the Carolinas. In North Carolina he again found Joe Johnston in his path, Davis having reinstated Johnston out of desperation. It was to Sherman that Johnston surrendered his outnumbered and bedraggled army as the war came to a close.

Sherman spurned all requests that he run for President, saying he'd rather spend four years in the penitentiary than in the White House. His ambitions reached no higher than the office of general-in-chief of the army, to which he ascended in 1869. Sherman died of pneumonia at the age of seventy-one in February, 1891. Joe Johnston, then eighty-four, attended his funeral in New York City, standing bareheaded in the raw winter weather and taking a chill that led to his own death by pneumonia a short time later.

The controversial John McClernand, Lincoln's political general, left the Vicksburg battlefield under protest and appealed Grant's order to Washington, but nothing was done on his behalf. The following year he was assigned to a command in Texas, where he served for only a few months and then resigned his commission. Subsequently McClernand conducted a law practice in Springfield, Illinois; he died in 1900.

Admiral David Farragut, after his frustrating attacks on Vicksburg from New Orleans in 1862, continued to serve in the lower Mississippi and in the Gulf of Mexico, winning great fame for his defeat of the Confederate forces in Mobile Bay in 1864. The old sailor lived only six years longer, rounding out his sixty-year career by taking America's European Squadron on a grand goodwill tour of the continent's ports, being received everywhere with the highest honors.

Farragut's foster brother, Admiral David Porter, played a very active role in the Civil War till the end, his last service as commander of the North Atlantic Blockading Squadron. He escorted President Lincoln up the James River for a visit to Richmond when that city finally fell to Grant. After the war, Porter's various duties included a tour as superintendent of the Naval Academy at Annapolis.

In 1885, when he was seventy-two years old and his friend Sherman was sixty-five, Porter said of Vicksburg: "Nearly all the clever young officers who went on that expedition with me are dead and gone. . . . All are swallowed up who are not made of iron and steel. . . . Old Tecumseh and myself hold on, two tough old knots, with a good deal of the steel in us yet. . . ." Porter died on February 13, 1891—one day before "Old Tecumseh."

Samuel Byers, the Union soldier who penned the colorful portrait of Grant at Champion's Hill, was captured by the Confederates at Chattanooga. While in a Southern prison, he learned of Sherman's Georgia campaign and composed a song he called "Sherman's March to the Sea." It was to be sung in the North for several decades. Byers achieved prominence also as an author and as an American consul.

Another who was present at Vicksburg and later served the nation overseas was Confederate General Dabney Maury of Virginia. In the 1880s, once again an American citizen in good standing, Maury was appointed Minister to Colombia.

Charles Dana, the man sent from Washington to evaluate Grant, returned to newspaper work after the war, at the same time writing books, editing anthologies of poetry, and collaborating in the production of a set of encyclopedias. He died in 1897, having just completed his *Recollections of the Civil War*.

Union diarist Osborn Oldroyd turned to bookselling upon his discharge from the service. A great admirer of Lincoln, whom he had met during the Lincoln-Douglas debates in 1858, Oldroyd lived in a way that he must have found very rewarding. This is explained in his book *A Soldier's Story of the Siege of Vicksburg*, published in 1885, which includes an afterword addressed to the veterans of the war:

"The author of this book makes his residence in the old home of Abraham Lincoln at Springfield, Illinois. He has devoted a large portion of the building to the display of a very extensive collection of personal and historical relics of the martyred President, and articles of various kinds connected with the war of the rebellion. The different portraits, medallions, busts, engravings, autograph letters, papers, books, pamphlets, etc., of Mr. Lincoln alone number into thousands. No such collection as this exists anywhere [else] in the wide world, yet you are invited to call at any time when visiting the State Capital and examine this collection *free of charge*. If anyone has . . . any . . . relics of the war which they would like to add to this museum, their offering will be received with thanks, and proper credit given the donor."

Oldroyd later moved to Washington and became custodian of the house opposite Ford's Theater in which Lincoln expired. Oldroyd himself died in Washington at the age of eighty-eight in 1930. This was the man who had found himself in "delicate health" at the outbreak of the war in 1861.

Joseph Stockton, the diarist from Chicago, worked his way from major to brevet brigadier general before the war ended. Returning to his home city, he became a railroad official and a citizen dedicated to public service. He was one of the founders of Lincoln Park. During the great fire of 1871 Stockton led a corps of workers that saved many valuable city records and much of the household property of people who were burned out. His own home was turned into a refugee center.

In 1906 the old general returned to Vicksburg for a visit. Says his grandson Walter T. Stockton, a retired architect still very much alive at this writing: "I remember going over the battlefield with him, and he recognized much of the original terrain." General Stockton died the following year.

Confederate Sergeant Willie Tunnard settled in Shreveport, Louisiana, at the war's close, beginning at once the writing of a memoir of his regiment, one of the best to be done on either side. He spent much of the rest of his life in newspaper work, at the same time maintaining a very active membership in the local camp of the United Confederate Veterans. In good health to an advanced age, Tunnard died in 1916, simply going to bed one night and never waking.

Corporal Ephraim Anderson, the Confederate from Missouri, returned there after the war and, like Tunnard, wrote an excellent "historical and personal" memoir. Anderson tried newspaper work for a time, then turned to farming, which gave him "contentment and happiness." He died in a Confederate soldiers' home at the age of seventy-five. Anderson was the man who had thrilled to his first love under a magnolia tree south of Vicksburg.

One Southerner who made a deliberate retirement into obscurity after Appomattox was Isaac Brown, the courageous commander of the *Arkansas:* "I took to the plow as a better implement of reconstruction than the pen." Brown, however, made a brief emergence in the 1880s to write an article on his famous vessel for the *Century Magazine.*

Samuel Lockett, the engineer who designed a great part of Vicksburg's defenses, also reappeared at this time to give the magazine his story. His postwar pursuits appear to have gone unrecorded.

Mary Livermore, Annie Wittenmyer, and Jane Hoge, the Union hospital workers at Vicksburg, continued in fields of public service. Mary Livermore won inclusion in late-nineteenth-century encyclopedias as a reformer. Lecturing on woman suffrage, the female role in the war, and temperance reform, she achieved fame both at home and abroad. The indefatigable woman wrote several books about her life and work. She was eighty-three when she died in 1905.

Vicksburg citizen Emma Balfour, the physician's wife, remained in the city for life, first enduring the Yankee occupation and then playing a role in the struggle toward revival. Outliving her husband by a decade, Emma was nearing seventy when she died in 1887. Her diary became a valued family relic.

The Reverend Dr. William Lord and his wife and children left Vicksburg a few weeks after the Yankees moved in, going first to Mobile, Alabama, and then to Charleston, South Carolina, on the Atlantic coast. Then the Yankees captured Charleston, and the Lords fled inland to Winnsboro. After the war Dr. Lord returned to Vicksburg to become pastor of a newly constructed church, but he eventually accepted a call to Cooperstown, New York, the region of his birth, where his peregrinations ended.

Dora Miller, the Union sympathizer from New Orleans who spent much of the siege in her cellar writing in her diary and reading Charles Dickens, returned with her husband to the Crescent City. "H." had but a little more than two years to live after watching the Union banners raised over the Vicksburg courthouse and exclaiming that he felt at home again in his own country. The young widow, left with two infant sons, turned to schoolteaching, continuing in the profession for many years, at the same time doing some writing for newspapers and magazines. Dora outlived both her sons, dying during World War I at the age of seventy-nine.

As for cave-dweller Mary Loughborough: Being denied permission to accompany her husband when the prisoners left Vicksburg, bound for Mobile, she and a number of other women in a like fix went up the Mississippi to Saint Louis, Missouri, which placed them in Yankee territory. One day Mary showed her Vicksburg journal to a friend, who urged her to try to have it published. Mary promptly wrote to a New York publisher, who agreed to look at the manuscript and who accepted it at once. *My Cave Life in Vicksburg*, released in 1864, was well received by the

Northern public, even though it was dedicated to "M.," Mary's rebel husband, who had returned to active duty.

After the war, Mary and her husband settled in Arkansas. M., who had worried so much about Mary's security during the siege, soon died. In 1882 Mary secured the publication of a Southern edition of her book. In its preface she said: "The second edition, like the first, is dedicated to M.—to one then absent—now gone before—reverently and tenderly—to a memory."

An advertisement in the back of the book announced that the author was preparing a novel to be published that same year. In 1884 Mary founded one of the nation's first women's magazines, the *Arkansas Ladies' Journal*. Three years later she died, not yet fifty-one years old.

BIBLIOGRAPHY

Abbott, John S. C. *The Life of General Ulysses S. Grant.* Boston: B. B. Russell, 1868.

Anderson, Ephraim McD. *Memoirs: Historical and Personal; Including the Campaigns of the First Missouri Confederate Brigade.* Notes and foreword by Edwin C. Bearss. Dayton, Ohio: Morningside Bookshop, 1972. First published in 1868.

Angle, Paul M., and Miers, Earl Schenck. *Tragic Years: 1860–1865.* 2 vols. New York: Simon and Schuster, 1960.

Annals of the War. Philadelphia: The Times Publishing Company, 1879.

Battles and Leaders of the Civil War. 4 vols. Robert Underwood Johnson and Clarence Clough Buel (eds.). New York: The Century Co., 1884–1888.

Bearss, Edwin C. *Rebel Victory at Vicksburg.* Published by the Vicksburg Centennial Commemoration Commission. Little Rock, Ark.: Pioneer Press, 1963.

Bill, Ledyard. *The Life, Campaigns, and Battles of General Ulysses S. Grant.* New York: Ledyard Bill, 1868.

Bowman, S. M., and Irwin, R. B. *Sherman and His Campaigns.* New York: Charles B. Richardson, 1865.

Brown, Alonzo L. *History of the Fourth Regiment of Minnesota Infantry Volunteers During the Great Rebellion.* St. Paul, Minn.: The Pioneer Press Company, 1892.

Browne, Junius Henri. *Four Years in Secessia.* Hartford: O. D. Case and Company, 1865.

Cadwallader, Sylvanus. *Three Years with Grant.* Edited by Benjamin P. Thomas. New York: Alfred A. Knopf, 1955.

Catton, Bruce. *Grant Moves South.* Boston and Toronto: Little, Brown and Company, 1960.

———. *The Centennial History of the Civil War.* 3 vols. Garden City, N.Y.: Doubleday and Company, 1961–1965.

Chase, Edward. *The Memorial Life of General William Tecumseh Sherman.* Chicago: R. S. Peale & Co., 1891.

Civil War Naval Chronology. Compiled by Naval History Division, Navy Department. Washington, D.C.: Government Printing Office, 1971.

Commager, Henry Steele. *The Blue and the Gray.* Indianapolis and New York: The Bobbs-Merrill Company, 1950.

Coppée, Henry. *Grant and His Campaigns.* New York: Charles B. Richardson, 1866.

Dana, Charles A. *Recollections of the Civil War.* New York: D. Appleton and Company, 1898.

Davis, Jefferson. *The Rise and Fall of the Confederate Government.* 2 vols. Cranbury, N.J.: Thomas Yoseloff, 1958.

Deming, Henry C. *The Life of Ulysses S. Grant.* Hartford: S. S. Scranton & Co., 1868.

Duyckinck, Evert A. *National History of the War for the Union.* 3 vols. New York: Johnson, Fry and Company, 1868.

Evans, Clement A. (ed.). *Confederate Military History.* 12 vols. New York: Thomas Yoseloff, 1962.

Everhart, William C. *Vicksburg:* Historical Handbook No. 21. Washington, D.C.: Government Printing Office, 1961.

Farragut, Loyall. *The Life of David Glasgow Farragut.* New York: D. Appleton and Company, 1879.

Fiske, John. *The Mississippi Valley in the Civil War.* Boston and New York: Houghton, Mifflin and Company, 1900.

Frank Leslie's Illustrated History of the Civil War. New York: Mrs. Frank Leslie, 1895.

Garland, Hamlin. *Ulysses S. Grant: His Life and Character.* New York: Doubleday & McClure Co., 1898.

Grant, U. S. *Personal Memoirs.* New York: Charles L. Webster & Company, 1894.

Greene, Francis Vinton. *The Mississippi* (Campaigns of the Civil War, vol. 8). New York: Charles Scribner's Sons, 1882.

Guernsey, Alfred H., and Alden, Henry M. *Harper's Pictorial History of the Great Rebellion.* 2 vols. Chicago: McDonnell Bros., 1866, 1868.

Harper's Encyclopaedia of United States History. 10 vols. New York: Harper & Brothers, 1915.

Harper's Weekly; May 4, 1861, to May 13, 1865 (reissue). Shenandoah, Iowa: Living History, Inc., 1961–1965.

Headley, P. C. *Life and Campaigns of General U. S. Grant.* New York: Derby & Miller, 1868.

Hoehling, A. A. *Vicksburg: 47 Days of Siege.* Englewood Cliffs, N.J.: Prentice-Hall, 1969.

Hoffman, Wickham. *Camp, Court, and Siege.* New York: Harper & Brothers, 1877.

Hoge, Mrs. A. H. *The Boys in Blue.* New York: E. B. Treat & Co., 1867.

Howland, Edward. *Grant as a Soldier and Statesman.* Hartford: J. B. Burr & Company, 1868.

Johnson, Rossiter. *Campfires and Battlefields.* New York: The Civil War Press, 1967. First published in 1894.

Johnson, W. Fletcher. *Life of Wm. Tecumseh Sherman.* Edgewood Publishing Company, 1891.

Johnston, Joseph E. *Narrative of Military Operations.* New York: D. Appleton and Company, 1874.

Jones, Archer. *Confederate Strategy from Shiloh to Vicksburg.* Baton Rouge: Louisiana State University Press, 1961.

Jones, John B. *A Rebel War Clerk's Diary.* Edited by Earl Schenck Miers. New York: Sagamore Press, 1958.

Keim, DeB. Randolph. *Sherman: A Memorial in Art, Oratory, and Literature by the Society of the Army of the Tennessee, with the Aid of the Congress of the United States of America.* Washington, D.C.: Government Printing Office, 1904.

King, W. C., and Derby, W. P. *Campfire Sketches and Battlefield Echoes of the Rebellion.* Springfield, Mass.: W. C. King & Co., 1887.

Larke, Julian K. *General Grant and His Campaigns.* New York: J. C. Derby & N. C. Miller, 1864.

Lewis, Lloyd. *Captain Sam Grant.* Boston: Little, Brown and Company, 1950.

————. *Sherman: Fighting Prophet.* New York: Harcourt, Brace and Company, 1932.

Livermore, Mary A. *My Story of the War.* Hartford: A. D. Worthington and Company, 1889.

Long, E. B. (with Barbara Long). *The Civil War Day by Day.* Garden City, N.Y.: Doubleday & Company, 1971.

Lossing, Benson J. *Pictorial Field Book of the Civil War.* 3 vols. New York: T. Belknap & Company, 1868.

Loughborough, Mary W. *My Cave Life in Vicksburg.* Little Rock, Ark.: Kellogg Printing Company, 1882.

Maclay, Edgar Stanton. *A History of the United States Navy.* 2 vols. New York: D. Appleton and Company, 1898.

McClure, Alexander K. *Abraham Lincoln and Men of War Times.* Philadelphia: The Times Publishing Company, 1892.

Mahan, A. T. *Admiral Farragut.* New York: D. Appleton and Company, 1897.

Maury, Dabney H. *Recollections of a Virginian.* New York: Charles Scribner's Sons, 1894.

Merrill, James M. *William Tecumseh Sherman.* Chicago, New York, San Francisco: Rand, McNally & Company, 1971.

Miers, Earl Schenck. *The Web of Victory: Grant at Vicksburg.* New York: Alfred A. Knopf, 1955.

Moore, Frank (ed.). *The Rebellion Record.* 12 vols. New York: G. P. Putnam, 1861–1871.

————. *Women of the War.* Hartford: S. S. Scranton & Co., 1866.

Northrop, Henry Davenport. *Life and Deeds of General Sherman.* Waukesha, Wis.: World Publishing Co., 1891.

Oldroyd, Osborn H. *A Soldier's Story of the Siege of Vicksburg.* Springfield, Ill.: Published for the author by H. W. Rokker, 1885.

Pemberton, John C. *Pemberton: Defender of Vicksburg.* Chapel Hill, N.C.: The University of North Carolina Press, 1942.

Porter, David D. *Incidents and Anecdotes of the Civil War.* New York: D. Appleton and Company, 1886.

————. *The Naval History of the Civil War.* New York: The Sherman Publishing Company, 1886.

Richardson, Albert D. *A Personal History of Ulysses S. Grant.* Hartford: American Publishing Company, 1868.

Robins, Edward. *William T. Sherman.* Philadelphia: George W. Jacobs & Company, 1905.

Sherman, William T. *Memoirs.* 2 vols. New York: D. Appleton and Company, 1875.

Stockton, Joseph. *War Diary (1862–1865).* Chicago: Privately printed, 1910.

Struggle for Vicksburg. From the editors of *Civil War Times Illustrated.* Gettysburg, Pa.: Historical Times, Inc., 1967.

Taylor, Richard. *Destruction and Reconstruction.* New York: D. Appleton and Company, 1879.

Tenney, W. J. *The Military and Naval History of the Rebellion.* New York: D. Appleton and Company, 1865.

The Soldier in Our Civil War. Edited by Paul F. Mottelay and T. Campbell-Copeland. 2 vols. New York: G. W. Carleton & Company, 1886.

Tomes, Robert, and Smith, Benjamin G. *The Great Civil War.* 3 vols. New York: Virtue and Yorston, 1862.

Tunnard, W. H. *A Southern Record; the History of the Third Regiment, Louisiana Infantry.* Preface, notes, and roster by Edwin C. Bearss. Dayton, Ohio: Morningside Bookshop, 1970. First published in 1866.

Under Both Flags: A Panorama of the Great Civil War. Chicago: W. S. Reeve Publishing Co., 1896.

Vilas, William Freeman. *A View of the Vicksburg Campaign.* Wisconsin History Commission, 1908.

Walker, Peter F. *Vicksburg: A People at War.* Chapel Hill, N.C.: The University of North Carolina Press, 1960.

War of the Rebellion: A Compilation of the Official Records of the Union and Confederate Armies. Series I, Volume XXIV, in three parts. Washington, D.C.: Government Printing Office, 1889.

Webb, Willard (ed.). *Crucial Moments of the Civil War.* New York: Bonanza Books, 1961.

Williams, T. Harry. *Lincoln and His Generals.* New York: Alfred A. Knopf, 1952.

Wilson, James Grant, and Coan, Titus Munson. *Personal Recollections of the War of the Rebellion.* New York: New York Commandery of the Loyal Legion of the United States, 1891.

Wittenmyer, Annie. *Under the Guns: A Woman's Reminiscences of the Civil War.* Boston: E. B. Stillings & Co., 1895.

INDEX